Library of
Davidson College

Next to God . . . Poland

Next to God... Poland

Politics and Religion in Contemporary Poland

Bogdan Szajkowski

St. Martin's Press, New York

© Bogdan Szajkowski 1983

All rights reserved. For information write:
St. Martin's Press, Inc., 175 Fifth Avenue, New York, N.Y. 10010
Printed in Great Britain
First published in the United States of America in 1983

ISBN 0-312-57233-6

Library of Congress Card Catalog Number 83-40151

For us, next to God, our first love is Poland. After God one must above all remain faithful to the Homeland, to the Polish national culture. We will love all the people in the world, but only in such an order of priorities. And if we see everywhere slogans advocating love for all the peoples and all the nations, we do not oppose them; yet above all we demand the right to live in accordance with the spirit, history, culture, and language of our own Polish land—the same which have been used by our ancestors for centuries.

(Cardinal Stefan Wyszyński, Sermon in St. John's Cathedral, February 1974)

. . . and in the spirit of traditional Polish tolerance, we consolidate a situation in which there is no conflict between the Church and the State. We are willing to co-operate in the attainment of our great national goals. A cause uniting all of us—as we emphasized together with the Primate of Poland, Stefan Cardinal Wyzyński—is the concern for the prosperity of our homeland, the Polish People's Republic.

(Edward Gierek, Address during his visit to the Vatican, 1 December 1977)

In view of the experience of several decades, it is necessary to state that the relations between the Church and the State, as a result of fundamental ideological differences, have never been, are not, and will not be ideal . . . Poland will remain a lay State, and the Marxists will actively work toward the preservation and strengthening of exactly that characteristic of the People's State. Any change from that position would not be acceptable as it would be contrary to the established interests of the socialist State and the nation.

(Mieczysław Rakowski, *Polityka*, 10 March 1979)

POLAND: Diocesan boundaries

Contents

Preface	ix
Introduction	1
1 Church–State Relations 1944–1970: Conflicts and Co-existence	9
2 The Church and Dissent: 1970–1980	29
3 The Triumph of Solidarity	87
4 Tribulations under Martial Law	155
5 A New Coalition	221
Appendix I:	229
Appendix II: Cardinal Stefan Wyszyński to the Members of the Main Council of the Polish Episcopate, Warsaw, 22 May 1981	235
Appendix III: 'Theses of the Primate's Social Council in the Matter of Social Accord'	240
Selected Bibliography	249
Index	253

Preface

When I left Poland in the summer of 1967 on flight LO 361 bound for Copenhagen, I was convinced that the dark clouds that were gathering over the country of my birth would be dispelled in no more than a few months. It seemed inconceivable that the nation in which I was born and raised would not after all the centuries of trials and tribulations find its rightful way to prosperity, happiness and peace. Today, more than a decade later, after further betrayals by Poland's rulers which brought more misery, suffering and humiliation to the proud, brave and ingenious people of Poland, as an optimist I feel that new prospects might just possibly be in the offing through the oldest Polish institution, the Roman Catholic Church. This book is devoted to an analysis of the political role of the Church in Poland since 1945 and its constantly growing impact on Poland's politics.

Many people have helped me with this book; none are responsible for its content. I would like to thank especially David Nicholas, the Managing Editor of the Independent Television News, Maggie Eales, ITN's Senior Foreign Editor for sending me to various European capitals in order to collect material, some of which became extremely useful in writing this book, and my other colleagues at ITN for their helpful guidance on the sources available at ITN.

This book is partially based on a lecture course on Modern Poland given at the Adult Christian Education Centre at the United Reform Church, Windsor Place, Cardiff. I wish to thank the Centre for persuading me to give the course, and my students for their penetrating questions. I also wish to thank my own Department of Sociology at University College, Cardiff for the use of facilities and in particular Martin Read for his help and advice on the use of computers which speeded up the preparation of the manuscript.

My thanks also go to Witek Klimaszewski who very kindly translated Cardinal Wyszyński's last address printed in Appendix II, and to

PREFACE

Tom Keenoy who read parts of the manuscript, for his most useful comments and suggestions.

I am grateful to my good friends in Rome, Warsaw, Paris, Oslo, Belgrade, Geneva, Brussels, New York, Washington, Vienna and Prague who were able to assist me in small ways in writing this book.

Finally I want to thank my wife Martha and three daughters Vara, Sophie and Nadia for their constant encouragement, patience and thick skins throughout the months which I spent writing this book and for whom indeed it is written.

Dinas Powis
3 July 1983
Bogdan Szajkowski

Introduction

The Roman Catholic Church in Poland has for centuries been a national institution. Embedded in the national fabric, Polish Catholicism represents not only a system of religious beliefs and sacramental acts but also the embodiment of Polish cultural values and traditions. Therefore it has always exerted a considerable impact on popular attitudes towards political ideologies and institutions. Poland's national identity has for some time now found its modern form from and in conflict with the State, which has been continuously weakened since the end of the seventeenth century. The Polish State eventually ceased to exist with the third partition of Poland in 1795. But if the partitions weakened the authority of the State, they strengthened immeasurably that of the Church, which over the period of two hundred years had become the most important national institution, surpassing in its influence even that of the State.

The fact that the religions of the two most repressive and culturally aggressive partition powers, Prussia and Russia, were respectively Protestantism and Orthodoxy, made it remarkably easy for the indigenous population to identify Roman Catholicism with Polish nationality. During the years of Poland's occupation, the Church had been the guardian of the nation's language, history, traditions and culture. But even earlier it had developed a strong constitutional role. Following traditions dating back to the twelfth century and earlier to counter threats to the integrity of the Polish State, in the absence of a nationally accepted monarch, the Primate of the Roman Catholic Church replaced the person of the king in the interval between two reigns.[1] Thus in more recent times the State has been continuously faced with a rival authority whose national role stretches back to the Middle Ages and whose roots in society are very deep.

Since the end of the Second World War, attempts to legitimize the Communist regime in Poland encountered several obstacles, two of which appear to be particularly relevant here. Firstly, Communism came from the East and was brought by the Russians, a people whose state had been in competition with Poland since the sixteenth century. More recent memory was, however, particularly painful. Poland regained its independence in 1918. Two years later, during the Russo-Polish war, the Red Army occupied a sizeable part of eastern Poland and at one stage even threatened the capital. Somehow the exasperated Polish Army managed to defend Warsaw and eventually expelled the Soviet troops. The victory in the battle of Warsaw has since been referred to in the Polish unofficial history as the 'miracle on the Vistula' performed by the Black Madonna of Częstochowa, the Queen of Poland, again acting as she did in the seventeenth century during the Swedish occupation of Poland.[2] The icon of the Black Madonna has remained for centuries not only a religious symbol, but also a symbol of Poland's resistance to foreign tyranny, and few Poles would wish to draw any distinction between the two.[3]

During the Russo-Polish war of 1920, the Polish Communists, clinging rigidly to Rosa Luxemburg's programme of Social Democracy, supported the invading Red Army whose victories in the Second World War extended Soviet rule over Eastern Europe to the River Elbe. They regarded an independent Polish State as merely a transition to Poland's submersion in the 'international camp of social revolution where there is no problem of national borders.' Solutions like autonomy, independence and self-determination were merely connected 'with the evolution of a capitalist world'. The Polish Communists therefore, quixotically, refused to have anything to do with the newly re-born Polish State.

The second obstacle to the legitimization of the Communist regime in Poland was the fact that it had been installed in 1945 by the Soviet Union which is at least formally guided by Marxism–Leninism, an outlook whose principles are fundamentally at odds with those of Catholicism.

The Catholic Church in Poland has always been the strongest Church in Eastern Europe. After its victory during the Counter-Reformation in the seventeenth century, it ruled unchallenged over the souls of the Polish people. The Church enjoyed exceptional influence and wealth, accommodating itself to changing political currents and circumstances. The move of the Polish borders some 500 kilometres westwards meant that for the first time in Polish history, and uniquely in Eastern Europe, the Polish nation was religiously and ethnically homogeneous.[4] The

INTRODUCTION

Church represented great power, uniting some 90 per cent of the population[5] within its organization and behind its ideology.

When the country fell under Communist rule a new era began of direct encounter between the Catholic Church and Communism. The Church had a coherent, uniform organization,[6] more efficient and certainly not inferior to that of the ruling Communist Party. Most importantly, however, the Church had a broader basis of social support than the Communists. The peasants, who formed the majority of the population at that time and who had originally benefited from the agrarian reform carried out by the new regime almost immediately after its formation, soon became aware of the real agricultural policies of the regime. As they opposed forcible collectivization of their newly acquired land, they became the target of abuse, persecution and victimization. They have remained the strongest and most faithful ally of the Church.[7] The workers, a great percentage of whom were of peasant stock, in whose name the Communists claimed to have seized and wielded power, were soon disillusioned because of the ineffective economic policies of the new Government. The overwhelming majority of the intelligentsia, which to a great extent consisted of the members of the former landed gentry, and which after the war absorbed the remnants of that class, was naturally opposed to the Communist regime. Even for those who were by no means religious, the Church offered the only opportunity of openly expressing their disapproval of the Government by attending Sunday mass. The Church pulpit became a unique source of the uncensored word, of a voice eminently concerned for the material and non-material well-being of the people of Poland.

Very many Poles, perhaps the majority, looked to the Church not only for spiritual guidance but also for political direction. The Church decided to avoid violent confrontation with the new regime and tried to realize ideological goals by gradual methods. Over the years of uneasy State-Church coexistence since 1945, there have been periods of sharp dramatic struggles followed by spells of tranquility and compromise. On the whole the Church has held her ground in the defence of both her own spiritual mission and her place within Polish society. Indeed the moral authority of the Church grew even greater and was recognized not only by the faithful but by non-believers as well.

The symbiotic relationship between Polish national, cultural and

INTRODUCTION

democratic political traditions embodied in Polish Catholicism have in the past three decades been reflected in another trend: that of political realism and to a considerable extent opportunism. In recent years the Church had openly joined the overwhelming current of dissent and since the late 1970s became its main spokesman, as well as arbiter between the Communist regime and the majority of the population. It also gained access, unprecedented in any Communist country, to the centres of formal political power. At the same time, contrary to expectations from the faithful, the Church still continues to insist that it cannot be directly involved in politics or assume the role of an opposition group. Since the declaration of martial law, however, the Church has embarked on unprecedented social, political and economic initiatives which if successful would change fundamentally the nature of Communist rule in Poland and have far-reaching impact on big power relations in the strategic part of the European continent.

An illustration of these themes is the main object of this study.

Notes

1. Under Polish law at that time the Primate was the first among the country's senators and as such he presided over the Senate. After the death of a monarch he handled domestic and foreign policy in his capacity as *interrex*. He further received foreign envoys, conveyed and supervised the progress of electoral sessions of Parliament and officially announced its choice of the new king. The rulers of Poland were also crowned and had their matrimonial unions blessed by the Primate, the latter taking precedence even over cardinals. After 1918 Poland's constitution and the new code of Canon law changed the legal position of the Primate. Nevertheless, in the public mind he remained head of the Church in Poland and the work of primates Edmund Dalbor (1918-26), August Hlond (1926-48) and Stefan Wyszyński (1948-81) went a long way towards perpetuating this image.
2. On 18 November 1655, the Swedes started their siege of Jasna Góra with several thousand soldiers. The monastery was defended by 150 noblemen and seventy monks led by Prior Father Augustyn Kordecki. After forty days of abortive attempts, general Müller gave up the siege on 26 December 1655. That fact spurred the nation on to a victorious struggle. On 1 April 1956, King Jan Kazimierz vowed to entrust the country to the authority of the Mother of God recognizing Her as the Queen of Poland.
3. According to tradition the icon of the Black Madonna was painted by St. Luke on the table used by the Holy Family. Then it was transported to Constantinople and afterwards to Ruthenia, from where Prince Władysław Opolczyk brought it to the monastery of Jasna Góra in 1383. Historically it is known that in 1430 Hussites from the border region of Bohemia and Moravia

INTRODUCTION

attacked Jasna Góra, tore out the picture from the altar, and attacked it with sabres. The back board of the picture broke into three parts. The damaged picture was taken to Kraków, where King Władysław Jagiełło ordered its conservation. According to the latest research, the boards were then glued together, the missing parts were refitted, the surface was levelled, the new layer of canvas was stuck on and the new picture was painted in distemper. Research has shown that the original picture, destroyed in 1430, dated back to the first centuries of Christianity. The present picture (82.2 centimetres wide, 122.2 centimetres high and 5.5 centimeters thick) depicts the Virgin Mary holding the Infant on her left arm. Face complexion is brown. On the Virgin's right cheek are two evident smudges painted in memory of the picture's profanation. Traces of the real slashes are left under the canvas. The icon has witnessed major national events. Jan Długosz (1415-80), a Polish historian, writes that the picture presents 'the most dignified Queen of the World and Ours'. Since the early fifteenth century, the Virgin Mary was referred to as 'The Queen of Poland and the Poles'.
4. There are no official statistics on ethnic minorities in Poland since the war. It is estimated, however, that in 1961 minorities formed approximately 2 per cent of the population. Among the largest were the following: 180,000 Ukrainians; 165,000 Byelorussians; 140,000 Germans; 31,000 Jews; 23,000 Czechs and Slovaks; 19,000 Russians; 12,000 gypsies; 10,000 Lithuanians; and 10,000 Greeks and Macedonians. Since then the number of Jews has declined to an estimated 3,000 due the expulsions and 'encouraged emigrations' after 1968. Similarly after 1970 a great many Germans took advantage of the opportunities to emigrate to West Germany.
5. The active number of churchgoers is difficult to estimate on the basis of available evidence but a study conducted by Adam Podgórecki shows that in 1964 81 per cent of the urban and 90.1 per cent of the rural population defined themselves as believers. Subsequent research carried out in 1966 (based, as was the previous study on a representative sample of the adult population) shows that 72.5 per cent of the urban and 82.8 per cent of the rural population claim to be believers. On the other hand research carried out in 1971 dealing with what might be called the middle-level intelligentsia (young people undergoing occupational training in institutions of further education, teachers and local government employees—a total of 1,115 people) shows that 64 per cent of those investigated defined themselves as believers. See Adam Podgórecki, 'The global analysis of Polish Society (a sociological point of view: the problem)', *Polish Sociological Bulletin*, no. 4 (1976) p. 25.

According to official Church sources the average percentage of Roman Catholics in Poland is 93.3. The lowest are in the dioceses of Drohiczyn, 78.1 per cent; Lublin, 87.2 per cent; Łódź, 88.2 per cent and Warsaw 88.7 per cent. The highest are in the dioceses of Lubaczów, 99.1 per cent; Łomża, 98.3 per cent and Gniezno 98.3 per cent. See *Kościół katolicki w Polsce, 1945-1978* (The Catholic Church in Poland, 1945-1978), Poznań-Warsaw, Pallotinum, 1979, p. 21.
6. Only limited statistical data on religious denominations has been published in Poland since the war, an impression of the Roman Catholic Church's strength may be ascertained from figures for 1976 in Table 1.

The first of the non-Catholic denominations was the Orthodox Church active in Poland as early as the fourteenth century. Lutheranism and Calvinism

INTRODUCTION

Table 1. Religious denominations

Churches and religious denominations	Parishes, congregations, etc.	Churches, chapels, prayer houses	Priests, ministers
Roman Catholic	6,716	14,039	19,456
Polish Orthodox	223	301	216
United Evangelical	207	65	206
Polish Baptists	127	53	60
Seventh Day Adventists	124	126	66
Augsburg-Evangelical	122	356	100
Jehovah's Witnesses	108	18	305
'Epiphany' Movement	80	146	405
Other national Christian sects	149	169	180
Other international Christian sects	146	80	84
Jewish	16	24	–
Muhammadan	6	2	6

Source: *Rocznik Statystyczny – 1977*, Główny Urząd Statystyczny, Warsaw: 1977, p. 23.

appeared in the sixteenth century and the nineteenth and twentieth centuries brought in the Protestant freedom movements as well as Methodists, Mariavites, the Polish National Catholic Church and others. Table 2 illustrates the strength of denominations belonging to the Polish Ecumenical Council.

On 18 October 1978 the official Polish Press Agency released the set of figures on the Roman Catholic Church in Poland shown in Tables 3, 4 and 5. In addition there are two Catholic institutions of tertiary education; the Catholic University of Lublin and the Academy of Catholic Theology in Warsaw. During the academic year 1978–9 the Catholic University of Lublin employed 267 teaching staff and was attended by 2,309 students (1,372 lay students and 937 priests and nuns). During the same academic year the Academy of Catholic Theology employed 106 staff and was attended by 870 students (522 lay students and 348 priests and nuns).

7. It is interesting to note that mass migration of the peasant population to towns has taken place in Poland since 1945. It is estimated that 20 per cent of the inhabitants of Warsaw were born in the countryside, and in Wrocław no less than 40 per cent. In other towns in the Recovered Territories and new towns like Nowa Huta the proportion is even higher. Polish sociologists refer to this phenomenon as the 'ruralization of the towns' or the 'ruralization of the working class', because the bulk of the migrants from the countryside became workers. A survey conducted in 1970 showed that 63 per cent of the blue-collar workers and 37 per cent of white-collar workers who had taken up residence in towns in the preceding decade, had come from the rural areas. For an overview of the social changes of Polish society between 1945 and 1970 see R. F. Leslie (ed.), *History of Poland since 1863*, Cambridge, Cambridge University Press, 1980, pp. 444–57.

INTRODUCTION

Table 2. Members of the Polish Ecumenical Council

Denomination	Bishops	Clergy	Believers	Dioceses	Parishes
Polish Autocephalous Orthodox Church	6	320	500,000		230
Polish Catholic Church	7	120	33,000	3	86
Old Catholic Mariavite Church	3	25	25,000	3	41
Evangelical-Augsburg Church		107	80,000	6	122
Evangelical Reformed Church		5	5,000	5*	9
Methodist Church		38	4,100		63†
Polish Church of Baptist Christians		64	7,000	7*	57†
United Evangelical Church		247	13,900		114

Source: Press Office of the Secretariat of the Polish Episcopate, 1979.

*Districts
†Communities or Congregations

Table 3. Parishes and buildings

Parishes	8,316
Monastic parishes	420
Ecclesiastical buildings	14,039

Table 4. Clergy and nuns

Clergymen	15,095	Nuns	27,646
Monks	4,790	Female orders and convents	101
Monastic orders and male congregations	42	Nunneries	2,487
Monasteries	553		

Table 5. Educational establishments

	Diocesan seminaries	Number of students	Monastic seminaries	Number of students
Senior	24	3,607	20	1,451
Junior	2	130	9	432
Total	26	3,737	29	1,883

1 Church-State Relations 1944-1970: Conflicts and Co-existence

During the Second World War the Church shared the fate of the nation and the trials of occupation. The clergy joined the resistance movement. Four bishops and no less than 3,000 priests, almost a third of the Polish clergy, lost their lives; some perished in German concentration camps. When the war ended the Soviet-installed Communist regime set out to break what it saw as a formidable opponent of its doctrine. The regime concentrated on three principal areas: breaking the Church's relations with Rome; undermining the homogeneity of its clerical structures and lay organizations; and the speedy secularization of Polish society.

When the Polish Committee for National Liberation formed the first Government under the leadership of the Polish Workers' Party,[1] on 22 July 1944 in Chełm, it guaranteed, among other things, in its statement known as the Lublin Manifesto, freedom of conscience and respect for the rights of the Church.[2] The decree on land reform of 6 September 1944, which expropriated all estates in excess of 124 acres, excluded some 450,000 acres of land belonging to the Church. But as early as 12 September 1945, the Government of National Unity terminated the Concordat of 1925.[3] This abolished some outdated privileges of the Catholic Church, and since then the relationship between Church and State has remained basically unregulated.

The Leninist claim to power demanded the Party's right to the monopoly of organization within the society, with the elimination of all independent and rival social groups as a prerequisite. The mission of the Catholic Church, and the manner in which it pursued that mission, which was accepted by the overwhelming majority of the population, stood in the way of this totalitarian pretension.

According to Vatican sources,[4] the ultimate aim of the Communist religious policy was to create in Poland a schismatic national church which, separated from Rome, was to submit more easily to political controls. It should be remembered that external circumstances provided a conducive atmosphere for the Communist anti-Vatican offensive. The Cold War, in full operation at that time, strongly accentuated the division of Europe and this had severe repercussions on communications between the Church in Poland and Rome.

However, it appears that the Vatican was prepared for such an eventuality. Already in 1945, Pope Pius XII invested the Primate of Poland, Cardinal August Hlond, who was returning to Warsaw from his exile during the war, with special prerogatives which entitled him to exercise extensive powers should the Polish Church become isolated from Rome. Although the text of the document was never published, it is reasonable to assume that it did not preclude negotiations and agreements with the regime.

On his return to Poland in July 1945 Cardinal Hlond stated that:

> Catholics expect that the new government will reflect Christian ideas, the genius of the Polish nation and the national aspirations. After centuries of pain Catholics are anxious to feel in the new Poland the masters of their own destiny without sadness and divided consciences. Christian Poland will be the love and pride of its citizens.[5]

In order to have a direct political input into the new political situation the Church attempted to re-create the pre-war Catholic Workers' Party as a political party that would represent the vast majority of Catholics. However, after several months of negotiations and political wrangling the idea was formally dropped in December 1946.

In the immediate post-war period the Communist regime's attitude to the Catholic Church was that the co-existence of Catholicism and Marxism in Poland was not only feasible but even highly desirable, provided Catholics supported the Communists in their endeavours to build the new Poland. It was argued that both sides could profit from each other's experience. An open debate on the controversial aspects of Church–State relations ensued in the official mass media.[6] The Party made numerous gestures designed to appease the Church: worship was freed from interference, Communist dignitaries attended public religious ceremonies, numerous church buildings were reconstructed with State assistance, and even the army was ordered to assist Corpus Christi processions.

CHURCH-STATE RELATIONS 1944-1970

During this period two lay Catholic groups, one centered in Kraków and the other in Warsaw, attempted to see their way through the new, complicated situation. They represented two tendencies within Polish Catholicism, which have dominated the scene until the present. One, closely related to the Episcopate, tried to reflect the semi-official social and political views of the Church authorities *vis-à-vis* the regime. The other, more accommodating and more opportunist, was consistently used by the regime for its own purposes.

The first, the Kraków group, originated in the immediate post-war years when two Catholic periodicals were launched there with the support of the Cardinal of Kraków, Adam Sapieha. One was a popular weekly *Tygodnik Powszechny* (Universal Weekly), the other a more intellectual monthly *Znak* (The Sign). Co-operating with one another, these two periodicals provided a rallying point for Catholic intellectuals. Originally the people who joined the group shared no uniform political views, representing to a certain extent conflicting political traditions. However, after some years of exhausting debate, the differences lessened and gradually a closely-knit group of Catholic laymen with a similar political outlook emerged.

Political realism dominated their actions and outlook. Seeing no imminent changes in the political situation, they attempted to create a forum for the expression of Polish Catholic opinion in a Communist Party state. Their primary attention at first centered on religious rather than social or political problems. Yet, in the same way as any group coming into the open in post-war Poland, they had to endorse the existing political system. They did this in a somewhat reticent way by declaring to seek some *modus vivendi* with the Marxists on the basis of 'exchanging unbiased opinions'. At the same time, however, they reaffirmed their determination to derive solutions to essential problems in individual and social life from the Catholic Dogma.[7]

Throughout the years 1946-55 they remained faithful to these principles. In the post-war years of struggle between the Communists and anti-Communists they refrained from taking one side or the other. In the subsequent years of Stalinist repression they declined to soften their stand towards Communism and, in spite of persecutions, clung to their beliefs. This led to outright suppression in 1949 when *Znak* was closed down.[8]

The Warsaw group known as Pax centred on a weekly, *Dziś i Jutro*, and was a closely-knit political group. Most of its leaders came from the pre-war 'national radical' organization known as 'Falanga',[9] which originated in the 1930s as a splinter group of the extreme right-wing of the National Democratic Party. Led by the ambitious Bolesław Piasecki,[10] this group sided with the State in the ongoing Church-State dispute. At every stage of the prolonged struggle whether it was the restrictions of the Episcopate's charitable activities, the confiscation of Church property, the removal of religious instruction from schools, or the campaign of intimidation against the clergy, this group of so-called progressive Catholics supported the regime and denounced the hierarchy. At the same time they kept loudly affirming their allegiance to the Church. By the early 1950s, when the persecution of the Church reached its climax, Pax, in contrast, enjoyed the most prosperous period of its existence.

Cardinal August Hlond died in 1948 and his successor as the Archbishop of Gniezo and Warsaw and Primate of Poland was the 47-year-old Bishop of Lublin, Stefan Wyszyński.[11] It must be assumed that the special powers vested by Pius XII in Cardinal Hlond were now transferred to Wyszyński, who was faced with increasingly deteriorating Church-State relations.

By 1948 the monopoly of power in the hands of the Polish Workers' Party, which after the merger in December of that year with the Polish Socialist Party was renamed the Polish United Workers' Party, became almost complete. By that time also Catholic printers had been placed under State control and Catholic books, periodicals and newspapers had been prohibited in public libraries. The regime restricted the activities of the Church to religious areas only.

The issue that had led to further deterioration of Church-State relations was that of Church administration of the Recovered Territories in western Poland, which had formerly become part of Poland under the Potsdam Agreement of 2 August 1945. The failure of the Vatican to recognize the Polish hierarchy in the Western Provinces, gave the regime new incentives for attacks against the Vatican and the Catholic hierarchy. Although Cardinal Hlond and Archbishop Wyszyński had always stated that the former German lands formed an integral part of Poland, and therefore also Polish Church administration, the Vatican refused to appoint regular diocesan bishops there before the final signing of a peace treaty.[12]

CHURCH-STATE RELATIONS 1944-1970

One other event contributed to the deterioration of an increasingly difficult and complex situation. On 13 July 1949 the Vatican excommunicated those Catholics in Poland who belonged to the Communist Party. The Warsaw regime denounced the decree, calling it an 'act of aggression against the Polish State'.

On 5 August 1949 the Government passed a law providing prison sentences of up to five years for anyone refusing the sacraments to citizens because of political or scientific opinions or activities. Moreover, all religious orders and associations were to register within three months, and religious processions were made dependent on government permit. The Catholic hierarchy instructed the heads of religious orders not to comply with the law and tried in vain to settle the matter with the Government. The three-months' deadline passed, with the orders failing to register.

The regime's policy was tightened through the censorship of Church publications; disbanding of the Church youth associations; the seizure on 23 January 1950 of the Church's largest welfare institution, Caritas; the suspension of Church radio broadcasts; and the nationalization of hospitals. Finally, on 6 March 1950 the greater part of Church land was expropriated.[13] The regime began the destruction of some of the most important connections between the Church and the nation.

At that time it looked as though the Church and State were heading for full head-on confrontation. Then suddenly on 16 April 1950 an official government communiqué announced that two days earlier on 14 April the regime and the Catholic hierarchy had signed an agreement on some of the contentious issues. The agreement, unprecedented in Eastern Europe, and the only one of its kind, has served as a model for Church-State relations in other 'people's democracies' and safeguarded the Church's position in Poland.

In the agreement both sides made far-reaching concessions. On the sensitive and important question of the Recovered Territories the Accord stated:

> The Polish Episcopate affirms that economic, historical, cultural and religious rights as well as historic justice enjoin that the Recovered Territories belong to Poland for all time. Taking the view that the Recovered Territories form an inseparable part of the Republic, the Episcopate will make representations to the

Apostolic See to have jurisdiction enjoying the rights of residentiary bishoprics reconstituted into permanent episcopal ordinaries.

The Episcopate will, within the limits of its powers, counteract activities hostile to Poland, especially the anti-Polish and revisionist actions of part of the German clergy.[14]

The Episcopate, the Accord stated, would be guided by the Polish *raison d'état*.[15]

Accepting the concept that the Church's mission can be implemented within various socio-economic structures established by secular authority, the Episcopate will explain to the clergy that it should not oppose the development of co-operatives in rural areas because all co-operatives are essentially based on the ethical concept of human nature.[16]

The hierarchy was to 'oppose the misuse of feelings for anti-State activity' and combat the operations of anti-government resistance groups, and punish all clergy guilty of such affiliation. In addition the bishops agreed to teach the faithful respect for State authority and State laws and to exhort the faithful to intensify their efforts in the reconstruction of Poland. The agreement most importantly acknowledged the Pope as the supreme authority of the Roman Catholic Church in Poland in matters of faith and ecclesiastical jurisdiction.

The Government on the other hand agreed to the continuation of the activities of the Catholic University in Lublin, and that Catholic associations would enjoy the same rights as they had before. The Catholic press and publications were to have the same privileges as others. Public worship was to be free from interference. Military authorities, after consultation with the Episcopate, were to draw up regulations governing the work of chaplains, and religious care in penal institutions and hospitals would be given to those who requested it. The Government also promised not to restrict the existing programme of religious education in schools. In carrying out its decree on the expropriation of Church land, the Government pledged that it would take into consideration the need of both clergy and ecclesiastical institutions. Finally, the Catholic welfare organization, Caritas, was to be re-established and recognized as the Association of Catholics.

CHURCH-STATE RELATIONS 1944-1970

The Accord was not a concordat but rather a *modus vivendi*, a technical instrument. The motives that induced the Polish bishops to seek such an agreement may be reduced to political realism or political opportunism. Nevertheless, the agreement proved beneficial to the Church. It also imbued the hierarchy, and especially Archbishop Wyszyński, with a sense of their own independence in coping with domestic problems, including Church-State relations. Although the Church had compromised on certain important points, most importantly it had preserved its doctrinal independence.

The agreement did not, however, prevent further deterioration in the Church's position. On 23 October 1950, soon after the signing of a protocol with the German Democratic Republic recognizing the Oder-Neisse line as the inviolable and permanent border between Poland and the GDR, the Polish Government sent an ultimatum to the hierarchy demanding abolition of the provisional ecclesiastical administration in the Recovered Territories. The Government decree that followed, on 26 January 1951, provided for the liquidation of the provisional status of Church administration, along with the apostolic administration there, and for the removal of priests who were acting as apostolic administrators. The regime proceeded with the election of its own administrators, the Capitular Vicars, and the appointment of parish priests as permanent managers of their parishes. On 18 February 1951, the Polish Primate simply granted canonical jurisdiction to the elected Vicars.

During the 1952 elections to the Polish Parliament, the first elections since the end of the war, the bishops urged the faithful to fulfil their civic duties. Also although suggesting amendments, they took a positive attitude towards the preparation of a new constitution of the Polish People's Republic.

In spite of the Episcopate's conciliatory efforts, a violent offensive against the Church was launched at the end of 1952. On 9 February 1953, a decree was issued by the Council of State on the occupation of Church administrative offices, by which the authority of Rome was subordinated to the State, thus limiting the formal powers of the Pope in matters of Church jurisdiction. The decree made it obligatory to swear allegiance to People's Poland and gave the regime the right to remove clergy from their posts. This proved to be a useful pretext for the government to replace bishops and priests with the so-called 'patriotic priests', with the intention of establishing a national church independent of Rome. The principle of separation between State and Church, proclaimed in the April 1950 agreement and the Constitution of 1952,[17] was now supplanted by State intervention in ecclesiastical affairs.

The forcible elimination of the Church from public life did not end even after Stalin's death on 5 March 1953. The repressive State apparatus did not initially undergo any political or structural alterations. It was a prisoner of its own dogmas. Any liberalization in Church-related policies during the uneasy battle for succession after Stalin's death could have been interpreted as a sign of the weakness of the Polish Communists. It is significant that after March 1953 the violent campaign against the Church reached its peak. Stalin's death revived rival factions within the Communist leadership and each turned against the Church in order to seek a scapegoat and preserve its position.

How critical the situation was for the Catholic Church was symbolized by the arrest on 25 September 1953, of Cardinal Stefan Wyszyński,[18] the Polish Primate, who was prohibited from performing his ecclesiastical functions. This action was taken on the basis of the February 1953 decree permitting removal of clergy who 'act against State interests'. The Cardinal was officially accused of failing to fulfil the 1950 Church-State Accord and interned in four remote monasteries. By the end of the same year eight bishops and 900 priests were in prison.[19]

Further administrative measures threatened the continuation of the Church's mission: some of the seminaries for priests and the holy orders were dissolved; pressure on the Catholic University of Lublin was stepped up; Catholic faculties of Polish Universities were dissolved at the beginning of the winter semester 1954-5; religious instruction in schools was forbidden in January 1955.

In addition to this there was an attempt to weaken the Catholic Church from within. 'Patriotic priests' acceptable to the State were placed in key positions within the Church. The authorities gave particularly strong support to the Pax movement, which benefited both financially and politically during the closing stages of the Stalinist period in Poland.

Stalinism in Poland began to crumble after the workers' first revolt in Poznań in June 1956. The protesters who marched on the provincial headquarters of the Communist Party shouted 'We want God and bread'. The formerly disgraced and humiliated Władysław Gomułka was brought back on 21 October from internal political exile to lead the divided and deeply demoralized Polish United Workers' Party. In the explosive internal and international situation, when Russian tanks were rolling across Poland, the new leadership turned to the Church for support. Cardinal Wyszyński was released from house arrest on 28 October and brought back to Warsaw in triumph. The following day he addressed a crowd gathered in the courtyard of the Primate's Palace and appealed for calm and caution saying: 'Our motherland demands now from you much calm, much caution, and many, many prayers'. However, a week later in his first sermon after release he stated the Church's expectations from the faithful more explicitly.

> Poles know how to die magnificently . . . But, beloved Poles also need to know how to work magnificently. A man dies but once and is quickly covered in glory. But through work he gives long years in trouble, hardship, pain and suffering. This is a greater heroism.[20]

In exchange for support from the Catholic hierarchy the Government agreed to give the Church certain privileges. A new agreement between the Government and the Episcopate was concluded in 7 December 1956 The communiqué issued after the signing of the agreement summarized Church-State relations as follows:

> The Joint Commission of representatives of the Government and the Episcopate discussed a number of unresolved questions concerning relations between the State and the Church. In the course of the conversations, the representatives of the Government emphasized their readiness to remove the remaining obstacles to the realization of the principle of full freedom for religious life.

> The representatives of the Episcopate stated that as a result of changes in public life aimed at the consolidation of legality, justice, peaceful co-existence, the raising of social morality and the righting of wrongs, the Government and the authorities would find in the Church hierarchy and clergy full understanding for these aims.

The representatives of the Episcopate expressed full support for the work undertaken by the Government aiming at the strengthening and development of People's Poland, at concentrating the efforts of citizens in harmonious work for the good of the country, for the conscientious observance of the laws of People's Poland and for the implementation by the citizens of their responsibilities towards the State.

The agreement abolished the decree of 9 February 1953 and reinstated the Church's jurisdiction over its own affairs including the exclusive right to establish dioceses and parishes as well as to alter their jurisdiction according to the Church's internal rules. Those acts merely required prior consultations between appropriate Church and State agencies. Furthermore, the agreement also confirmed the Church's traditional prerogative derived from Canon law, to select its bishops and priests providing that those appointments did not encounter 'justified objections' from the State against individual candidates. All officially accepted appointees had to pledge loyalty to the State.[21] Two Catholic periodicals *Tygodnik Powszechny* and *Znak* were revived and five members of their editorial boards were put up as the official Catholic candidates in the forthcoming elections to the Parliament. Thus for the first time the Catholic laity was accorded a certain degree of political influence in internal affairs. In return, the hierarchy threw its support behind the parliamentary candidates of the Polish United Workers' Party. Monks and nuns were allowed to return to their monasteries and the Capitular Vicars who were appointed by the State on its own authority in the Recovered Territories in 1951 were removed from their posts.

Although the improved Church-State relations lasted only a few months and some of the concessions made to the Church were withdrawn once the political crisis passed, the 1956 precedent became a pattern. In all subsequent crises the Church would give the regime support and in return regain certain privileges lost during the 1945-56 period; thus gradually edging its way to the pre-1939 situation of genuine political influence.

On 14 January 1957, a week before the parliamentary elections, Cardinal Wyszyński met Prime Minister Józef Cyrankiewicz to discuss Church-State relations. This, the first meeting on the highest level for more than three years, began a new pattern of direct consultations between the heads of government and the Catholic hierarchy at times of acute political crisis. From then on this pattern has remained a regular feature of Polish politics. The exact content of the Wyszyński-Cyrankiewicz meeting is not known. But the Primate must have felt satisfied with its outcome. Within hours of the meeting the Episcopate issued a statement appealing to Catholics to 'fulfil their duty of conscience and participate' in the forthcoming elections to Parliament. In this way the Church expressed unequivocal support for the authorities. In terms of legitimizing the Gomułka regime through the elections to Parliament, which until then was for most Poles merely a rubber stamp for the Communist Party decisions, the Church's support was crucial.

From then on the relationship between the Roman Catholic hierarchy and the leadership of the ruling Polish United Workers' Party changed from that of dangerous enemies fighting an everlasting battle for the control of Polish souls, to that of indispensable allies. Although in the ensuing decades the battle and wasteful squabblings would continue, neither side would overstep the unwritten rules of the game. The realization that if the Church pushed too hard and destabilized the balance the Communist regime would be restored by outside Soviet or joint Warsaw Pact intervention; or that if the regime undermined the Church's political position too far, the hierarchy might call on 'the Pope's divisions', resulted in a peculiar check-mate truce. Though both sides from then on would have their little victories, they realized that neither could win an outright one. And both would explain to their respective constituencies that this was in the interest of Poland; the faithful and non-believers alike. The withdrawal by either side of their essentially contractual consent would destroy both.

In the January 1957 elections five prominent lay Catholics from the hierarchy-supported *Tygodnik Powszechny* and *Znak* were elected to Parliament. In the Sejm they were joined by four other deputies who had been elected as non-party candidates. Together they formed their own parliamentary caucus known as the Znak Circle,[22] and one of the deputies, Jerzy Zawieyski, for the first time in People's Poland was appointed a member of the Council of State—the collective presidency.

At the same time, an important outlet for broader participation by lay Catholics in political life was the establishment in Warsaw, and later in several other cities, of the Clubs of Catholic Intelligentsia. Although, formally, each club was independent they nevertheless co-operated closely with each other. The main objective of these clubs was to create a forum for discussion of topics ranging from religion and philosophy to social and political problems. As such the clubs provided a meeting ground for Catholics who held different political opinions ranging from the former members of the pre-war Catholic Labour Party to the supporters of *Tygodnik Powszechny*. The clubs provided a fairly effective link between the Znak parliamentary caucus and the more vocal representatives of Polish Catholicism.

In May 1957 Władysław Gomułka declared that he saw a necessity for the coexistence of believers and non-believers, Church and socialism, and the Catholic hierarchy and people's power. The Church made use of the improvement in its position to once more gain access to the State-controlled mass media.

All these were lasting gains for Poland, the Church and the regime of patriotic co-operation in the months following the national crisis in 1956. But the relaxed relations between State and Church did not last for long. After a period of relative weakening of Communist Party domination, the bureaucratic reaction of the authorities and the Party to the Catholic challenge set in. The monastery of Jasna Góra at Częstochowa, the most sacred shrine of Polish Catholicism, was raided by the police in 1959 in search of illegal publishing equipment and there were scuffles between the police and pilgrims.

During the preparations for the elections to the Sejm on 16 April 1961, the regime declared that Polish atheism had to fight with the Catholic hierarchy for control over the souls of the whole nation.[23] By 15 July of the same year, religious instruction in schools had already been eliminated by the new School Law. In response to this, the Church constructed a fine network of so-called cathechetic points, which contributed substantially to a raising of the *niveau* of catechism over the last twenty years, and strengthened the link between Church and nation again. The abolition of religious instruction therefore had precisely the opposite to the desired effect.[24] It not only increased the determination of Catholics to defend their educational role but also stimulated further the process of development of the Church as an autonomous organization within the society.

CHURCH-STATE RELATIONS 1944-1970

The State refused to license many projects for new churches,[25] and one such refusal touched off a violent riot on 27 April 1960 in Nowa Huta, the socialist model town built in 1950s and centred on the giant Lenin steel works, with a population of 200,000 and not a single church.[26]

The two most bitter confrontations in the mid-1960s centred on the celebrations of the millenium of Christianity and statehood. While the Church's emphasis was on the thousand years of Christianity in Poland, the regime underlined the secular aspect of the same occasion and emphasized the thousand years of Polish statehood. Since the founding of the state and the coming of Christianity occurred together in Poland in 966, the separation of the foundation of the state from the so-called baptism of Poland by the regime was just as artificial as was the undervaluation of the Polish Christian tradition, Polish character and sense of national identity, as both clearly bear the stamp of Christian culture in the official histories of Poland.

The Church began preparing for the celebrations in 1957 in the form of a Novena, an idea conceived and planned by Cardinal Wyszyński during his internment. The preparations were extensive and involved an elaborate programme of prayers, thematic sermons, liturgical celebrations and a visitation in some parishes by a copy of the icon of the Black Madonna of Częstochowa. The picture was brought in procession through a town or village to the parish church and worshipped there for a day before being transported to the next destination. The visitation of the icon was always a festive occasion for the local faithful. The expressions of religious fervour and the periodic mobilization of the population became a major irritant for local and central Communist authorities. The icon was scheduled to travel across the country from parish to parish but was confiscated several times by the security police while on route,[27] which resulted in confrontations at local as well as at central level between, on the one hand, the clergy and faithful and the police and Communist officials on the other.

Another crisis came in November 1965, when in preparation for the millenium celebrations, the Polish Episcopate sent a letter to the West German bishops in which they suggested mutual forgiveness for the wrongs each nation had inflicted on the other. The letter was a simple offer of Christian reconciliation between the two traditionally antagonistic nations. It offered pardon for the atrocities inflicted by the Germans

21

on Poles throughout Polish history and particularly during the Second World War. In return the Polish bishops asked for forgiveness for the forced eviction of some three million Germans who used to live on the Recovered Territories which became part of Poland in 1945. For a while Catholic opinion in Poland was shaken by the bishops' letter. Hatred of the Germans for their atrocities during the 1939-44 occupation was still intense in Poland and a great many people could not agree that the removal of the German population from lands regarded as historically Polish could somehow be equated with five years of genocide which the Germans had imposed upon Poland.

Gomułka pounced on the chance. A furious propaganda campaign was launched against the Polish bishops' letter. The bishops were presented as a group unreliable towards the nation and even as traitors to the Polish *raison d'état*. The situation was made additionally difficult for the Polish Episcopate because it had to wait in vain for an equally generous gesture of reconciliation from the German bishops.

Cardinal Wyszyński was denied a passport and Pope Paul VI, who had intended to travel to Poland for the millenium celebrations was refused an invitation. Gomułka's campaign, however, misfired. As soon as the party attacked the Episcopate, Catholic opinion swung strongly back to the Church's side. The central celebrations of the millenium which were held on 26 August 1966 at Jasna Góra in Częstochowa became an impressive manifestation of popular backing for the Church. Over a million people from all over the country converged on Jasna Góra on that day. The original icon of the miraculous Black Madonna was for the first time in centuries removed from its chapel and paraded among the crowd and later placed on a platform where open air liturgical ceremonies took place. Beneath was an empty seat with a bouquet of red and white carnations—a symbol and a tribute to the absent Pope. Relations between Church and State remained tense for the next two years, even to the point where the meetings of the joint Episcopal-Government Commission, held at regular intervals since July 1949, were now abandoned.

One other issue that had begun to complicate Church-State relations in Poland in the 1960s was the emergence of Vatican Ostpolitik which in practice compromised the interests of the Polish hierarchy in its dealings with the authorities. Even during the reign of Pius XII there had been a strong current of opinion in the Vatican's Secretariat of

State that the possibility of establishing a *modus vivendi* with the Communist regimes should be explored. Vatican policy towards Eastern Europe and the Soviet Union changed dramatically, however, with the accession of John XXIII. In February 1963 the Soviet government released from detention the head of the Ukrainian Uniate Church, Archbishop Josyf Slipyi.[28] The following month Krushchev's son-in-law Alexei Adzhubei and his wife visited the Pope. The encyclical *Pacem in Terris*, issued by Pope John XXIII in April, which had laid the foundations for dialogue and co-operation between Catholics and Communists, was very positively received by the Soviet and Eastern European regimes. This trend was further strengthened by Pope Paul VI's encyclical *Ecclesiam Suam* of August 1964. The agreement of 29 June 1966 on establishing diplomatic relations between the Vatican and Yugoslavia, which directly affected the Catholic Church's work in that country and in particular in the strongly nationalist Croatia, was the first far-reaching understanding between the two hitherto implacable opponents. But when the Pope desired to employ his Yugoslav gambit in Poland, he encountered strong opposition from Cardinal Wyszyński, who believed that the Church in Poland was strong despite or because of its opposition to the regime. His view was that direct Vatican initiatives could only lead to a deterioration in the painfully constructed precarious understanding.

The architect of the Vatican's Ostpolitik and its executor was Archbishop Agostino Casaroli—secretary of the Council for Public Affairs of the Church—special nuncio for contacts with the Communist regimes. Casaroli was particularly interested in establishing direct contacts between the Vatican and the Communist regimes in order to fill vacant bishoprics, thus rebuilding the crumbling formal structures of the Church in the Communist countries. For this he had to have the support of the respective regimes, and this inevitably meant accepting at times government nominees for Church posts, some of whom were 'patriotic priests'.

Understandably Cardinal Wyszyński was unsympathetic to Casaroli's ideas. In spite of this Casaroli travelled to Poland for the first time in February 1967.[29] His visit was followed by the Pope's conciliatory decision in May 1967 vesting four administrators of dioceses in the Recovered Territories with the authority of residential bishops under the direct authority of the Holy See. This paved the way for the final

CHURCH-STATE RELATIONS 1944-1970

recognition by the Vatican of the Western borders of Poland; something the Cardinal had been unsuccessful in pursuading the popes to do for two decades. He now realized that if the direct Warsaw-Vatican contacts continued to be so successful he might become merely a passive observer. This forced him to seek another round of *modus vivendi* with the regime. The opportunities arose after the next workers' revolt in December 1970, which forced Gomułka's resignation and began the Gierek era in Polish politics that was to last a decade.

Notes

1. The Polish Workers' Party founded in 1942 in occupied Warsaw was a successor of the Communist Party of Poland liquidated by Stalin in 1938.
2. Manifest Polskiego Komitetu Wyzwolenia Narodowego, in Norbert Kołomiejczyk and Bronisław Syzdek, *Polska w latach 1944-1949*, Warsaw, Państowowe Zakłady Wydawnictw Szkolnych, 1971, pp. 289-93.
3. The Concordat of 1925 had established a general framework of Church-State relations on an essentially threefold basis. First it provided for mutual recognition of the full sovereignty of both Poland and the Vatican in the international arena. This implied a definition of the Church's ecclesiastical units (dioceses) within the territory of the Polish state and furnished the basis for the establishment of diplomatic relations between Warsaw and the Holy See. Second, the Polish state explicitly accepted the autonomous character of the Church's internal organization, derived from traditional rules of Canon law, and pledged respect of and support for ecclesiastical jurisdiction in religious matters. At the same time the State was assured a large degree of influence over the selection of bishops by maintaining the right to veto individual candidates. Finally, the Church received a formal guarantee by the State for the free exercise of its religious and moral functions in society as well as for unhindered management over its economic and educational establishments. The decision by the Government of National Unity to renounce the Concordat cut the entire system of legal ties between the Church and State organizations.
4. Oskar Halecki, *Eugeniusz Pacelli, Papież Pokoju*, London, Hosianum, 1951, p. 229.
5. 'Kościół katolicki wobec zagadnień chwili', homily during the ceremonies of Christ the King in Poznan on 28 October 1945.
6. See for example 'Can There Be Co-operation Between Catholics and Marxists?' *Poland Today*, Warsaw, January 1947.
7. *Znak*, July 1946.
8. Similar was the fate of *Tygodnik Powszechny*. When in 1953 its editors refused to commemorate Stalin's death with an eulogy, the weekly was taken away from the group and handed over to the Warsaw group.
9. Falanga was strongly influenced by Italian fascism. Its programme was anti-liberal, anti-Communist and strongly anti-Semitic.
10. During the war Piasecki was one of the leaders of a small underground organization whose armed units fought German and Communist partisans

CHURCH-STATE RELATIONS 1944-1970

alike. He was captured by the Soviet security forces in 1944, but in spite of his past record re-emerged on the Polish political scene a year later, after agreeing to organize a Catholic splinter group which would co-operate with the regime.
11. Stefan Wyszyński was born in 1901 in the village of Zużela in the province of Białystok, the son of an impoverished nobleman working as a village schoolteacher. He studied at the Catholic University of Lublin and entered the priesthood at the age of 24. After ordination he became a curate at Włocławek Cathedral and later between 1931 and 1939 taught sociology at the Włocławek Theological Seminary. As the founder, in 1935, of the Catholic Workers' University and author of numerous studies dealing with social questions he became known as the 'worker priest'. During the Second World War he was forced to go into hiding and was active in the underground resistance movement against the Nazis. After the war he was appointed resident Bishop of Lublin where he served until 1948.
12. Ryszard Marek, *Kościół rzymsko-katolicki na ziemiach zachodnich i północnych*, Warsaw, Państwowe Wydawnictwo Naukowe, 1976, pp. 1-77.
13. This meant the application of the land reform of 1944 which appropriated all estates in excess of 124 acres.
14. *Poland Today*, May 1950. See also Jan Zaborowski, *The Catholic Church on the Odra and Nysa*, Warsaw, Novum, 1976, p. 38.
15. This meant the unquestioned acceptance of Poland's place within the Soviet sphere of influence and Soviet-Polish alliance as a dominant foreign policy factor.
16. Zaborowski, *The Catholic Church on the Odra and Nysa*, p. 38.
17. The Constitution of the Polish People's Republic, promulgated in 1952 and ammended in 1976, in paragraph 82.2 states the complete separation of Church and State. At the same time it guarantees (paragraphs 67.2; 81.1 and 82.1) freedom of belief and conscience. Many conflicts have stemmed from the adoption of these two related but inherently contradictory principles which left unresolved an important issue of the legal status of the Church. It should be remembered that the Constitution gives the State the exclusive right to rule on the legal and economic status of religious institutions and to control their activity in society. The State itself is defined as an explicitly atheistic organization dedicated to the propagation of socialist ideas and to the establishment of a society which would be immune to religious influences and free of religious beliefs. The intended effect of these measures has been to solidify the domination of the State over religious institutions to such an extent as to reduce them to relatively insignificant movements with constantly declining social appeal.
18. Archbishop Wyszyński was appointed Cardinal on 12 January 1953.
19. Between 26 September and 12 October 1953 Cardinal Wyszyński was held in Rywałd in northern-central Poland. For the next twelve months between 12 October and 6 October 1954 he was detained in Stoczki near Lidzbark Warmiński in north-western Poland. As a result of deteriorating health he was on 6 October 1954 moved to Prudnik Śląski in the south-west of the country, where he was detained until 27 October 1955. The fourth place of his detention was a convent, Komańcza, in south-eastern Poland where he was kept between 27 October 1955 and 28 October 1956. During the three years of his imprisonment Cardinal Wyszyński kept notes which

were published in 1982 under the title *Zapiski więzienne* (Prison Notes; Paris, Editions du Dialogue). The Notes, in addition to being a mine of detailed information, are also a remarkable document of contemporary history written by an even more remarkable man.
20. *Słowo Powszechne*, 5 November 1956.
21. On 31 December 1956 the Council of State passed a new decree on the staffing of Church positions, replacing the one of 9 February 1953. In the 1953 decree, the State acquired extensive influence over the personnel policies of the Church. For example, article 6 of the decree stated that, 'any social activity against the law and public order by a person holding a pastoral position in the Church, will lead to the dismissal of this person by the superior Church organ or by the request of the State organs'. This was changed in the new decree. Article 7 read: 'If an ecclesiastic engages in activity harmful to the State, the appropriate State organ will appeal to the superior Church authority to issue appropriate orders; and in case of inefficacy of such orders, the State may ask that the ecclesiastic be dismissed from his position'.
22. In the 1961 and subsequent elections the number of Znak deputies was reduced to five.
23. See for example the political and ideological preparations for the campaign for the Sejm elections at the Seventh Plenum of the Central Committee of the Polish United Workers' Party (20-1 January 1961) in *Nowe Drogi*, no. 2, 1961.
24. *Historia kościoła w Polsce*, vol. 2, part 2, Poznań-Warsaw, Pallotinum, 1979, p. 221.
25. The issue of an inadequate number of consecrated buildings has dominated Church-State relations since the late 1940s. Table 6 gives a detailed breakdown of the number of churches and chapels built between 1945 and 1979.
26. Nowa Huta, 'New Foundry', was built with a special purpose. Its location as a satellite of the historic city of Kraków was not motivated by economic consideration, such as the vicinity of iron ore, coal, or particularly cheap transport facilities. Rather it served a purely ideological purpose—to act as a counterweight to the old city's traditional conservative image. In November 1956, at first signs of ideological and political liberalization, the workers sent a delegation to Warsaw to request permission to build a church. The permission was granted, and in early 1957 a citizen's committee was established in Nowa Huta to supervise construction and raise the necessary funds. By March of that year a site had been allocated by the municipal planning authorities, and a 12 meter-high cross was erected to mark the location of the church. The construction plans initially agreed by the authorities were unexpectedly subjected to review, however, and in October 1959 the permit was formally withdrawn on the grounds that the site was needed for a school. The situation became explosive in the spring of 1960 when removal of the cross was ordered, and there was serious unrest in the city during which the People's Council office was set on fire. On 27 April an infuriated crowd stoned the police, who responded with tear gas and water cannon. But not even the massive arrest that followed prevented the population from sticking to their demands. The party secretary held responsible for the incidents was dismissed and the cross remained on the site— if only as a symbol, because a school was built where the church was to have

CHURCH-STATE RELATIONS 1944-1970

Table 6. Building of Churches*

Years	New churches†	Rebuilt churches	Enlarged churches	New chapels	Enlarged chapels
1945-50	59	551	–	–	–
1951-55	57	–	–	–	–
1956-60	94	177	–	–	–
1961-65	63	–	–	–	–
1966-70	37	143	–	–	–
1945-70	352‡	871	–	–	–
1971	17	–	4	1	–
1972	24	–	3	5	5
1973	26	–	6	6	2
1974	39	–	13	13	14
1975	12	–	17	10	3
1971-75	118	–	43	35	24
1976	14	–	22	9	6
1977	34	–	32	24	10
1978	20	–	53	33	12
Total	538	871	150	101	52

* As at 1 January 1979.
† Some churches still in the process of construction.
‡ Included in this figure are 17 churches in the diocese of Opole not included in data given for specific years, and 25 churches which are still under construction.

Source: Materiały Sekretariatu Episkopatu Polski. (Materials of Secretariat of Polish Episcopate).

stood. Years elapsed during which large crowds of believers gathered every Sunday to attend Mass celebrated in the open. These public manifestations of religious fervour ultimately became too much for the authorities, and in September 1965 they finally agreed to grant the long-sought building permit. Two years later, on 14 October 1967 the Archbishop of Kraków, Karol Wojtyła symbolically dug the first spadeful of earth for the foundations, and on 18 May 1969 he laid the cornerstone, which had been cut from Saint Peter's Basilica in Rome and donated by Pope Paul VI. The project was finally completed on 15 May 1977 when the church was consecrated by Cardinal Wojtyła.

27. After one such arrest on 26 June 1966, the copy was kept till September in Warsaw Cathedral. The clergy then attempted to move it to Katowice where it should have arrived on 4 September for a tour of the parishes of that see, but it was intercepted by the state authorities and redirected to Częstochowa. The picture resumed its journey after five years in August 1972.

28. The Ukranian Uniate Church was in 1946 forcibly incorporated into the Russian Orthodox Church. Although the Soviet authorities do not admit its existence the remnants of the Church operate clandestinely in the Ukraine even today.
29. It should be recalled that following Casaroli's first visit to Poland the Archbishop of Kraków Karol Wojtyła was awarded a cardinal's hat on 26 July 1967. There was a wide-spread assumption that he was chosen by both the Vatican and the Polish Government as a counter-balance to Wyszyński. In the following years he was clearly chief executor of the Vatican's policy of *rapprochement* with the Polish regime. After Casaroli's visit Cardinal Wojtyła became a member of four important Vatican congregations: for Eastern Churches; the Clergy; Catholic Education; and the Liturgy. He also became a consultant in the Council of Laity and a member of the secretariat of the Synod of Bishops. While Cardinal Wyszyński was allowed by the regime to visit only Rome, Wojtyła travelled extensively to Belgium, Switzerland, Luxembourg and West Germany in November 1970, the USA and Canada in September, October and November of 1969 and again in August 1976. In February 1973 he visited Australia, Papua New Guinea and New Zealand; and in June 1977 West Germany.

2 The Church and Dissent: 1970–1980

Poland entered the 1970s in a critical state. After fifteen years of inept management the economy was showing severe strains. The much needed reform of the economic system had been delayed so long that by 1970 drastic measures had to be introduced, inflicting severe hardships on the population. The Poles, however, after over two decades of extensive industrialization and limited consumption, were in no mood to accept further deprivations and instead demanded to have their sacrifices tangibly rewarded by an improved standard of living. After the disappointment of 1956 they now demanded actions rather than mere promises. The country was like a volcano that might erupt at any moment. The explosion came sooner than many people expected.

On 12 December 1970, in an extraordinarily insensitive move less than two weeks before Christmas, which is traditionally the most important religious as well as family holiday in Poland, the Gomułka regime announced sweeping increases in food and fuel prices without any corresponding increases in wages and salaries. The increases were approved by the Central Committee on 14 December. The workers in the Lenin Shipyard in Gdańsk went on strike in protest against the new prices and staged a demonstration in the city centre. The militia's attempt to disperse the protesters precipitated a violent clash. The crowd attacked eighteen buildings and set on fire the voivodship headquarters of the Party. The following day the disorders continued and spread to the neighbouring city of Gdynia. That day the authorities in Warsaw authorized the use of firearms by the police and the deployment of army units to quell the disorders. The army, equipped with tanks, went into action that night. Workers, who in response to appeals to go back to work arrived by commuter trains in the morning, found themselves confronted with firing squads.[1] The first victims were three workers from the Lenin Shipyard, as they came out of the main gates. Enraged workers then marched to the city centre and there was more shooting and before the day was over the hospitals on the Baltic coast were crowded with the injured. According to official figures 28 people died, 1,200 were wounded and 3,000 arrested.[2] On 16 December the disturbances spread to Elbląg, and the following day violent demonstrations broke out in Sopot, Gdynia, Słupsk and Szczecin where, again according to official figures, 17 people were killed. Although the army had restored order in the coastal cities by midnight on 18 December, the situation was not wholly under control. The ruthless use of force and Gomułka's blank refusal of any dialogue with the strikers, whom he considered 'counter-revolutionary', had enraged workers in Warsaw and other industrial cities.

The unexpected climax of the workers' protest was the ousting on 19 December of Gomułka and his replacement as the First Secretary of the PUWP by the Silesian Party leader, Edward Gierek, who quickly admitted on 20 December that 'the working class was provoked beyond endurance' and that the Party had lost contact with the nation. He also appealed in the by then customary way, to the workers and to the whole nation, party and non-party members, believers and non-believers, to every citizen to take part in solving the important problems which faced the country. Echoing Gierek's reference to believers and non-believers, the Prime Minister Piotr Jaroszewicz promised in his first speech to the Sejm on 23 December that the Government would 'be aiming at full normalization of relations between the State and the Church, expecting at the same time that the efforts of the Government' would be met 'with proper understanding among the spiritual and lay Catholic centres'.

These appeals were promptly answered on 24 December by Cardinal Wyszyński in his Christmas Eve Sermon at Warsaw's St. John's Cathedral. After referring to the recent events, a tragedy, which in his words, was 'almost unique, unprecedented in our history' he appealed:

> We beg of you, do not accuse. Show understanding, forgive, feel compassion, put your hands to the plough so that there can be more bread in our Motherland, and justly distribute the slice of bread first of all to the children of the nation, working mothers and fathers, because they have the first right to this bread which grows on Polish soil.

The Primate said that if he could, he would take on himself responsibility for all that had happened.

THE CHURCH AND DISSENT: 1970-1980

Perhaps I have not cried out enough, I have not admonished enough, perhaps not warned and begged enough—although it is known that my voice was not always listened to and has not moved every conscience, not inspired each will, each thought.

There was also clearly a conciliatory, but dignified tone in the following passage:

> We bishops and priests in our free Motherland, for whose independence and prosperity we work, struggling on the sector assigned to us of spiritual renovation of the nation—we feel joint responsibility and we beg the families of those who were beaten to accept our confession and our plea for forgiveness.

The Cardinal implied that the joint responsibility and therefore co-operation extends beyond the clergy by saying:

> We are capable of, and we can afford, true democracy in Poland, because this has existed in the traditions of the Polish people since the times of the kings. We can afford to exact from our Christian spirit more active co-operation with the children of God in the whole nation.

But neither Cardinal Wyszyński's pleas nor the chance of leadership brought an end to the protests. After the Christmas break, continuous mass meetings and breaks in production, especially on the coast, showed that the workers were in the mood for more definite guarantees. It was only after 24 January, the day of a dramatic, unannounced personal appearance of Edward Gierek at the Warski Shipyard in Szczecin, during which he begged the workers to return to work, that slowly the workers began resuming normal work in Szczecin. The following day he went to Gdansk to plead at the Lenin Shipyard to persuade the workers to trust him. The prices question still festered, however, until the women of of the Łódź textile mills struck in mid-February. Only after that, with reports of still more unrest from other factories did the government back down and restore the old food prices.

For the Church the mass upheavals of December and January were to signal the necessity of much more direct involvement in the area of civil and human rights. The area was not one without difficulties.

Two parallel arguments could be advanced on this issue. Those opposed to direct engagement reasoned that the apostolic mission of the Church consisted in promoting the Kingdom of God which is not of this world. Others, in favour of involvement, stressed that there exists an inextricable connection between the spreading of the Gospel and an active pursuit of justice on earth. In taking a stand on the issue of human and civil rights, the Church remained on its own immemorial ground of Christianity, which always maintained that man enjoys certain inviolable and inalienable rights, not to be granted by a government to a community, but due to the fact that he is a human being. The Christian mission has by its very nature a political dimension, since the salvation it preaches encompasses the elimination of the socio-political causes of evil.

Whatever the rationale, the Polish Episcopate took a firm and decisive position in defence of the workers' rights. On 29 December 1970, the Main Council of the Episcopate issued a letter to 'All Compatriots of Our Common Motherland', which spoke about the recent events, shortly before Christmas, that 'painfully affected our country, especially the cities of the coast'.

> The recent events have made it amply apparent that the nation's right to existence and independence must include: the right to freedom of conscience and freedom of religious life, with full normalization of relations between the Church and the State; the right of our nation to free cultural activity, consistent with the spirit of the Christian principles of social co-operation; the right to social justice, expressing itself in the fulfilment of justified demands; the right to truth in social life, to truthful information, and to freedom of expression regarding opinions and demands; the right to material conditions that assure a dignified existence for every family and citizen; the right of citizens to be treated without abuse, unfair injury, or persecution. Both the central authorities and the entire state administration, and especially those charged with the maintenance of order in society, are responsible for the assurance of these rights. All citizens of the State are to share in this responsibility.

The letter went on to refer to the encyclical *Pacem in Terris* which was so favourably received by the Communist regimes, and which emphasized the respect of civil and human rights as a condition of peace in social life. The letter continued:

> The use of coercion does not contribute to the maintenance of peace in social life, especially when innocent men, or even women and children, are not spared. The life of the nation cannot develop in an atmosphere of fear; it must be led to peace in the spirit of justice and social love.

On 27 January 1971, when the country was still in a mist of uncertainty about the future direction of the workers' upheaval, the Episcopate issued another letter which was even more explicit in its condemnation of the old regime and in listing its expectations from the new one. Part of the letter read:

> In the painful December events, firearms were used imprudently. This had tragic consequences! The streets of the coast were stained with blood, and the whole nation suffered a profound shock . . . During the last years we have suffered a sea of troubles and humiliations. We have witnessed conceit and indifference to every free thought, to every postulate—even the most just—and to every presented demand. Our tragedy is a consequence of these humiliations suffered by the entire nation and society; they have also affected the Church in Poland.
>
> We can do much to promote the victory of good and reason, to introduce a reign of social justice and respect for man, and, as a consequence, to promote internal order and peace, which insures the existence and freedom of our Motherland. For where there is no social peace, independence is threatened! Only within the limits of peace, order, and internal freedom can we speak about the independence of the Motherland. The search for ways of introducing peace and order is everyone's responsibility.

The emphasis in both of these pronouncements on free cultural activity, freedom of information, freedom of expression, freedom from persecution, social justice and respect for man were not new for the Episcopate. This time, however, they were presented in stronger language than ever before and in the new context of a rising tide of increasingly well organized popular discontent. Also the Church's demands echoed substantially those of strike committees in many trouble spots in the country. Thus it appears that a new and direct bridge between those making the demands and those who could articulate, propagate and legitimize them at the highest level was now established. The tragic events of December created a nucleus for the link and subsequent structures between the Church and dissent which would dominate the next decade of Polish policies.

As in the past the new rulers of Poland in order to legitimize their rule needed the support of the Church hierarchy. On 3 March 1971, Cardinal Wyszyński met the Prime Minister, Piotr Jaroszewicz—the first such a meeting since 1960. After the meeting Jaroszewicz stressed the necessity of normalization of State-Church relations. As an outward sign of the change of policies, the Government in June 1971 returned ecclesiastical property in the former German territories to the Church. This property had, *de facto*, been operated by the Church since the end of the Second World War. On 22 February 1972 the regulations requiring the Church to keep a complete inventory of all its property were abolished. The possibility of a Papal visit to Poland which was vetoed by Gomułka in 1966 was once again discussed at the highest Church-State levels. The government also granted some thirty permits for the construction of new churches.[3] In another open gesture of accommodation the authorities helped to airlift some 1,500 Polish pilgrims to Rome for the beatification ceremonies in October 1971 of the martyr of Auschwitz, Father Maksymilian Kolbe.

At the same time Warsaw-Vatican talks re-started between Archbishop Casaroli and the head of the Office for Religious Denominations, Aleksander Skarzyński.[4] In a clear attempt to estrange the Curia in Warsaw, and Wyszyński in particular, from Rome in order to reach agreement over his head, the regime in Warsaw stated that it considered it necessary to 'conduct parallel talks with the Church hierarchy in Poland on the one hand and with the Vatican's Secretariat of State on the other'. These talks were conducted at a strictly governmental level and did not involve Church-State problems in Poland.

One direct and extremely important result of these talks was the Vatican's normalization of the status of the Polish Church's administration on the Recovered Territories. How much this was to be proof that direct Vatican-Warsaw talks may be more successful is a matter for conjecture, since Cardinal Wyszyński and the Polish Episcopate had always strongly argued for the Holy See's recognition of the

Western borders of Poland. On 28 June 1972, the Vatican, making its own contribution to *détente*, normalized the Church administration in the Western Provinces. This move followed the ratification on 3 June 1972 of the 1970 treaty between Poland and the Federal Republic of Germany. The decision involved both the appointment of resident bishops, who until then were only apostolic administrators[5] and the determination of diocesan boundaries to bring them into line with Poland's present frontiers. This also meant that for the first time since the end of the second World War the Vatican recognized *de facto* and *de jure* these territories as a part of Poland.

However, the Pope's decision did not speed up the expected full Vatican-Warsaw normalization. The Holy See was given to understand that any further progress must be preceeded by the liquidation of the embassy of the Polish government-in-exile at the Vatican. Indeed on 19 October 1972 the embassy of the 'Republic of Poland' was closed and the ambassador Kazimierz Papee lost his accreditation.[6] But even this did not improve matters and the talks dragged on intermittently for the next decade.

As the Vatican-Warsaw negoations continued a number of problems in Church-State relations remained unsolved. One of the most important issues became the great reluctance of the authorities to issue permission for the construction of new churches. Cardinal Wyszyński estimated that at least 1,000 new churches should be built in order to catch up with the movement of the population over the past twenty years.[7] The Church hierarchy was pressing continuously for new permits but without much success. The Government's reply has always been that there was a shortage of building material. Although in the first quarter of 1971 seventeen permits were granted this was an exceptional case immediately after the events of December 1970. Even when such permits had been granted the actual construction in any cases was held up by local party officials. As if the delays in the construction of new churches were not enough, on 22 March 1972 a provisional chapel in the village of Zbrosza Duża, thirty miles south of the capital was demolished by a group of some 150 militiamen and the tabernacle, containing consecrated hosts, was seized.[8] Similar actions by the authorities against unauthorized sacred buildings were taking place also in other parts of the country.[9] This issue later became one of the rallying points for the various Believers' Self-defence Committees.

THE CHURCH AND DISSENT: 1970-1980

Church-State relations began to deteriorate visibly in late 1972. In October 1972, in contravention of the 14 April 1950 Accord, seminary students were again beginning to be conscripted into the army.[10] In October the following year the Sejm passed a bill on the socialist education of school children. The school curriculum was to be organized so that the children would be detained at school in the afternoon. This meant that they would not be able to attend classes in religious instruction offered in churches. The educational system was now based on atheistic premises and the Church was completely excluded from it. It also meant that in practice, school education was against the system of upbringing of the Catholic family and consequently a serious violation of Catholic parents' rights.

The Church, though an institution deeply concerned with problems of education and upbringing and one which represents the views and wishes of millions of Catholic parents and pupils, was not regarded as a partner for discussion on this issue. Its objections to some of the measures could only be aired in pastoral letters drawn up at various episcopal conferences and subsequently read in churches. On several occasions the Episcopate attempted to express in the form of memoranda its point of view on the bill before it was submitted to the Sejm, especially with regard to the dangers it presented to religious instruction and the exclusion of any alternative ethical and moral views in education, which tended to reduce the Church's influence over young people.

Speaking even before the bill was read to the Sejm Cardinal Wyszyński charged in August 1973:

> We know that this is not a Polish invention, that it does not originate in the spirit of our people. Importations of this type can only harm the nation, and must, therefore, be distrusted.

The bishops emphasized that the education bill contravened civil rights of parents who were believers and who wanted to educate their children in the spirit of religious principles.

In a general feeling of frustration with the authorities people began to take into their own hands the organization of their religious life. Since 1972 a movement of religious renewal (to be known later as the Light and Life Movement) has developed and has organized summer camps for children, students and even parents. The movement, which totally contradicted the official state model of a Church 'confined within the four walls of the sacristy', became an object of systematic harrassments and persecution by the authorities.[11]

Another example of independent action from Catholics was the construction of churches without State permits. This movement was particularly strong in the diocese of Przemyśl where some hundred churches were built over the next seven years; the peasants while building them pretended they were constructing farm buildings. There were constant clashes with the police: whole areas were cordoned off and electricity and water supplies were cut off. Priests in Przemyśl diocese were heavily fined but their energetic bishop, Ignacy Tokarczuk, persistently encouraged them to defy the authorities and would himself often come at night to consecrate the newly-built churches.[12]

In March 1973 the hierarchy expressed its deep concern at the merger of the non-political organization, the Polish Students' Association, with the Socialist Youth Union and the Socialist Rural Youth Union into a monolithical organization, the Socialist Union of Polish Students, directly subordinate to the party. At the Catholic University of Lublin (KUL), the only independent university in Eastern Europe, students saw this move as an attempt to infiltrate an institution that had hitherto been free from internal government control. They decided to form their own representative body elected from every department. This move represented a major change in attitude on the part of the students, since until now any opposition to official ideology at the university had always been discreet. The KUL student organization was the first of the independent student unions that emerged in other Polish universities in subsequent years.

By 1974 the regime's ideological offensive was again operating fully but in spite of the increasing difficulties encountered by the Church in Poland the direct Warsaw-Vatican negotiations not only continued but intensified. The Polish Foreign Minister Stefan Olszowski held a meeting with Archbishop Agostino Casaroli during the Helsinki Conference on Security and Co-operation in Europe in June 1973. This was followed by Olszowski's visit to the Vatican in November that year, during which he was received by Pope Paul VI and later by the Vatican's Secretary of State Cardinal Villot. He also held talks with Archbishop Casaroli during which the papal visit to Poland in 1975 was discussed. Afterwards he said that his talks with Casaroli 'will lead to normalization of relations' between Poland

and the Vatican. As for a possible papal visit, Olszowski stated: 'I am convinced that a *modus vivendi* and a normalization of Church-State relations are obviously a pre-requisite for the Holy Father's visit to Poland'.

The pressure on Cardinal Wyszyński to conform was now obvious and it was coming from both sides of the negotiations in which he was not included. Wyszyński went to Rome at the end of November, where he stayed for three weeks. On his return to Warsaw he delivered three sermons over the Christmas period (24, 25 and 30 December 1973) in which he made his position clear. In the first place, the Primate stated, the problems between Church and State had to be settled within Poland before any permanent system of relations between the Holy See and the Polish government could be established. Before a concordat could be concluded, Poland's 'more than thirty million believers' had to be granted not only full religious freedom, but also a due role in the country's social, cultural and business life. This could not happen, he said, until a satisfactory solution had been found for at least the following problems.

1. In the first place, the Catholic Church must be free to educate the nation's youth 'in the spirit of the Gospel', and, the present attempts at forced laicization and atheization must be abandoned. 'The nation remains, the parties change', he emphasized.
2. The current discrimination against 'Catholic citizens' in public and professional life had to come to an end. 'We cannot be pariahs in the homeland for which we too work honestly', he said.
3. The centuries-old Catholic civilization in Poland must be given a 'wider margin'; Catholic writers and artists should have access to the information media, theatres, etc.; and an independent Catholic press should be established; Poland should not be a country for non-believers only.
4. The problem of the construction and repair of church buildings had to be settled satisfactorily.

These then were the four, hard hitting and clearly stated demands from the Primate in return for his support for Casaroli's designs for Warsaw-Vatican normalization. They in fact were not new, and had been mentioned by the Episcopate in various contexts before. But presented in such a forthright way by the head of the Polish Church they almost amounted to an open challenge. But perhaps the most interesting aspect of these sermons was that the demands were unquestionably political in nature and strongly emphasized the aspect of civil rights for Catholics in Poland in the social, professional, economic and political spheres.

Archbishop Casaroli arrived again in Warsaw on 4 February 1974, this time on the invitation of the Foreign Minister Stefan Olszowski. During the three days of the official part of his visit he was received by the Polish Prime Minister, Chairman of the Council of State and other ministers. The Polish Primate was conspicuously absent from the capital during the official part of Casaroli's visit. However, on the evening of 7 February from the pulpit of St. John's Cathedral in Warsaw, in the presence of Casaroli, he delivered a sermon in which he was more critical than ever of the Warsaw regime. When Casaroli was given the translation of the sermon, he was dumbfounded. He had hoped to bring the negotiations with Warsaw to a successful conclusion, but Wyszyński had virtually torpedoed any possibility of an agreement. The time had come to give the embattled Cardinal a serious warning. A few months earlier the Pope had sent into exile to Austria another stubborn Archbishop, the Hungarian Primate Cardinal Mindszenty. Wyszyński had to consider seriously the Pope's decision regarding Mindszenty. In October 1974 Paul VI summoned Wyszyński to Rome in order to persuade him to be more co-operative. The 'Iron Cardinal' with his vision of the Polish Church's role in Polish society and its commitment to it, constituted the last obstacle to an agreement between Warsaw and the Vatican. In order to avoid any surprises on the part of Wyszyński in Poland, it was decided that the talks between the Vatican and Warsaw should be conducted in Rome. Kazimierz Szablewski at the Polish Embassy to the Quirinale was appointed as deputy minister with an assignment to conduct the negotiations with the Holy See.[13]

Although Cardinal Wyszyński became isolated *vis-à-vis* the Vatican his standing and popularity among his bishops, clergy and faithful was increasing. Also by 1975 it was becoming increasingly apparent that the regime was clearly on a collision course not only with the Catholic hierarchy but also with intellectuals and workers. The former climate of guarded support and moderation had largely evaporated and the stakes were increasing on both sides. Cardinal Wyszyński and the hierarchy now also responded to the overwhelming current of dissent in the society.

The battle-ground became the proposed changes to the Polish Constitution, which were revealed to the Sejm on 19 December 1975. Three proposals in particular aroused concern; the Constitution was to confirm the historic fact that the Polish People's Republic is a socialist state in which the power belongs to the working people of the towns and villages and the leading force is the Polish United Workers' Party. The second proposal concerned the principle of Poland's foreign policy; its participation in a world socialist system and Poland's unshakeable fraternal bond with the Soviet Union. The third proposed amendment stipulated that citizens' rights be inseparably linked with honest fulfilment of their duties.

These proposals caused an avalanche of protests,[14] objections and petitions from intellectuals, students, artists, the Church hierarchy and the general public. This marked a turning point in the history of dissent in Poland and the beginning of its concerted action.

The Episcopate lodged two memoranda on 9 and 26 January 1976 with the authorities and various bishops summarized the Church's position in their sermons. It appears that these and other protests had made some impact. When the final version was approved on 10 February 1976[15] the controversial clauses had been toned down. The party's role was defined as that of a 'guiding political force in the construction of socialism'. The clause concerning foreign policy was amended to a statement that the Polish People's Republic 'strengthens its friendship and co-operation with the USSR and other socialist countries'. On citizens' rights the official version states that 'citizens of the Polish People's Republic should honestly fulfil their duties towards the Motherland and contribute to its development, but it no longer made civil rights a privilege dependent on such conduct'.

Nevertheless, responding to the growing current of dissent the hierarchy returned to the question of Constitutional amendments in an Explanatory Statement by the Secretariat of the Episcopal Conference regarding the proposed changes to the Constitution, issued in March 1976.[16] Referring to the position of the party as a leading organ in the State, they drew attention to the danger resulting from a division of citizens into two categories and subjecting the life of the nation to the materialistic outlook unacceptable to believers. Freedom of the Church —the Statement said—and individuals' freedom of conscience and of religious practice both public and private are the prerequisites for social harmony in the life of the nation and the State. 'The constitution should guarantee that the State be able to carry out its duties by means of the appropriate institutions of Parliament, Government, independent judiciary system and civil service, free trade unions; the Government must be aware of its obligations to all sections of the nation and fulfil them equitably and without hindrance. Parliament should be assembled by free elections and should be the guardian of all civil rights and duties'. Interestingly the statement also recalled the social and economic rights of private farmers 'who constitute an important section of society from the point of view of land cultivation and the provision of food'.

On the issue of foreign policy the bishops drew attention to the fact that the Constitution may not contain anything that could limit the sovereignty of the nation and of the Polish State. Recalling the principles of sovereign equality, inviolability of frontiers, and non-interference in internal affairs, which are contained in the UN Charter and confirmed at the Helsinki Conference, the bishops emphasized that the nation cannot be absorbed into any supranational or state body; and that the Constitution should emphasize the right of the nation and the State to preserve complete sovereignty in the domains of national culture and economic freedom.

Finally, the statement also stated: 'The State has a duty to respect and safeguard every Person-Man-Citizen. Indispensable civil rights may not be conditioned on the fulfilment of duties'.

Several bishops in their sermons joined in the popular barage against the beleaguered regime. Thus for example, Ignacy Tokarczuk, the bishop of Przemyśl in his sermon in Przemyśl Cathedral summed up Poland's situation in the following terms. Polish citizens, he said, had to live with lies, they were said to have elections but these only involved confirming candidates; they were said to be equal, but some people were more equal than others; despite official declarations about the normalization of Church-State relations, Polish Catholics could not build churches freely or publish freely, and believers were under pressure to give up their faith. There was in Poland state capitalism which was worse than capitalism. In Poland workers were not allowed to strike and employers controlled the unions and the courts, in short, everything.[17]

The uproar which the constitutional amendment evoked amongst a substantial section of the population[18] gave the Church an opportunity to present its first comprehensive statement on all the important issues of contemporary Polish society and the anxieties felt by people for many years and which had remained latent until the outburst of organized dissent brought them to the surface. The mention of free elections, the plight of farmers and pronouncements on foreign policy caged the Church into a position of a clearly identifiable political opposition force, being able to check the Party's performance openly. Behind the façade of the regime's polite words and the bishops' insistence that they were not undermining the political system by speaking vociferously and openly on the rights of citizens and the nation, the political and ideological conflict was intensifying. In May 1976 Kazimierz Kąkol the Minister for Religious Affairs summed up the Party's view in a speech to trusted Party activists:

> Even though as a Minister, I have to smile to gain the Church's confidence, as a Communist I will fight it unceasingly. I feel ashamed when comrades from other countries ask me why so many Poles go to Church, I feel ashamed when guests congratulate me on the spread of religion in Poland. Normalization of relations with the Church is not capitulation. We will not make any compromises with the Church. It has only the right to carry out its observance within the confines of the sanctuary. We will never allow it to evangelize outside those walls. We will never permit the religious upbringing of children. If we cannot destroy the Church, we shall at least stop it from causing harm.[19]

While the controversy aroused by the Constitutional amendments still continued, another spell of workers' riots broke out in June 1976, sparked by a new attempt to increase food prices.[20]

On 24 June the Prime Minister Piotr Jaroszewicz gave details of the price increases.[21] On the same day almost the entire labour force of the Ursus Tractor Plant on the outskirts of Warsaw went on strike. The protesters demanded consultations with the highest authorities and on being refused stopped a number of trains on a nearby railway line, in order to let as many people as possible know of their strike. In Radom, the Walter Metal Works went on strike and later ransacked and set on fire the voivodship Party headquarters. Stoppages and protests took place in Płock, Grudziądz, Łódź, Gdańsk, Nowy Targ,

Warsaw, Starachowice, Poznań and other centres. On the evening of 25 June Piotr Jaroszewicz reappeared on television to say that, in view of 'valuable amendments and contributions' put forward by the working class the price increases were being withdrawn until a later date. After his announcements, in almost all cases the strikes and protests stopped immediately. It was then that the militia and Security Services launched a campaign of indiscriminate reprisals. Several hundred of the protesters were summarily dismissed from work; over 2,000 arrested; several hundred sentenced to periods of detention and fines by Petty Offences Tribunals or courts. In Radom alone twenty-five people received longer sentences, up to ten years' imprisonment. Many of those detained especially in Ursus and Radom were beaten and systematically tortured by the militia, the Security Service and the prison wardens on a scale unprecedented since 1956. Some of the victims dispatched well-corroborated complaints to various state organs, most frequently to the office of the Public Prosecutor General or to Parliament. The first to rally in support of the workers were the intellectuals who on 26 June in a letter to the Sejm called for an authentic dialogue between the authorities and the people. Among the fourteen signatories to this letter were two priests.

The events of 25 June changed the complexion of Church–State relations. The gulf between the rulers and ruled became very apparent and the leadership was visibly insecure. Such an explosive situation could have resulted in further unrest, which might have been harmful to Poland's interests as a whole. Recognizing this situation, the line adopted by the Church hierarchy was at first one of prudent silence. On 16 July, however, Cardinal Wyszyński appealed to the authorities against harsh sentences and dismissals from work. But because of the sensitive nature of the affair this was not admitted until mid-August. A further evidence of the two-pronged approach to the price protest question was the Communiqué of the Plenary Session of the Episcopate held between 8-10 September.

The bishops called upon the people to 'increase efforts and solid work and even be ready to make sacrifices for the common good and to preserve the social order'. 'Solid work is a moral obligation and ability to make sacrifices a Christian virtue', the communiqué continued. 'It is only by a common effort that we can overcome the difficulties the country is facing'. To the Government, the bishops issued the following appeal: 'The Plenary Conference of the Episcopate asks the State authorities to cease its oppression of workers who took part in the anti-Government protests. Workers who participated in the protests should have their rights and their social and professional positions restored. They should receive compensation for their losses. Those sentenced should be given amnesty'.

The evenhandedness of this communiqué indicates the Episcopate's desire to calm the domestic situation and help both Party and people to find a way of resolving the nation's difficulties. It was also a masterful political stroke on the part of the Episcopate to make its first official call for amnesty and reinstatement in a hallowed plea for sacrifices from all sides for the good of the Polish nation.

Almost all national newspapers published the first part of the bishops' appeal—something almost unknown in People's Poland. This selective quote was intended to substantiate Gierek's claim made on 3 September that there were no tensions between Church and State. But the call for amnesty was left out of the media reports on the Conference, and this selectivity served to heighten rather than lessen the tensions the Party leader had denied. By late September Cardinal Wyszyński had begun contradicting Gierek's words in his sermons, demanding amnesty in unequivocal terms. On 27 September, he declared, 'It is painful when workers must struggle for their rights from a workers' government'.

On 23 September a group of fourteen intellectuals issued *An Appeal to the People and Government of Poland*.[22] The Appeal announced the formation of the Committee for the Defence of Workers (KOR) with the purpose of initiating all forms of defence and help for the imprisoned, dismissed and persecuted workers and their families. This included financial, legal and medical aid as well as dissemination of information concerning victimizations. The Appeal which was sent to the Sejm shortly before one of Cardinal Wyszyński's tough sermons also demanded complete amnesty for those imprisoned and reinstatement of workers dismissed after the June events 'concurring in this with the Resolution of the Conference of the Episcopate of Poland of 9 September 1976'. It also called upon people to support these persons by making financial contributions and providing information about the June events.[23]

Interestingly the KOR Appeal clearly supported the Episcopate's

THE CHURCH AND DISSENT: 1970-1980

Communiqué of 9 September. There was only one priest among the founding members of KOR—Father Jan Zieja, veteran of the Warsaw uprising and chaplain to the underground Home Army during the war —but other members praised the Church's commitment to the cause of civil and human rights in Poland.[24]

After the formation of KOR, a certain division of labour seemed to develop between the intellectuals and the Church. Although there certainly was never any formal or even informal co-operation between KOR and the hierarchy, there appears to have been unintentional co-ordination. Their actions seemed to complement each other. During October KOR issued several communiqués documenting the facts of the June events and the trials which followed. The communiqués concentrated on cases where workers' rights were disregarded and brutal methods used to repress the protests.

On 16 November the Committee handed in a letter to the Sejm asking for an official inquiry into the charges of brutality. Two days later the Episcopate, complaining that its earlier appeal for amnesty had gone largely unheeded, announced that 'giving aid to people and families deprived of their work and means of livelihood is the duty of all people of good will and especially of a Christian community'. Collections for the persecuted workers were taken only in churches where the protests took place, so as to avoid the impression of a nationwide Church campaign in defiance of the authorities. But this formality could not disguise the fact that the Episcopate had decided to support KOR tactics.

The Church and KOR shared a concern for the imprisoned workers and the general question of civil and human rights in Poland. But there were also essential differences between them. Most of the Committee members were left-wing intellectuals, and several were Marxists and ex-Communists. Their opinions and personal philosophy were more overtly political than that of the Church, and there were many points upon which the two groups differed. For the intellectuals the Church's tacit support of their efforts for civil and human rights was crucial, because without it they represented too small a group to effectively pressure the regime into making concessions. The Church, however, was careful to keep a certain distance from the intellectuals, not only for reasons of opinion but also to avoid the impression that the Episcopate was engaging in overtly political activity. This subtle interplay between

THE CHURCH AND DISSENT: 1970-1980

Church and KOR became particularly evident in the weeks before Christmas 1976. On 28 November an Episcopal letter stating that 'one can constantly feel a secret conspiracy against God' identified Church complaints against government's policies. In private interviews, individual members of KOR supported the Church's demands, but no public statement was made for the group. On 6 December Cardinal Wyszyński added his voice to the demands for an inquiry into charges of police brutality against the strikers. The inquiry demand drew wider and wider support in December and January, including 185 priests from Przymyśl diocese, who on behalf of their parishioners appealed to the speaker of the Sejm to propose a motion to set up a special Parliamentary commission to 'investigate impartially the allegations of police brutality'.[25] The Church leadership, however, refrained from further pronouncements on this issue. There seemed to be no doubt that the Episcopate shared the Committee's opinion about the brutality charges. But in conjunction with its image as protector of both faith and people it was wary of becoming too closely identified with groups it felt did not have the same relationship to the people, no matter how sympathetic some of their views might be. It also had to guard against being linked with one particular segment of political opinion. The Church always believed that it could and must be able to carry out its mission in any socio-political system, provided that it is not deprived of the basic freedoms and means necessary for fulfilling its task.

Nevertheless, there was an increasing dialogue, perhaps better defined as an exchange of values between the Church and the secular Left represented by KOR. This relationship is analysed by one of the founding members of the Committee, Adam Michnik, in his book *Kościół, lewica, dialog*,[26] written in 1976 and published a year later. There he agrees that what he until recently held to be his secular ideas of human dignity, personal freedom, respect for individuals, are not in fact a secular invention but have their roots in the Christian teaching and tradition. In a remarkable passage he quotes Dietrich Bonhoeffer who noted how, in the hour of need in Nazi Germany, the persecuted secular values, long alienated from Christianity, again had recourse to and sought protection in the fold of their forgotten mother, the Church. Referring to a similar situation in contemporary Poland Michnik wrote:

THE CHURCH AND DISSENT: 1970-1980

The children of the Church, who had grown up and departed from her, in the hour of danger returned to their mother. And although in the course of their long alienation they have changed a great deal, though they look different and speak a different language, at the decisive moment mother and children recognized each other. Reason, law, civilisation, humanism—whatever they are called—have sought and found at their source a new meaning and new strength. This source is Jesus Christ.

Michnik's explicit commitment to what he recognized as ultimately Christian values is all the more interesting because he was a part of a growing movement of vociferous and articulate dissident groups.

The Church's behaviour in the aftermath of the June 1976 riots once again illustrate an established pattern of its actions at a time of national crisis—willingness to refrain from criticism when the domestic situation is tense. But the Episcopate has also shown that it expects concessions in return for its responsible stance and that it can switch to the offensive if it feels its demands are not being heeded, as it did on 18 November with the collection call. This action was clearly taken because of the lack of response to the Church's demands for amnesty. Cardinal Wyszyński in December gave his backing for KOR's call for an official investigation into charges of police brutality.

As was only to be expected, after the June protests, the regime's policies towards the Church had eased. By now it was necessary to placate the hierarchy to stabilize the situation. A special gesture was made on 3 August 1976 when Wyszyński reached the critical age of 75. According to Canon Law the Cardinal had to submit his resignation to the Pope. One might have expected the Warsaw regime to put strong pressure on the Vatican to retire the Cardinal. On the contrary, on his seventy-fifth birthday he received a bouquet of seventy-five roses from the Prime Minister. When the Vatican reconfirmed the old Cardinal in office Bishop Bronisław Dąbrowski, the Secretary of the Episcopate, while congratulating Wyszyński in the name of the hierarchy emphasized that the Pope had been asked not only by the Polish Church, but also by the government, to retain the Primate in his post.

By now also the Vatican's Ostpolitik towards Poland was more or less dead, although official Warsaw-Vatican contacts continued and Archbishop Luigi Poggi the Holy See's special nuncio for permanent working contacts with the Polish Government made several routine visits to Poland.²⁷ There was now only weak talk of establishing diplomatic relations since Cardinal Wyszyński ruled such out until the internal Church-State affairs were settled to the Church's satisfaction.

The fast-growing organized dissident movement in the later 1970s introduced a third force in Church-State relations. The numerous groups which had mushroomed since 1976 in Poland began producing unofficial newsletters, petitions and periodicals outside the State censorship system. They revealed the enormous damage inflicted on economic, social and cultural life by thirty years of misleading propaganda. Irrespective of their political preferences all the opposition groups agreed that the process of social disintegration had to be resisted through moral revival. By fighting for a moral and national revival, the dissidents found that they were defending the same values as those championed by the Church. It is interesting to note that copies of the many letters of protests and petitions were quite often deposited with Church authorities or sent for notification to Cardinal Wyszyński and local bishops. Local priests became active in organizing and giving advice to various dissident groups and not surprisingly a strong relationship was forged between dissent and the Church at a grass-roots level.

During 1977 the Gierek regime belatedly attempted to reach a new deal with the Catholic hierarchy. In Gierek's view as long as the Church would use its influence to encourage hard work, honesty and the notion that the prosperity of the nation was the joint responsibility of Catholics and Communists, the regime would recognize the authority of the Church in the moral field. As long as Church leaders refrained from attacking the political leadership, the State would avoid harassing its legitimate activities. Alarmed by the convergence between the opposition movement and the Church, in a worsening economic situation and after the ratification of the Helsinki agreement, he thought that the Government could deal effectively with the dissidents only if the Church remained uninvolved. But it was too late.

The initial trickle of a few dissenting voices became an unstoppable movement and a permanent feature of Polish society. In addition the ruling group had to face provocations from disturbed lower rank hardliners in the Party and the members of the security apparatus who had become weary of their own positions. One such provocation, tragic in consequences, added considerably to the already explosive situation.

THE CHURCH AND DISSENT: 1970-1980

On 7 May 1977 Stanisław Pyjas, a philosophy student at Kraków University and KOR activist was found dead on the stairway to his lodgings. His death was attributed to the security services. His funeral became a mass demonstration of some 5,000 students who announced the formation of the Students' Solidarity Committee; 'an authentic and independent representation of students' in place of the government sponsored Socialist Union of Polish students.

Pyjas's murder brought a sharp reaction from the Archbishop of Kraków, Cardinal Wojtyła, who in his sermon condemned all regimes which will commit such acts for political reasons and referring to a wider context than the Polish crisis said:

> We are still very far from the liberation of the workers for which they themselves have fought for one and a half centuries. Having liberated themselves from the capitalist pagan economy, they have fallen prey to the materialistic pagan economy, and the people, just as they were slaves before, remain slaves today.

These were strong words from the future Pope and spoke volumes about his political and social ideas.

Another example of the escalation of the protest movement and the strengthening of the informal alliance between the new opposition and the Catholic Church was the hunger strike in May 1977 by fourteen people in St. Martin's Church in Warsaw in protest against the arrest of nine members and supporters of KOR and the continued detention of five workers jailed after the price protests in June 1976. Among the hunger strikers were one priest and two prominent Catholic intellectuals, Bohdan Cywiński and Tadeusz Mazowiecki. Recalling the examples of Mahatma Gandhi, Martin Luther King and the hunger strikers in Spanish churches against dictatorship and for freedom and democracy, the activists announced that for them the hunger strike was a form of prayer. The choice of a sanctuary was both symbolic and pragmatic, since Polish police are not empowered to enter a church in order to arrest persons, and the Church did not give way to Government pressure and refused to evict the demonstrators. This new form of protest, which threatened to mobilize the intellectual community as well as jeopardize the regime's policy of *rapprochement* towards the Church, proved successful. A few days later the arrested KOR members were freed and the release of the five workers followed afterwards.

By the middle of 1977 the Episcopate showed another example of its determination to speak out publicly against what it considered to be discriminatory measures against Catholics, and denounced a number of abuses that continued to cause widespread social discontent. The occasion was the Day of the Mass Media. On 15 June 1977 the bishops issued a pastoral letter read to congregations all over the country, which harshly criticized the country's official press, radio and television, accusing them of promoting 'godless ideology' and 'total dictatorship' and called on the authorities to make radio and television available for religious broadcasts including the Mass and homily on Sundays and holidays. Pointing out that the mass media were entirely in the hands of people guided by principles of militant atheism and an ideology hostile to all religion, the bishops urged the faithful to be critical and selective in their reading, listening and viewing and not to hesitate to protest to the editors and producers responsible for publications and programmes that were spiritually and morally offensive. Such a direct appeal for action was bound to produce popular response in various segments of Polish society, as we will see later when discussing the emergence of other dissident groups and in particular the believers' self-defence committees.

But if this were not enough for people to think about and react to, Cardinal Wyszyński issued a pastoral letter on 25 September 1977, even more poignant in the circumstances. In it he criticized the authorities for their disregard for human requirements and blamed them for being interested solely in 'top performance of production' while totally ignoring the 'most essential needs of the people'. Calling for a substantial improvement in living conditions in Poland, the Cardinal recalled the 'daily humiliations' undergone by those who have to queue daily for their food or are ejected from their home to make room for more office buildings. The letter also referred to the plight of all who have lost their jobs and been deprived of their means of livelihood because of their beliefs.

By now the Gierek regime, in an increasingly hopeless social and economic situation, realized that it could do little except woo the Church. An outward sign of this was a meeting between the First Secretary of the Polish United Workers' Party, Edward Gierek and Cardinal Wyszyński on 29 October 1977. The meeting, the first of its kind between the two leaders[28] took place in the Parliament building and lasted two hours. An official communiqué, issued afterwards and broadcast in every newscast for twenty-four hours in order that nobody in Poland should miss the news, spoke of an 'exchange of views on the most important problems of the nation and the Church, which are of great significance for the unity of Poles in striving to shape prosperity for the Polish People's Republic'.

The meeting on Gierek's part was a dramatic effort to seek a truce with the Church in the face of a worsening internal situation. As for Wyszyński, he explained his reasons during a sermon on 6 November: 'I decided, after long reflections over several years, that in situations which are especially difficult, the bishops and Primate of Poland must clearly see the demands of Polish *raison d'état*'. The talks were 'directed by the command of my conscience as a bishop and a Pole, in the hope that the good Lord will draw from those fruits which are so essential to our nation'.

No other details concerning this meeting were ever released, however it should be noted that subsequent to it the regime gave up its plans for educational reforms and so children could, if they wished, go to church in the afternoons to have their weekly religious instruction. Also after a long struggle, the Government gave permission for some new churches to be built.[29] These acts of courtesy provided a setting for Gierek's visit to the Vatican. This visit was a dramatic attempt on the part of the regime not only to seek further co-operation from the Church hierarchy but also from the majority of the population.

On 1 December 1977 Edward Gierek paid an official call on Pope Paul VI. It was the first meeting between a pontiff and a Polish leader in the thousand years of Polish Christianity. During the meeting both leaders delivered speeches which summarized their respective positions.[30]

Gierek, to underline the absence of conflict between the State and the Church, emphasized the unity of the Polish nation, saying:

> The entire Polish nation is united in its work for Poland for her development and prosperity. This patriotic unity rises above differences in outlook, in a historic imperative and supreme good for our nation and for the political forces at the helm of our State. With such motivation, and in the spirit of traditional Polish tolerance, we consolidate a situation in which there is no

conflict between the Church and the State. We are willing to co-operate in the attainment of our great national goals. A cause uniting all of us—as we emphasized together with the Primate of Poland, Stefan Cardinal Wyszyński—is the concern for the prosperity of our homeland, the Polish People's Republic.

The Pope, in reply, encouraged such co-operation and recalling the Church's contribution outside the purely religious sphere, in particular in the cultural area, in moulding the moral resistance of the nation, emphasized that the Catholic Church 'does not ask for privileges, but only for the right to be itself and to carry out its religious mission unimpeded'. And then he delivered a list of clearly expressed demands.

We expressed in the course of [our] talk the wish and—on our part—the strong wish, for co-operation, so that in a suitable climate of relations between the Church and the State, marked by mutual trust, given the recognition of the proper role and the mission of the Church in the contemporary situation in the country, we would act in favour of that 'unity of Poles in the cause of building the prosperity of the Polish People's Republic' which is also the wish of the Episcopate.

It is, after all, only in this manner that the Church will be in a position to make the contribution she wishes to make and which is expected of her. The better are the other conditions conducive to a high moral standard of the society—beginning with the education of youth at school and in State institutions, and ending with the environmental and socio-economic conditions of the country and its population—the greater the prospects of that contribution proving effective. We expressed with all our heart the wish that the difficulties met in these areas can be speedily and satisfactorily overcome, for the good of the Polish nation.

The Pope thus produced a list of demands familiar from the countless complaints made by the Polish Episcopate. They included problems of religious instruction for children; the problem of religious work among university youth; the possibility of running summer camps for Catholic youth; discrimination against believers attaining certain levels in their professional careers; restriction of the

Catholic press; possible representation in socio-political life—to name a few. The Pope's backing for these demands was as important as the circumstances in which they had been listed. Cardinal Wyszyński's triumph was now complete. He had survived attempts of Vatican diplomats to by-pass the Polish hierarchy in dealings with the regime. He made sure that Casaroli's *Ostpolitik* would not succeed in Poland.[31] In addition, by constructing dialogue, however informal, with dissident groups he elevated the Church to the apex of the effective power in Polish politics. Wyszyński was now acknowledged by the regime as 'an eminent Polish patriot' and his authority implicitly and sometimes even explicitly recognized by the Government's representatives.

This complex arrangement was full of pitfalls and the balancing act the Church had to perform was dangerous both theologically and politically. The Church had constantly to preserve its own image of a transcendental arbiter of salvation which prohibited it from playing the role of a political party or from overt identification with liberation theology. It had to continue its pacificatory role because should an open conflict arise its place would have to be on the barricades with the workers. At the same time it had direct and unique access to the very centre of formal power in a situation which both the Party and the State were very visibly showing the strains of incipient paralysis and disintegration. This gave it not formal but more importantly informal access to supreme political structures, which had enabled it effectively to state the terms without having to account for decisions made either by the Party or the Government. And, interestingly, no one from either the regime or the dissident side would venture to criticize the Church openly for the next three years. The triangle of dissidents, the State and the Catholic hierarchy would dominate Polish politics until the memorable summer of 1980.

The Church now accelerated its demands. In a communiqué issued on 16 December 1977 the bishops stated that full normalization between Church and State and a lasting guarantee of these relations 'must be based on recognition of the public and legal character of the Church and on a corresponding bilateral agreement'. This in effect meant that the Church was requesting to be returned to a pre-war status. The recognition of the Church's legal status would allow the bishops to formally uphold the Church's constitutionally granted rights before the courts. More freedom in organizational and administrative matters including youth organizations and the construction of churches and auxiliary buildings as well as more effective protection of the interests of priests and other religious workers were also being requested, and last but not least, recognition of the Church's legal status would have lent momentum and authority to the Church's legitimate demands for a more generous measure of religious and human rights.

Above all the recognition would have meant that the Church is a public body entitled to the same rights and obligations as other sociopolitical organizations, including the Party. This issue was important and sensitive not least because legal recognition of social organizations ideologically opposed to Communist goals, has always been incompatible with Communist practice. Yet, it is worth remembering that the Catholic Church is the only major religious institution whose legal status as a corporate body has not been recognized by the Polish State. The legal status of more than twenty other churches, including several Protestant denominations, has been formally recognized by the State.

In addition the bishops demanded that retaliatory measures must be stopped against the practice of religion by people in important public posts, as well as against priests and people hiring out premises for religious functions. For the first time the communiqué also demanded social insurance for the clergy employed by the Church, which would have put them on the level of all State employees. Even more important, however, was the demand to create an independent Catholic student organization, since the existing Union of Polish Socialist Students, controlled by the State—the bishops said—stood in contradiction of the Christian upbringing of the majority of academic youth and thus could not represent their interests.

These tough demands issued so soon after the euphoria of the Wyszyński-Gierek and Gierek-Paul VI meetings, indicated the price the Church had been asking for in its co-operation with the regime. The mention of bilateral agreement indicated that co-operation demanded lasting foundation. In addition the Episcopate quite clearly denied and contradicted Gierek's speech during his audience with the Pope that there was no conflict between the Church and State. The bishops were saying that until these conflicts were settled to their satisfaction the Church's contribution to the surmounting of the nation's state of crisis would be impaired.

The Church's strong concern for the preservation of independent intellectual thought was best manifested in early 1978 after the formation of the Society of Academic Courses also known as the Flying University.[32] On 22 January 1978 sixty-two prominent scholars founded the Society of Academic Courses, the aim of which was to challenge the Party's monopoly over scholarship and education, particularly in the social sciences and in the humanities and to counteract the stifling effects of total censorship.[33] The authorities reacted strongly to the formation of the Society and police reprisals against lecturers as well as students became widespread.[34]

The bishops responded to these harassments in a communiqué from the 162nd Episcopal Conference issued on 9 March 1978, stating that for years there had been an attempt to impose a monistic, materialistic, and secular stamp on Polish culture that is alien to the Polish Spirit. The communiqué condemned 'all actions that hinder the human spirit in the free creation of cultural values'. In amplification of this basic position, the communiqué went on to declare:

> The restriction of science and research as well as artistic and religious activity through State censorship is regrettable. The existence of such censorship on such a far-reaching scale, is a harmful mistake. The Church will support those initiatives which strive to manifest the culture, products of the human spirit, and history of the nation in an authentic form, because the nation has a right to objective truth about itself.

In an implied warning to the regime, which was urgently seeking the Church's aid to overcome the by then chronic socio-economic difficulties and problems of public morale, the bishops stated:

> There is enough strength in the nation to overcome the difficulties apparent, particularly in the economic sphere, but satisfactory social and political conditions are necessary to put a spark to the people's energy.

This, then, was clear support for the Flying University and another overt link with a powerful and articulate dissident group ideologically and historically close to the bishops' heart. Apart from this, it was an additional demand in a long list of previously stated ones for the Church's co-operation with the regime. Needless to say it is difficult to envisage how the regime could have met the Church's request for relinquishing its monopoly over the educational system or substantially relaxing censorship which was already severely undermined by the regular appearance of at least twenty *samizdat* papers with a total monthly circulation of no less than 20,000. Since most of them according to instructions printed on them 'please pass on, don't destroy' would have been read according to opposition circles, by another ten to fifteen persons, the potential readership of these publications was several hundred thousand.[35]

Among the Catholic *samizdat* publications one of the most interesting was *Spotkania* (Encounters),[36] which published its first number in October 1977. Edited by a group of young Catholics in Lublin, the journal, according to its first editorial, wanted to initiate amongst Catholic circles an independent forum with the aim of laying the foundations of a new Catholic consciousness. At the same time *Spotkania* wanted to become yet another voice in the current social discussion.

> We are aware of the necessity of confronting various sociopolitical and world views which at present comprise the independent thought in the country. The necessity is dictated not only by the danger from the totalitarian regime *vis-à-vis* all independent thought, but also above all by the desire for mutual understanding and co-operation of all these currents. The fact that supra-national and supra-denominational problems exist, requires us to see and unite our own concerns with the concerns of all those fighting for democracy in the wider world context.[37]

In the Polish context the journal was radical in the ideas and views it put forward. It stressed for example the necessity to extend the Catholic faith to social principles, and to fight against the deliberate process of social disintegration. It strongly argued against the religious, moral and political unity between the State and Nation.[38]

Were the bishops' demands therefore becoming increasingly unrealistic and provocative? Perhaps both, but in the circumstances they reflected the desires and aspirations of a vast majority of the society and in accordance with the Church's traditional role in Poland this was

THE CHURCH AND DISSENT: 1970-1980

to be expected of her if she were to maintain her struggle for social position. Anything short of direct involvement would have meant not only abandoning victories won thus far but also the centuries old role as a custodian of Polish nationalism, independent thought and resistance to unpopular State authority. The battle lines between the regime and the society were by now drawn too clearly and too finally for the Church to be merely an independent observer or arbiter.

The issue of the Church role in Polish politics by the Spring of 1978 became a matter of concern among the Party's *apparat* and some rank-and-file members who felt confused and disorientated by the state of affairs and the Gierek regime's apparently new approach to religion. The matter was clarified by Mieczysław Rakowski in an article published in the party weekly *Polityka* on 25 March under the title 'Basic Premises of Co-operation and Dialogue'.

The article provided a broad historical and political context in which to place the recent Church-State relations. According to it, the early post-war policy of total negation and all-out confrontation between the Church and the international Communist movement was based on a false premise. Both sides expected their respective opponents to 'wither away' in time. However, neither Communist expectations that the remnants of religion would 'soon disappear' automatically, nor the Vatican's assumption of the merely 'temporary', transitory nature of Communist rule in Eastern Europe materialized. So, as time went on, both sides had to reconsider their respective policies, and to look for some viable mode of coexistence. The Communists—who admittedly up until then were 'radically atheistic' and determined to combat religion in any form, resorting to 'repression' rather than 'argument', gradually did away with these 'sectarian tendencies', opting for more flexible policies by the later 1950s. Concurrently, the Vatican started to realize the 'stable' character of Communist rule and especially since Pope John XXIII allowed its socio-political doctrine to evolve from total negation towards a *modus vivendi*. As yet more common interests emerged, where concrete co-operation became possible between Church and State authorities in combating such ills as hunger, wars, terrorism, drug addiction and so on, both sides 'extended hands to each other, impelled by a deep feeling of shared responsibility for the fate of the world'.

The article thus far suggested that the Church's role in contemporary Poland was a logical consequence of a world-wide development which provided rationale for an increase in direct co-operation. This somewhat narrow and restricted interpretation would have put at ease the minds of disgruntled Party members who were also reminded that co-operation must not, however, be mistaken for an attempt to 'blur ideological differences', let alone to give up each side's opposing views on the 'nature of the world'.

Rakowski's article also addressed a list of conditions to the Church for future coexistence. Accordingly the Catholics were expected to co-operate with the authorities in efforts to maintain social peace and order, to improve public morality, to strengthen family ties, work discipline and 'civil responsibility' and to avoid any 'conflicts and tensions'. More generally they were called upon by their non-believing compatriots to rally behind Gierek's programme to increase the material and spiritual wealth of the nation.

The article was interesting on several counts. It re-stated the obvious, often-repeated theme of necessity of co-operation between believers and non-believers. It offered no indication of what the Church could expect in return for future co-operation. The Church, again, instead of being granted, in Rakowski's scheme, more adequate conditions for its social and educational work, found itself once more restricted to purely religious activities, which it greatly resented. The article above all offered the Party faithful reassurance that in spite of what might seem, as far as the Party leadership was concerned, no major changes were envisaged in formal Church–State relations.

Rakowski's exposé provided more than adequate reason for the Episcopate to issue another statement on its position. The opportunity was presented by the annual Mass Communication Sunday on 17 September 1978. The bishops issued a pastoral letter which was a blistering attack on the official radio, television and the press.[39] The mass media—it said—are used in order to impose only one kind of view, one pattern of behaviour in order to hold power over the people. The Church, which from the beginning of Polish statehood has been the co-creator of national culture, was now not only deprived of the right to own mass media but also of access to it.

> People who have taken over today's press, radio, television and theatre consider only their own goals. Controlling the media, they feed us with their views.

As citizens in our fatherland we have rights which cannot be given up. We have the right to expect information that is rapid, honest, objective. We have the right and, indeed, we have the duty to pronounce criticism and to express our evaluation of the contents that are conveyed to us . . .

We have the right to expect that the criticism will be heard and taken into consideration . . . To ignore our opinion, the opinion of consumers, is an expression of our treatment as objects to be freely manipulated by those who have taken over the power of citizens, who have been deprived of the right to pronounce their views publicy.

. . . We have the right of respect and of serious consideration of our convictions, our national and Christian culture, our customs and those values which for thousands of years have been the pride of our nation.

The tone and ferocity of these demands was almost without precedent. The emphases were on civil rights which Catholics or citizens should enjoy under the Constitution. Equally important was the fact that the demands themselves and their formulation reflected ever growing social currents and the Church's commitment to them.

In the same letter the Episcopate addressed themselves in an equally determined way, again, to the question of censorship stating that 'social life requires openness and freedom for public opinion'. They now demanded the abolition of censorship which not only 'disinforms' but also 'frees some from responsibilities for the nation'. In addition the bishops demanded the broadcasting on the radio and television of a Sunday Mass together with a homily and concluded: 'We have the right to expect that the voice of millions of faithful citizens of our country will not be without response'.

This was the final salvo. The letter, which must be regarded as one of the most important documents in contemporary history, marks a milestone in Polish politics. Although addressed to only one, nevertheless extremely important, facet of everyday life, it synthesized not only amply but vividly the feelings and aspirations of the great majority of Poles. At the same time giving way to any of these demands on the part of the regime would have meant opening the way for an official plurality of views which were just under the surface and thus undermining

THE CHURCH AND DISSENT: 1970-1980

the Leninist principle on which its very legitimacy was based. And this in essence was what the bishops were asking for. Quite clearly the situation required speedy and resolute action, since the so called overt co-operation that Gierek (on his own terms) expected from the Church was not forthcoming.

Then, while rumours were circulating that a large-scale offensive was being prepared against the entire spectrum of the dissident movement, an event took place which entirely altered the balance of power between Church and State. On 16 October 1978 Cardinal Karol Wojtyła of Kraków was elected Pope.

The news was received in Poland first with disbelief, then amazement, then joy.[40] The election of Karol Wojtyła to the papal throne triggered off an unprecedented demonstration of national and civic awareness. The equation 'Pope-Pole' had a fascinating aura which affected even those who had kept their distance from the Church. A great pride gripped the nation. The accession of the Polish Pope was, even more than a religious event, an event of national significance for Poland. Adam Michnik assessed the impact of the election in the following terms:

> Today the Poles expect that the opening of the Catholic Church to the world will combine the universalism of its values with the inflexible defence of human rights . . . The Church offered the opposition forces not only wise guidance, but also understanding and support. As a result of this a broad resistance movement emerged; a movement which in my opinion is capable of leading our country away from a totalitarian form of government and towards a system of democratic relations; a movement characterized by a realistic appraisal of the facts, but also by determination in striving for the sovereignty of the people *vis-à-vis* the Government. The Poles—Catholics as well as non-Catholics—are known to share their most precious possessions in the world. Now it is the Archbishop of Kraków. What do they want in return? . . . They want neither ambrosia from the heavens nor military intervention; nor do they expect the Yalta agreements to be voided overnight. They do not expect any miracles. To them, Cardinal Wojtyła's rise to the highest office in the Roman Catholic Church was a Miracle.[41]

While the population spontaneously began hanging Polish flags and portraits of the new Pope outside their windows and crowding the churches for special thanksgiving Masses, the Party leadership went into emergency session. From it emerged a handsome message of congratulations signed by the PUWP First Secretary Edward Gierek, Chairman of the Council of State, Henryk Jabłoński and Prime Minister Piotr Jaroszewicz.[42] The message sounded the only note available to the Party at such a moment: nationalism. 'For the first time in the history of the papal throne, it is occupied by a son of the Polish nation, which is building the greatness and prosperity of its socialist fatherland with the unity and co-operation of all its citizens'—the message said.

An official Government delegation headed by Henryk Jabłoński attended the inauguration of the Pontificate of John Paul II on 22 October and the Polish radio and television broadcast a three and a quarter hours live relay of the ceremonies from St. Peter's Square. It was the first televised Mass since Communist rule began. For that one occasion at least the regime acceded to the Church's persistent demands for access in Poland to the media.

The election of John Paul II changed almost overnight a number of important dimensions in the Polish political situation. It transferred the leadership of the Polish Church from Warsaw to Rome thus bringing to an end the almost absolute authority of Cardinal Wyszyński. The regime could now hope that the Vatican would be willing to improve its direct relations on the governmental level and thus eliminate the stubborn resistance of the Polish Episcopate. But, at the same time the supersession of Wyszyński also meant that Poland's spiritual leadership was now outside Polish borders and that a great source of authority in Polish society was now no longer in Poland and no longer subject to direct influence from the Government. The Vatican had now also acquired the best expert on its *Ostpolitik*, whose authority could not be challenged by the prelates in the Curia.

On another plain the election of the Archbishop of Kraków gave a massive infusion of confidence among Poland's unofficial opposition groups in particular among young people and accelerated their concern and demands for political change. Following the example of lay dissident groups, believers began to organize themselves into self-defence committees. The first such committee was formed on 26 November 1978 in the village of Opole Stare which had a history of confrontations with the authorities over a chapel built without a state permit. Their aim was to prevent attempts to demolish the chapel and to fight for equal rights for believers in the country. They began collecting signatures for a petition demanding religious programmes on radio and television.[43]

A day after the election of the new Pope the Polish Episcopate issued a proud statement[44] which expressed the hope that John Paul II would take part in the ceremonies of the 900th anniversary of the Martyr Bishop Stanisław of Kraków, scheduled for May 1979 and the 600th anniversay of the icon of Black Madonna of Częstochowa scheduled for 1982.

Negotiations were soon started by the Vatican for a papal visit to Poland. Gierek was convinced that the best policy was a generous and welcoming approach to the new Pope. His arrival in the country, he thought, could be used to enhance the unity of the nation on the basis of a simple patriotic spectacle: the socialist fatherland receiving its most distinguished son. The publicity and the influx of Western journalists which would accompany the visit also offered an occasion to display the achievements of the regime and its understanding with the Church on the importance of these achievements. His approach, though shared by part of the leadership was not supported by others and in particular by lower members of the party's apparatus who by being more closely in touch with the population's feeling and therefore the undercurrent in our society, displayed particular apprehension.

The occasion of the papal visit was viewed by the Party's leadership as unacceptable. The Pope wanted to take part in the ceremonies commemorating his predecessor in the See of Kraków, Stanisław Szczepanowski, an eleventh-century bishop, patron saint of Poland, who fiercely defied the tyrannical rule of the king in defence of religious and moral ideas and was as a result killed by the sovereign while saying Mass. For Poles he remained for centuries a symbol of civil courage and religious zeal, as well as of national identity. While the Archbishop of Kraków, Wojtyła had launched in 1972 seven years of prayer (corresponding to the period Stanisław served as a bishop of Kraków) and wanted the ceremonies in 1979 to be of an international character with Pope Paul VI attending them. After his election to the papacy it became imperative that he himself should be there. The object of the visit became a serious source of friction within the Political Bureau of the Polish United Workers' Party. There were many among the leadership who had been against the visit from the start, but all without exception were opposed to the date. In their view since St. Stanisław opposed the King's policies (900 years ago) he acted against the interests of the Polish State. Therefore it would be 'inappropriate' now to attempt to focus public attention on a person who had been 'the symbol of division, rather than of co-operation' between Church and State—especially at the present stage of development, when all possible conflicts between the secular and spiritual power in Poland should be avoided.

The differing interpretations of the saint's role was also the subject of a censorship of the Pope's first Christmas letter to his old diocese in Kraków. The letter which was to be published in the Kraków based weekly *Tygodnik Powszechny* included the following passage which was removed by the censors.

> In accordance with 900-year-old tradition, St. Stanisław has become the patron of moral order in our country, of that moral order which is so needed in our times ... As bishop and shepherd of the Kraków Church, St. Stanisław defended his contemporary society from the evil which threatened it, and he did not hesitate to confront the ruler when defence of the moral order called for it. In this way he became a magnificent example of concern about people, which we have to compare with our indifference, our negligence and despondency and our concern with our own interests.
>
> The welfare of the people and of society is indivisibly linked with concern for the moral order. Using modern language we can see in St. Stanisław an advocate of the most essential human rights, on which man's dignity, his morality and true freedom depend.

Thus, to the Church, Stanisław died in defence of a sacred cause and once the paragraph was removed from the letter the editor refused to publish the truncated version of Pope John Paul II's Christmas message. The full text was then read from church pulpits nevertheless.

While the discussions about the visit continued within the Polish leadership on inter-governmental level the Pope on 11 January 1979 invited himself to Poland telling the Polish Government that he considered it his 'duty' to take part in the ceremonies to mark the anniversary of St. Stanisław's martyrdom. Another, this time four-hour, meeting took place on 24 January between Cardinal Wyszyński and Edward Gierek, followed by a visit in March (22–26) by Archbishop Casaroli. What emerged from these negotiations was a compromise. The Pope could come to Poland not in May for two days but in June 1979 for nine days and visit six cities rather than two cities.

After the official announcement of the date of the visit on 2 March the Polish mass media felt obliged to make clear that the Pope's visit would not in any way alter the principle of the Party's leading role in society or the strictly secular character of the Polish People's Republic. The editor-in-chief of the Central Committee's weekly *Polityka*, Mieczysław Rakowski, warned its readers against any illusions of this kind, and advised the Church that it should not 'meddle' in the area of social, economic or any other politics, but on the contrary should give support to the Party's measures in these areas.[45] Similar was the tone of remarks of the Party's monthly theoretical organ *Nowe Drogi*, which although stressing that the PUWP's ranks were not closed to those who believed in God but are class-conscious and politically active working people went on to say that nevertheless the Party seeks to foster its members in the spirit of Marxist ideology. Its members must understand that one of their political obligations in the event of conflict will be to stand together with the Party.[46]

The lay dissent groups shared with the nation the joy of John Paul II's forthcoming visit to his homeland. A statement issued by the Social Self-Defence Committee 'KOR' on 19 May welcoming the Pope, quoted extensively the recently published first encyclical *Redemptor Hominis*[47] as a reminder 'of the values we fight for and will continue to fight for'.

> We remember that 'the Church has clearly defined its position towards those social systems, which supposedly for some higher good which is the good of the State' (though history has shown that it is the good of a particular party which defines itself with the State), 'restricted the laws of the citizens, deprived them of their inalienable human rights' . . . . Holy Father, we see in you an advocate of the principles of social morality and freedom of all nations. We see in you a champion of human dignity, a spokesman for those 'who have the

courage to say No! or to say Yes! even when the price is exacted'.

The statement was a further example of *rapprochement* between the most powerful opposition group and the Church, *rapprochement* centred on a new concept of politics based on the primacy of ethical values and social solidarity.

The bargaining over the itinerary of the Pope's visit went on for several months and at least two places which it is known he wanted to go to were dropped. One was Nowa Huta where he wanted to say Mass in the Church of Our Lady the Queen of Poland consecrated by him after several years of battle in 1977. The other was Piekary Śląskie, about seven miles from the Silesian capital Katowice and site of an annual pilgrimage by Catholic men on the last Sunday in May in which the Pope had regularly participated.[48] The Government was sensitive about Church influence among working people in the region and strongly resisted the idea of a papal visit there.

Details apart, the regime resigned itself to accept the visit whatever the consequences. But the resignation was not complete. In order to present the visit in a particular light detailed instructions were issued in May by the Press Department of the Party's Central Committee to the media on how to cover the visit.[49] The document not only set out arrangements by which the foreign press accredited to the papal visit would be under continual surveillance and guidance but also envisaged that Polish journalists covering the visit will be expected to perform certain ideological and propaganda assignments throughout the visit. It laid down precisely what the different types of Polish publications would be allowed to print before, during and after the visit. Thus for example: 'On the first day of the visit the morning and afternoon papers will publish a photograph of the Pope, information on the start of the visit, a biography, a commentary from the Polish Press Agency (PAP) while the Party press will not print any picture, but solely information, a biography and a commentary from PAP', the official government press agency PAP was to have exclusive rights to provide information on the visit with the exception of the Catholic press. This was in any case subject to normal leadership procedures. Weeklies due to appear on the news stands at the start of the visit would publish no material about it. After the visit the dailies except for the Party newspaper *Trybuna Ludu* were to use PAP material, *Polityka* was to publish a report on the Pope's visit to the former concentration camp in Auschwitz and the remaining socio-political weeklies were expected to cover selected subjects according to instructions from the Press Department. The memorandum also stipulated that illustrated weeklies could not include more than four photographs in any article covering a specific aspect of the visit after its conclusion.

The document reflected the general state of the regime's nervousness about the visit and spotlighted one important aspect of the centrally engineered pattern of control over preparations for the Pope's return to Poland. More importantly, however, it also draws attention to the character and mechanics of the manipulation of information in Poland in general.

On the eve of the Pope's arrival Mieczysław Rakowski, generally regarded as the voice of Gierek, published another article in *Polityka*[50] making clear that it was still the Marxists who managed Poland, despite any pretensions the Church might nourish. He stressed the common interest of Church and State in achieving international peace and co-operation. Emphasizing the national aspect of the visit, Rakowski wrote: 'He is a Pole coming to his home country. We will welcome him as a Pole'. Rejecting suggestions that the regime was embarrassed by the election of Cardinal Wojtyła as a Pope he stressed that the State and Church shared common goals and that the new Pope had experience of encounters between Catholicism and Communism. The visit, he said, 'will strengthen the unity of Poland in realizing goals underlying our national identity'. There was also a warm tribute to Cardinal Wyszyński, who had 'led the Roman Catholic Church in Poland in sometimes difficult situations, making decisions worthy of a great statesman'. The article ended with what could be interpreted as official though conditional readiness to meet some at least of the Church's demands:

> If the leaders of the Catholic Church in Poland will continue the policy of the past few years, a policy of co-operation as opposed to confrontation, and if they will take an active part in building our socialist fatherland, then the Marxists will certainly be ready to help settle problems which still exist today . . . Conditions between Church and State cannot be static.

THE CHURCH AND DISSENT: 1970-1980

After months of bargaining John Paul II arrived at Warsaw airport on 2 June 1979. As he kissed the Polish soil the bells in all the churches throughout the land began to toll. For nine days the Poles flooded him with outpourings of love and manifestations of their faith. In response he preached to them in thirty-two sermons not only on matters of Catholic doctrine but also on the great issues of the day with subtle but nevertheless clear political undertones. He said in Poland what he wanted to say and left others to do what interpreting they wished. He never failed to put his message across to the estimated thirteen million people who turned up in various places to listen to him.

On the first day he met Edward Gierek and other State dignatories in the Belvedere Palace.[51] During the ceremony the Party's First Secretary, Edward Gierek, cited the alliance with the Soviet Union as a main factor in solving national problems.

> Basic social transformations, industrialization and urbanization have brought civilizational and cultural advantages to the widest circles of the population, to the entire nation, as well as new, decent living conditions opening broad development prospects.

The Pope in reply reminded him that 'a prosperous and happy Poland is in the interest of peace and good international co-operation among the people of Europe'; that peace and *rapprochement* among peoples could only be built on the principle of respect of the objective rights of the nation, including its right to freedom and to create its own culture. Emphasizing that the Church wishes to serve people also in the temporal dimension of their life, the Pope continued:

> Given that this dimension is realized through people's membership of various communities, national and state, and is therefore at the same time political, economic and cultural, the Church continually rediscovers its own mission in relationship to these sectors of human life and activity. By establishing a religious relationship with man, the Church consolidates him in his natural social bonds.

He thus re-stated the concept rigorously rejected by Marxists that the fundamental mission of the Church was to make man more conscious of his dignity, his rights and duties; more socially responsible, creative and useful; more devoted in his life to his family, social, professional and patriotic commitments; to make man more confident and courageous. 'For this activity', he said, 'the Church does not desire privileges, but only exclusively what is essential for the accomplishment of its mission'. Agreement on these lines with the State authorities had been sought for over thirty years. Now the Pope was saying that the Church was aware that the great majority of Poles were its children, was seeking such agreement as 'one of the elements in the ethical and international order' based on respect 'of the national and human rights'.

On the same afternoon during a Mass celebrated in Warsaw's Victory Square he declared that 'Christ cannot be excluded from man's history anywhere in the world, from any geographical latitude or longitude. Attempts to exclude Christ from man's history are directed against man. Without Christ it is also impossible to understand the history of Poland'. Dwelling on the role of the Pope as pilgrim, he suggested that Poland could claim to have become 'the land of particularly responsible witness' It was from here that the word of Christ must be spread. Tracing the cardinal importance of Christianity in Poland's history, he said that in 1944 Warsaw had engaged in an uneven battle with the invaders, a battle in which she had fallen under her own ruins. 'If we do not remember that under these same ruins lies Christ the Redeemer ... then it is impossible to understand the history of Poland'.

On the second day of his visit, in Gniezno, the cradle of Polish Christianity, while recalling the gradual expansion of Christianity through the ancient lands of all East and South European Slavs, which had created the spiritual foundation for religious and cultural links between then, he alluded to religious freedom and censorship not only in Poland but also outside its borders by saying,

> I hope, dear brothers, that they can hear us. I hope that they can hear me, because I cannot imagine that any Polish or Slav ear, in any part of the world would be unable to hear words spoken by a Polish Pope, a Slav! I hope that they can hear me because we live in an epoch where the freedom to exchange information is so precisely defined, as is the exchange of cultural values. Here we are reaching the very roots of these values.

During a Mass for the faithful of Opole and Lower Silesia, on the third day of his visit he brought up again the question of the rights of nations and alliances.

THE CHURCH AND DISSENT: 1970–1980

As respect for the rights of every member of a community, a nation or, for example, a family, is a condition for inner unity within each society or social body, so recognition of and respect for the rights of each nation is a condition for reconciliation among nations. This includes, first of all, the right to exist and the right to self-determination, then the right to one's own culture and to multi-directional development.

The allusions to Eastern Europe were only too clear.

On 6 June during his three-day stay at the monastery of Jasna Góra in Częstochowa he also met the students from his old University of Lublin. The real human being, he explained to them, needs to feel both solidarity and opposition; they must belong to society, yet they must think for themselves. The danger was that the first would overwhelm the second. That would in fact be bad for whatever ideology appeared to profit from it:

> Any man who chooses his ideology honestly and through his own conviction deserves respect. The real danger for both sides—for the Church and for the other side, call it what you will—is the man who does not take a risk and accept a challenge, who does not listen to his deepest convictions, to his inner truth, but who only wants to fit somehow, to float in conformity, moving from left to right as the wind blows.

To the students the implication was clear, the instinct for conformity could only push you towards the collectivist or Communist side. The function of a Polish university, therefore, was to foster the kind of independent thought which prompted Christian opposition.

As he spoke on 7 June 1979 over the ashes of more than four million killed in the Auschwitz-Birkenau concentration camps, 'the Golgotha of our times', the Pope turned a moving memorial service for the victims of Nazi extermination—the 'insane ideology'—into a ringing call for the rights of the living. He recalled that the first encyclical of his pontificate was devoted to the dignity of man and human rights,

> the inalienable rights of man which can be trampled on so easily and annihilated by man! It is enough to dress man in another uniform, to equip the apparatus of violence with the success of

destruction . . . It is enough to impose on him an ideology in which human rights are subordinated to the requirements of the system, subordinated in an arbitrary fashion so as to suppress them completely.

This was his most outspoken warning and appeal for universal respect of human rights, and his finger was unmistakably also pointing in a not too distant direction.

On 9 June, during the sermon at the Cistercian abbey in Mogiła, just outside the 'Socialist' model town of Nowa Huta which he was prevented from visiting, he told the faithful: 'Remember this: Christ will never agree to man being viewed only as a means of production, or agree to man viewing himself as such. He will not agree that man should be valued, measured or evaluated only on this basis. Christ will never agree to that!'

One of the Pope's most thoughtful and most important addresses of the entire pilgrimage was delivered on 5 June in Częstochowa to the 169 Plenary Conference of the Polish Episcopate. It contained a new formulation of the Vatican *Ostpolitik*. Recalling his own work of many years with the Polish Episcopate, he said, he had realized what a special and responsible place Poland, and especially the Church in Poland, occupied in the map of the modern world. The Church's hierarchical system had played a decisive part in the nation's history and at the same time, the nation's history had in some providential way been incorporated into the structure of the Church in Poland, giving it firm foundations.

> We can correctly define the importance of a problem which has been a topical one for several years in Poland, that is the problem of normalizing relations between Church and State. In our age, insight into the fundamental rights of man—among which the right of religious freedom has undoubted, central importance—speaks in favour of the process. Normalization is of practical respect for that right.

The Pope's address was in essence a justification of the Church's inescapable involvement in political affairs, domestic and international.

He stressed that authentic dialogue must respect the conviction of believers. It must ensure all the rights of citizens, and normal conditions for the activity of the Church as a religious community to which the vast majority of Poles belong.

We are aware that this dialogue cannot be easy, because it takes place between two concepts of the world which are diametrically opposed. But it must be made possible and effective if the good of individuals and the nation demands it. The Polish Episcopate must not cease to undertake, with solicitude initiatives which are important for the present-day church.

But these initiatives, he implied, must be carried in unity with the Apostolic See, within the hierarchical order of the Church. The Pope thus reserved for the Vatican undisputed competence in the negotiations, but left the Polish Episcopate the right of active participation and codetermination. In this way he instructed the Polish Church to subordinate itself in the hierarchical structure of the whole Church but at the same time he was passing to bishops the order to continue the dialogue with the State. In a nutshell, further initiatives but in conjunction with Rome. This formulation was particularly important against the background of the not so distant past when the Polish Episcopate had to be on a constant alert not to become the object of a bargain struck by the Vatican for the sake of what it might have considered a higher goal of the Church as a whole.

The new concept of the *Ostpolitik* was clearly worked out in response to the criticism of past Vatican behaviour *vis-à-vis* the Communist regimes, which had produced no change in the situation of the national Churches, although there might have been normalization of relations between the Vatican and the States concerned. The new arrangements aimed at a uniform action of national Churches and the Vatican in a dialogue with governments, whereby it was not so important whether a representative of the Vatican or a bishop of the local Church takes a position because both, as members of a hierarchical order speak with one voice and one will. Consequently, governmental exchanges and even diplomatic relations between the Vatican and the respective regimes would not mean the completion of the normalization process, which has worried several Church hierarchies in Eastern Europe, but would be their means. In other words, they would not imply recognition of the existing state of affairs, but would be an instrument for their improvement in the interest of the Church.

The new formulation implied stronger participation and decision on the part of the Vatican in relations between the Church and State but this did not indicate an intention to weaken the position of the local bishops. On the contrary, with the emphasis on the hierarchical structure of the Church and the bonds between Episcopate and the Holy See, the Pope had underlined the Church's universality. This in turn meant a departure from the established pattern of double-track relations, Vatican-Government and local Episcopate-Government which again did not indicate the Vatican's withdrawal from active participation in the overall normalization of relations. This double-track arrangement of relations was to be merely regarded as a technicality and of secondary importance.

The circumstances in which this new formulation was outlined and the Pope's particular encouragement of the initiatives undertaken by the Polish Church as well as his emphasis on the universality of the Church's experience, meant that the procedure outlined did not pertain to Poland only, where the Church is strong, but to all Churches of Eastern Europe. The Pope by making Poland a model of Vatican *Ostpolitik* implied that this example can clearly demonstrate the usefulness of the Church to other Communist regimes in situations when political instability or social disorders afflict their nations. To the bishops who had been critical of the Vatican *Ostpolitik* and argued that they do not need it, the Pope was saying that the Vatican requires these arrangements since its *Ostpolitik* is not limited to Poland. This was particularly evident when calling himself the Slav Pope. John Paul II made several allusions to the Slavs world-wide in his homily in Gniezno. With his background and experience John Paul, unlike his predecessor, spoke and acted on *Ostpolitik* from a position of strength. This new approach was a marked difference from the previous muddled and confused *Ostpolitik* of the Vatican.

This papal visit to Poland was a psychological earthquake, an opportunity for mass political catharsis. The Pope expressed in public what had been hidden for decades, the people's private hopes and sorrows, their longing for uncensored truth, for dignity and courage in defence of their civil and human rights. A whole generation experienced for the first time a feeling of collective power and exaltation of which they

THE CHURCH AND DISSENT: 1970-1980

had never dreamt. It gave them a sense of confidence, unity and strength to take up their causes even more decisively. It demonstrated that after more than three decades of Communist rule, and despite atheist indoctrination, the Church was still an overwhelming force in the nation. Moreover, it rendered the role of the party even less significant, showing that whatever its claims, the party was not the guiding force in the nation and that it had lost the battle for the hearts and minds of the Poles. The Party apparatus, with its omnipresent tentacles stretching into every corner of society, appeared in this brief historic moment as a mere cobweb. The visit demonstrated once again, what was in any case by then obvious, that the vast majority of the population had come to regard the Catholic Church, the only independent large-scale organization capable of standing up to the party, as a 'lobbyist' via which to pursue their interests. The Church's stature and role thus demonstrated the inability of the regime to integrate society into the established patterns of the party-dominated mass organizations.

The smooth organization and control of the million-strong crowds in all the meetings with the Pope also showed the Party that the Church was eminently capable of leading and guiding the Polish nation not only spiritually but also organizationally and without the use of force or coercion.

The visit became a powerful demonstration of the bond between the Polish people and the world of Christian culture, a demonstration of their solidarity with the Catholic church, of their national pride in the person of the Pope and of their yearning for freedom, the champion of which they saw to be their fellow countryman.

The significance of this demonstration, expressed so spontaneously and vigorously, was in its lasting effect on Poland, resulting in the maturing of historical processes sooner than most people expected. The Pope, in his sermons, hit precisely the self-image of the Poles, into whom he injected a new desire for self-assertion and a new courage, without which the events of the summer of 1980 would have been inconceivable. In view of this the party was obviously no longer in a position to arrest the evolution of social groups towards a greater self-confidence. The election of the Pope and his visit to Poland were milestones in the accelerating erosion of the domestic power basis of the Party. However, it should be remembered that in spite of continuous signs of this erosion during previous decades, the Church had never considered the destruction or incapacity of the Party as an alternative to existing conditions in the current situation of Poland's membership of the 'socialist commonwealth'.

The Pope in his pronouncements in Poland stressed the humanist nature of the Catholic doctrine, and thus effectively internationalized the national and religious demands of Poland. Since the Party also acknowledged humanist values, the Church became even less open to attack in domestic affairs. At the same time, Christian humanism had a stimulating rather than a calming effect on the country rocked by ever-deepening crisis.

Added to this there was also in the Pope's pronouncements a Christian-Slav messianism and emphasis on the unity of Europe regardless of its present block structures. It is interesting, in retrospect, that one of the first tangible results of the Pope's expression of his solidarity and concern for other Slavs was a letter signed by over three hundred Catholic intellectuals to the Conference of the Episcopate of Bohemia and Moravia sent on 14 July 1979 to Cardinal František Tomašek of Prague. Its signatories asked the Czech bishops to intercede on behalf of ten members of the Committee of the Unjustly Persecuted and supporters of Charter 77 who had recently been arrested in Czechoslovakia and charged with anti-State activities. 'These admirable people' —the letter said—'acted from deeply humanist motives, in agreement with the teaching of the Church. The Second Vatican Council called on those who are politically gifted or are capable of political action to stand up against oppression by an individual or against the despotism and intolerance of a political party'.

When the Czechoslovak Church authorities refused to intervene on behalf of the dissidents and the courts handed down heavy sentences, several members of staff and students of Toruń University issued in November 1977 an appeal to world public opinion calling for further testimonies of solidarity with the convicted signatories of Charter 77 and members of the Committee for the Unjustly Persecuted. Recalling the Pope's words in Gniezno the appeal spoke of the deep humiliation they felt as a result of Polish soldiers' participation in the Warsaw Pact invasion of Czechoslovakia in 1968.

Concern for the dissidents in Czechoslovakia inspired by the papal visit to Poland was the reason for another hunger strike, in October 1979, by a united KOR-Catholic group of people in the church of the

Holy Cross in Warsaw.[52] The protest, which lasted for seven days was aimed at highlighting the plight of individuals persecuted in Czechoslovakia: priests arrested in Slovakia for participating in the John Paul II pilgrimage to Poland and political prisoners. They chose a Catholic church, they said, 'since in the Polish People's Republic only the Church could give sanctuary to people of various persuasions, people who act in the defence of the inalienable rights of man'.

By the end of 1979 the believers' self-defence committees had grown to three,[53] prominently quoting, as a basis for their formation, article 82 of the Polish Constitution, article 18 of the international Covenant on Human and Civil Rights and the Final Act of the Helsinki Conference, the committees sent the announcement of their formation not only to the local bishop and the office of the Polish Episcopate but also to KOR and other dissent groups. What appeared to be emerging in Poland was an informal infra-structure of dissenting groups.

The temporary thaw in Church-State relations following the papal visit was shattered by the decision of the city authorities in Częstochowa to build a motorway close to the shrine of the Black Madonna. This project would have separated the monastery of Jasna Góra from the town of Częstochowa and the pilgrims, instead of having direct access to the shrine, would have been forced to go through a subway no more than 10 metres wide. Such a scheme would have also allowed the authorities effectively to control access to the monastery. Work on the motorway began in September 1979 without any consultation with the Church or prior notification from the authorities. It continued in spite of strong objections from the local bishop until it became a national issue. At the end of December Cardinal Wyszyński condemned the schemes as an 'indescribable act of barbarity' and a threat to the 'spiritual capital of Poland'. Special prayers were requested in churches in the diocese of Częstochowa for the intention that those responsible for continuing the work should find the courage to stop, and all church bells rang three times a day for ten minutes to remind the faithful to pray for free access to the shrine. Finally at the beginning of January, three people began an indefinite fast in front of the icon of the Black Madonna in the Jasna Góra monastery and the Pope himself made discreet representations to the Government for the work to be stopped.

Faced with such strong opposition the authorities capitulated in the middle of January. A compromise solution reached between Church and State representatives resulted in abandoning the idea of a subway and instead traffic lights were installed.

The initial decision to build the motorway can only be considered provocative. It must have been clear from the beginning that it would be met with hostility and that some sort of compromise would be necessary. Therefore a question arises; why such a high-handed move in the first place? The idea to build the motorway came from the hard-liners within the Party leadership in order to make relations with the Church more difficult and therefore undermine Gierek's authority before the forthcoming Party congress. It was a strong indication of how vulnerable his position had become in the aftermath of the papal visit and his constant attempts to reach the co-operation of the Church and Wyszyński personally.

The whole episode became known as 'the battle of Jasna Góra' and the approaching Eighth Party Congress in February 1980 became for the Church a background against which to re-state its position *vis-à-vis* the increasingly disorientated regime.

In a series of public pronouncements between January and May 1980, the Church hierarchy, although repeatedly stating its willingness to co-operate with the regime to combat widespread apathy and low public morale and to alleviate some of the basic social problems, also made it clear that to fulfil its mission properly the Church must be given the appropriate means to do so. Among the most urgent demands were the long-standing requests of access to the mass media; the setting up of an independent Catholic press and publishing houses; re-establishment of traditional Christian associations, and recognition of the Catholic Church as a legal entity. Although there was nothing new in these demands, their re-statement in the wake of the papal visit and in the newly revived atmosphere of strong religious fervour, was additional encouragement for the faithful to back the Church's demands. Indeed, in the case of at least one of the demands, the broadcasting of the Mass, a national petition was organized with the full support of the hierarchy and active participation of parish clergy.[54] By January some 100,000 signatures were collected under the petition.

On 6 January 1980, Cardinal Wyszyński delivered his traditional Epiphany service in Warsaw's St. John's Cathedral. In it he openly chided the regime for mismanaging the economy and creating class divisions, in spite of the allegedly 'democratic' social system. Referring to his letter sent to the authorities on 23 December 1979, in which he asked for definite economic measures to be taken immediately, the Primate called on the regime to 'put an end to these beggarly queues which are destroying human life' and 'isolating the elementary rights of man'. He challenged the administration to desist from its customary shortsighted and 'mendacious propaganda' methods and to be guided in its work by the spirit of 'justice and truth'.

The strong social content of Cardinal Wyszyński's sermon was later reiterated by the communiqué from the Conference of the Polish Episcopate, issued on 28 February 1980. In it the bishops appealed to the authorities to grant all citizens the opportunity to participate actively in solving the country's problems, whether moral, social, or economic, instead of leaving that responsibility solely within the jurisdiction of the Party. Stating that only through free organization and free exchange of opinions is it possible to achieve the much needed national unity and social accord, they demanded that 'all Poles should have the right to form their own organizations, and social and economic problems should not be solved by just one group. They also added that 'nobody should face reprisals or fear reprisals for holding his own views'. In apparent support for the dissident groups the bishops called on the Poles to 'defend every honest initiative which aims at the renewal of society'. The bishops also repeated the by now familiar demands of access to mass media, the Church's right to act in the area of social assistance, freedom for religious organizations, especially among the youth, and others.

The statement was important for several reasons. It was once again evident that in spite of official government statements to the contrary, Church-State relations were not in a satisfactory shape and that no progress had been made in the main areas of contention, despite optimistic expectations following the Pope's visit. Issued just after the Eighth Congress of the Polish United Workers' Party on 15 February 1980, and before the parliamentary elections on 23 March 1980, it summarized succinctly the Church's position at the time when it should have been the subject of wide discussion. By implication the bishops stated their political platform before the elections.

That the authorities had no intention of compromising became apparent when the list of parliamentary candidates for the forthcoming elections was released on 1 March 1980. The totally subservient Pax group, which until then had had five deputies in the Sejm was rewarded by the addition of a sixth seat. Another pro-Government group, the Christian Social Association, which had only two deputies was now to have five and the Znak quota remained at five. In spite of numerous protests the distribution of seats between the various groups was confirmed in the elections on 23 March 1980.

By the spring of 1980, a number of student Solidarity Committees existed in various centres of higher education throughout Poland. They were opposed to the official Socialist Association of Polish students, and the bishops gave tacit support to these unofficial committees. Re-emphasizing their earlier idea of an independent student organization, they stressed, in a communiqué on 29 February 1980, that the future of the nation and true social progress depended essentially on the moral health of the young generation whose upbringing should be firmly based on 'stable moral principles and healthy national traditions'.

> It is indeed not fitting that young believing Catholics should be pressed to join definite organizations and political groups that force on them a world outlook conflicting with the Christian attitudes of the overwhelming majority of Poles. These pressures lead to hypocrisy and opportunism that corrupt the character of the young.

It would appear that also by spring 1980 the concerned action by the Church and dissident groups began to produce some tangible concessions from the regime. On 4 April the official Vatican newspaper *L'Osservatore Romano* published its first Polish edition, as a monthly. Some 140,000 copies were sent to Poland for distribution by Church officials. Edited by Father Adam Boniecki, the monthly was the only newspaper distributed in Poland not subject to any censorship. In one way it was a means of satisfying the bishops' complaints about the Church's lack of access to the mass media. On 2 May 1980 in an ostensible gesture of good will towards some two hundred seminarians engaged in military service, the government released them from military service in the future, thus meeting one of the most longstanding grievances.

Another major concession on the part of the regime towards the

Church was the extension of state social security benefits to all those employed in Church offices and Church schools, including cooks, gardeners and even cleaning personnel. The benefits also covered nuns and monks teaching religious classes to school children, as well as those employed in editorial offices run by the Church.

All these concessions, which were almost unexpectedly granted to the Church in the spring of 1980, were however clearly limited to strictly non-political issues and in retrospect must be seen as a bid to win popular support for the planned austerity measures which were finally announced in July 1980.

The hierarchy, however, did not allow itself to be deluded by 'velvet glove' concessions. It continued to maintain its ethico-political posture and did not miss opportunities to re-emphasize the Church's postulates. Only days after the extension of social security was announced the bishops, in a communiqué from the 173rd Conference of the Episcopate on 8 May 1980, reiterated their urgent call to the regime to end the recently intensified reprisals against people holding non-conformist views. They also implicitly expressed their support for the Flying University. The communiqué contained a dramatic call for a 'climate of social peace' and mutual trust between the authorities and society as an essential condition for overcoming Poland's deepening social and economic *malaise*. As a clear indication of its willingness to restart the joint Government-Episcopal Commission, suspended since 1967, the hierarchy proposed to discuss the outstanding problems with the appropriate State authorities. In the bishops' view such a gathering would be a valuable contribution to the 'common effort of all Poles' in their work for the good of the country and would serve not only the Church's interests, but that of the State and society as well.

By the end of the Spring, no one seemed to have a clear concept of the future. The regime was under constant pressure from its own internal critics for allowing too many clearly visible gains to the Church and for not stamping hard enough on the fast spreading dissident movement, and was showing increasing signs of its incompetence and indecision. The dissident movement, having found a willing co-operator and protector in the Church and in spite of severe persecution and harrassment, was steadily gaining confidence and momentum. The Church, finding itself in the role of protector and adjudicator of both, assumed a position of unprecedented moral and political power. But none of the participants in the triangle had any clear sighted view, not only of the not too distant but even of the immediate future. There was, however, a desire for' dialogue, not out of willingness but out of necessity, since all three groups were well aware that in an outright confrontation, the winner might have to be someone from outside the borders of Poland. At the same time they wished to conduct the dialogue on their own terms. This, by its very essence, could not provide even a starting point for the cure of the social, political and economic ills of the Polish society. Worst of all, all the interested parties in Poland knew that the country was a powder keg and yet none was able to prevent the explosion.

Notes

1. Who was responsible for the order to shoot is still shrouded in mystery. The findings of an official investigation conducted soon after were kept secret in spite of repeated promises that all the facts about the brutal repression would be revealed. In November 1980 one of the protagonists in the drama, the then first secretary of the Gdańsk provincial Party committee and the man who arrived on the scene on 16 December, said that the order came from Warsaw and it was a political decision made by the 'principal figures' in the leadership. It was passed on to the Prime Minster at that time Józef Cyrankiewicz and then to the Chief of Security Forces. Cyrankiewicz refuted the charges in an angry letter. It should be remembered that the decision to use the army could not have been taken without the agreement of the Defence Minister, General Wojciech Jaruzelski.
2. These figures have been disputed by eye witnesses. However, the monument to the victims of the 'December events' unveiled in December 1980 has only twenty-eight names engraved.
3. According to the normally reliable communiqué of the Committee for the Defence of Workers the government issued the following number of permits for the construction of churches: 1974, 39; 1975, 12; 1976, 14; 1977, 34; total 99 (KOR Communiqué no. 21, 31 July 1978). However, on 18 October 1978 the official Polish Press Agency claimed that 'in 1971–78 permission was granted for the construction, re-construction or expansion of 385 churches and chapels'. See also note 3 to Introduction.
4. Archbishop Casaroli paid three visits to Poland in 1967. The first round of talks was held in Rome in April 1971, the second in Warsaw in November of that year.
   During this period the Vatican also used the offices of other high ranking prelates, including Cardinal Franz König, the Archbishop of Vienna, who visited Poland in April 1971, January 1972 and May 1972. In April 1973 Cardinal Araoz Arturo Tabera, Prefect of the Congregation for Liturgy, visited several cities and villages in Poland—his stay lasted two weeks.
5. The four existing titular prelates acting as apostolic administrators became

THE CHURCH AND DISSENT: 1970-1980

bishop-in-ordinary of the same dioceses: Bolesław Kominek 'titular bishop of Eucaita and apostolic administrator of the central part of the Archbishopric of Wrocław' became the Metropolitan of Wrocław: Franciszek Jop, 'titular bishop of Daulia and apostolic administrator of the southern part of the Archdioces of Wrocław' became the bishop of Opole, where regardless of his official title, he has, in fact, presided since 1956; and similarly Bishop Jan Oblak of Warmia, with its capital in Olsztyn. A new diocese of Gorzów was created from territory detached from the Archdiocese of Wrocław, the old diocese of Berlin, and the old Prelature of Schneidmuelh. The former apostolic administrator, Bishop Wilhelm Pluta remained as its head while his two former auxiliary bishops, Jerzy Stroba and Ignacy Jeż were named bishops of Szczecin-Kamierń and Koszalin-Kołobrzeg respectively (two new dioceses carved out of the old territory of Gorzów).

The church administration in Poland now consisted of twenty-seven dioceses. Four of these dioceses, Gniezno-Warsaw, Poznań, Kraków and Wrocław are metropolitan sees administered by archbishops, one of whom, traditionally the head of the Gniezno-Warsaw diocese, holds the title and functions of primate. Three dioceses are ruled by apostolic administrators, two—those of Białystok and Lubaczów—represent the remaining territories of the former metropolitan sees of Vilna and Lvov respectively, parts of which are now in the USSR. The third, in Drohiczyn, former diocese of Pinsk, the greater part of whose district is now also in the USSR. To date the Vatican has not formally recognized the administrative changes in the territories concerned and which occurred after the Second World War when the new eastern borders of Poland were determined.

6. Kazimierz Papee was the Polish ambassador to the Vatican since 1939. Since 1945 he represented the Polish government-in-exile in London. After the accession of Pope John XXIII in 1958 he was recognized only as a chargé d'affaires.
7. Since Poland has twenty-seven dioceses the estimate of 1,000 new churches does not appear to be exaggerated.
8. This was the second incident at this village, in July 1969 a provisional chapel was occupied by a group of fifty militiamen and later converted into a warehouse for agricultural machinery. The villagers having been unsuccessful in obtaining a building permit promptly erected another provisional chapel.
9. The best documented police raids on unauthorized chapels are: March 1972, in the village of Bredzowice (Katowice Voivodship); November 1974, in Warsaw; April 1976, in the village of Gorki—south-west of Warsaw in the Kampinos Forest.
10. Article IV of the Accord states: 'Implementing the bill on military service, the military authorities will defer the call up of members of theological seminaries in order to enable them to complete their studies, while ordained priests and monks who have taken vows will not be called up, but will be transferred to the reserve and assigned to the auxiliary services.' This Accord was in fact broken on many occasions by Gomułka from 1960 onwards, but never formally cancelled. Seminarians were drafted as a form of reprisal against bishops who in one way or another had incurred the wrath of Gomułka. The practice was stopped after the fall of Gomułka in 1970.

THE CHURCH AND DISSENT: 1970-1980

Poland's theological students had always been at a disadvantage with their counterparts in other disciplines so far as military service is concerned. Under Ministry of Defence regulations of 21 July 1959, students attending certain universities and colleges (the list included over seventy institutions) were not called up, but studied military subjects as part of their academic curriculum. A later regulation dated 7 August 1973, extended this privilege to certain 'nonacademic' schools in which the Council of Ministers had introduced military training. Seminaries were not included on either list.

11. Background to the movement, its analysis and related documentary material is given in an article by Grażyna Sikorska, 'The Light-life Movement in Poland', *Religions in Communist Lands*, 11, (forthcoming, 1983).
12. Quoted after Alexander Tomsky, 'Poland's Church on the Road to Gdansk', *Religion in Communist Lands*, 9 (1981), p. 35. For a detailed and most interesting account of this movement see Adam Boniecki, *Budowa Kościołów w Diecezji Przemyskiej*, London, Biblioteka Spotkań, 1980.
13. Szablewski was appointed by the Polish Prime Minister at the suggestion of the Ministry of Foreign Affairs. He was formally accredited neither to the Italian State nor the Holy See and his status was similar to that of the United States permanent representative at the Vatican.
14. The texts of main protest letters and their analysis are published in *Dissent In Poland: Reports and Documents in Translation, December 1975-July 1977*, London, Association of Polish Students and Graduates in Exile, 1977.
15. The only MP to abstain from voting on the proposed amendments was the leader of the Znak Circle Stanisław Stomma. He was dropped from the list of candidates for the parliamentary elections in March 1976.
16. For complete text see *Dissent in Poland*, pp. 20-3.
17. Quoted by Alexander Tomsky in 'Poland's Church on the Road to Gdansk', pp. 35-6.
18. The various letters of protest against the Constitutional amendments were signed by over 40,000 people. The government official spokesman Włodzimierz Janiurek admitted during a press conference on 5 February 1976 that 'one in a thousand' of the population remain critical of the draft constitution. A more authoritative admission of dissent came from the chairman of the Council of State, Henryk Jabłoński who in his 10 February presentation to the Sejm of the final document, stated that the document was not totally endorsed by the population.
19. Quoted by Alexander Tomsky, p. 36.
20. It is frequently said that food prices remained stable in Poland since the events of 1970. But in fact, hidden increases in the price of many articles including foodstuffs were not infrequent between 1970 and 1976; articles were often repacked, renamed or reclassified as better quality, and in each case the end result was the same; higher prices in shops. In the same period, 1970 to 1976 nominal wages and salaries rose from average of 2.235 zlotys in 1970 to 3.546 zlotys in 1975; although the increase was much less in real terms. The Government was forced to subsidize food prices to the tune of 22 thousand million zlotys in 1970 and over 100 thousand million in 1975. The market supply situation worsened; many articles, food in particular, were in short supply and the queues in front of shops visibly lengthened.
21. The increases were larger than expected: the price of sugar was to go up by

THE CHURCH AND DISSENT: 1970-1980

100 per cent, of meat and fish by 69 per cent, of butter and better quality cheeses by over 50 per cent, of poultry and vegetables by 30 per cent. The effect would be to increase the household expenditure by 16 per cent. To compensate for these increases, wage and salary supplements were proposed, ranging from 240 zlotys a month for low-earners to 600 for high-earners. However, should the contract of employment be dissolved, either by the employee, or through his fault by the employer, the supplement would be permanently forfeited.

22. For complete text of the Appeal and other related documents see Peter Raina, *Independent Social Movements in Poland*, London, London School of Economics and Political Science, 1981. See also *Dissent in Poland*.
23. For complete text see: *Dissent in Poland*, pp. 135-6. In September 1977 after all those arrested during the June 1976 protests had been released and the majority of those who lost their jobs had been reinstated, KOR decided to broaden the scope of its human rights activities to include all those who had been persecuted for their political views and who were seeking help in the defence of their rights as citizens. KOR also changed its name. From then it was known as the Committee for Social Self-Defence or 'KOR'.

    For complete text of KOR'S 29 September 1977 Statement see: B. Szajkowski (ed.), *Documents in Communist Affairs—1977*, London, Butterworth, 1982, pp. 276-8.
24. Later in the Committee's Communiqué no. 4 dated 22 November 1976, KOR explained that it would consider that it 'had no further role to play, when the appropriate institutions started performing their proper duties when an amnesty was declared, the victimized workers were rehabilitated and re-instated in their old jobs on full pay and without loss of continuity of employment, when the scale of reprisals was made public, and when officials responsible for the abuse of law and for the use of torture were brought to court'.
25. Jacek Kuroń, one of the spokesmen for KOR said in an interview with *Le Monde* published on 29 January 1977 that Marxists like himself should not depend totally on the Church as a focus of opposition to the Government, since it had become 'the fundamental adversary of the system', but he indicated that he appreciated the Episcopate's stand on human rights. Another KOR member, Adam Michnik, described in November 1976 the Church's support for the Committee's goals as 'precious'.
26. Adam Michnik, *Kościół, lewica, dialog*, Paris, Institut literacki, 1977.
27. Archbishop Poggi was appointed the Vatican special nuncio for permanent working contacts with the Polish Government, subsequent to the joint Vatican-Polish communiqué of 6 February 1974 issued by Foreign Minister Stefan Olszowski and the Secretary of the Council for Public Affairs of the Church Archbishop Agostino Casaroli. His first trip to Poland in his official capacity took place between 25 February and 25 March 1975 during which he handed his credentials to the Foreign Minister. The second visit was from 23 April to 18 May 1976 and third between 4 and 26 March 1977.
28. Cardinal Wyszyński met Gierek's predecessor Władysław Gomułka in January 1958, January 1960 and April 1963. In addition, unofficial contacts between the regime and the Episcopate were also maintained on a lower level, until 1966.

29. Thus, for example, in Warsaw churches were built in six parishes and permits granted for the construction of two others and the rebuilding of one which had been destroyed.
30. For the complete texts of both speeches, see Szajkowski, *Documents in Communist Affairs—1977*, pp. 255-9.
31. By now also Casaroli was beginning to admit some doubts about the Christian-Marxist dialogue. During a lecture at the Austrian Institute of International Relations in February 1978 he suggested that the contradictions between Marxist and Christian principles could not be overcome. As a major obstacle he singled out the atheistic indoctrination of the youth which was alien to Catholic teaching. He also informed his listeners, in a veiled way, that any positive results of the *Ostpolitik* were insignificant and that he was sceptical about future developments.
32. The name Flying University comes from an academic society created in 1885 in Russian-occupied Poland which aimed at helping Poles to preserve national identity and to enable young people to enrich their knowledge through self-education. It offered uncensored courses in higher education, especially in the field of social, political and economic sciences which were secretly conducted by well known scholars in private homes.

During the Second World War in occupied Poland only elementary education existed for Poles but secondary and even higher level courses, organized underground by the Flying University were available on a limited scale. After 1945 with very few exceptions organized educational activity, independent of the state was almost non-existent. The only notable exceptions were the Catholic University in Lublin and seminaries for training priests. In 1956 the Crooked Circle Club—a discussion club for the intellectual elite emerged in Warsaw but was dissolved by the authorities in February 1962 together with several smaller clubs in other cities which attempted to copy it. Afterwards various semi-private seminars appeared periodically. These were usually run by eminent academics in their homes for the benefit of young lecturers and senior students. Other attempts at independent education were small usually short-lived study/discussion groups, which were the product of the intellectual curiosity of the young. Perhaps the best-known of these was the Contradiction Seekers' Club in the early sixties, otherwise known as 'Michnik's Club'. Organized independent activities in post-war Poland began to emerge only in 1977 and should be seen against the background of general increase of dissent. One of these is the Independent Discussion Club in Łódź founded on 29 October 1977. Its declaration issued on that day stated the Club's aims as: free discussion, the exchange of views, self-educational activity in the form of seminars, discussions and lectures, meetings with eminent writers and artists. In October 1977 a group of intellectuals began a series of lectures in Warsaw, devoted primarily to the social sciences and history. The lectures took place in private flats and were attended mainly by students of the various higher educational establishments in Warsaw. This initiative also called the Flying University soon led to the formation of the Society for Scientific Courses.

From the second year of its activities, the Flying University frequently used churches for its lectures which allowed many more people to participate in their activities. Thus for example in October 1978 over 1,200 attended

THE CHURCH AND DISSENT: 1970-1980

Professor Władysław Bartoszewski's lecture on 'Attitudes towards Totalitarianism' in Wrocław Cathedral.
33. From the beginning a number of professors from the Catholic University of Lublin took part in giving talks on various subjects, including Irena Nowakowa (sociologist), Czesław Zgorzelski (historian), and Irena Sławińska (sociologist). Other prominent Catholic intellectuals such as Tadeusz Mazowiecki, the chief editor of the monthly Więź (Bond), and Jacek Woźniakowski from the monthly Znak (Sign) also took a very active part. Cardinal Karol Wojtyła allowed the academic chaplaincy in Kraków the use of a monastery for a similar course of public lectures between November 1977 and March 1978.
34. For documentary material on the society of Academic Courses see Raina, *Independent Social Movements in Poland*, pp. 334-69.
35. A pamphlet published by the Department of Ideological Training of the Polish United Workers' Party Central Committee in May 1978 listed nineteen illegal journals with a total single print run of 20,000 copies.
36. In addition to *Spotkania* three other Catholic *Samizdat* publications appeared regularly in Poland: *Zgrzyt* (Grind); *Krzyż Nowohucki* (The Cross of Nowa Huta); *Wspólny Dom* (Common Home). For background to the emergence of *Spotkania* and analysis of its content see: Piotr Jeglinski and Alexander Tomsky, 'Spotkania—Journal of the Catholic Opposition in Poland', *Religion in Communist Lands*, 7, (1979), pp. 23-8; Alexander Tomsky '*Spotkania* Revisited', *Index on Censorship* (forthcoming).
37. *Spotkania* (London edition), no. 1, October 1977, p. 9.
38. Twelve numbers of *Spotkania* appeared in Poland between 1977 and 1981. Eight numbers have been re-published in London. One issue of the journal appeared under martial law. Its editor, Janusz Krupski, was picked up by the police only after ten months in hiding.
39. For complete text see B. Szajkowski (ed.), *Documents in Communist Affairs—1979*, London, Butterworth Scientific, 1982, pp. 465-8.
40. An interesting account of the reactions in Poland to Cardinal Wojtyła's election is printed in *Spotkania* (London edition), no. 8, pp. 155-69.
41. *Der Spiegel*, 23 October 1978.
42. For full text see Szajkowski (ed.), *Documents in Communist Affairs—1979*, p. 492.
43. The suggestion to form committees for the defence of believers was made in a letter from forty-two deans of Przemyśl diocese sent to the local *voivode* on 13 October 1978, in protest against government policy of taking seminarians from their studies by drafting them into the army: 'just as other Polish citizens are not called up during the time of their higher studies. We do not want to threaten anybody. All we want to do is to defend the lawful civic rights of the believers. At the same time we emphatically declare that if our requests are not heeded, we will resort to all suitable means towards this end, including the formation of the Believers' Self-defence Committees and organization of hunger strikes in various countries in the diocese'.
44. For complete text see Szajkowski (ed.), *Documents in Communist Affairs —1979*, pp. 493-4.
45. See *Polityka*, 8 March 1979.
46. Wiesław Mysłek, 'Kościół i władza', *Nowe Drogi*, no. 5, May 1979, pp. 34-7.

THE CHURCH AND DISSENT: 1970-1980

47. *Redemptor Hominis*, London, Catholic Truth Society, n.d.
48. In protest against the authorities' refusal to let the Pope visit Piekary Śląskie, two free trade-union activists from Katowice, Kazimierz Świton and Mirosław Szydło, and a student from the Catholic University of Lublin, staged a hunger strike in the church in Piekary Śląskie. Their protest lasted for thirteen days and ended only after intervention from the Bishop of Katowice.
49. For complete text see Radio Free Europe, Munich. Background Report 151, 6 July 1979.
50. See *Polityka*, 1 June 1979.
51. For the complete texts of both speeches see B. Szajkowski, ed., *Documents in Communist Affairs—1980*, London, Macmillan, 1981, pp. 231-8. Subsequent quotes of the Pope's pronouncements in Poland are taken from *Return to Poland. The Collected Speeches of John Paul II*, London, Collins, 1979.
52. See Szajkowski (ed.), *Documents in Communist Affairs—1980* op. cit., pp. 252-3.
53. The second committee was formed on 4 August 1979 in Przemyśl and the third on 9 December 1979 in the village of Cisów in south-east Poland. For details see Raina, *Independent Social Movements in Poland*, pp. 397-406.
54. The petition was started in August 1979, chiefly by dissident circles associated with the Social Self-Defence Committee, 'KOR'.

3 The Triumph of Solidarity

The Polish workers' revolt in the summer of 1980 was the culmination of a long process of dissent in which a range of movements participated, some of which have been analysed in the preceding chapters.[1] At the same time it should be stressed that the mass solidarity which surfaced in the summer of 1980 and which was chiefly political in nature could not have been achieved without the discreet but determined encouragement from the Church in the past. Equally important was the fact that after thirty-five years of socialism in Poland religious symbolism had become the only language capable of expressing the ideals of social emancipation. Included in this symbolism was the continuity of Polish cultural heritage, the ancient struggle for national independence and the identity of the individual. It was based on the Church's ideology, its moral and ethical values which enabled it to retain the role of custodian of Polish nationalist tradition, commitment to values of hard work and social humility, establish a *modus vivendi* with the Communist regime and interact with the secular Left. All these factors played equally important roles not only in retaining but enhancing the Church's position *vis-à-vis* both the regime and the faithful. The common good of the country and the maintenance of order in the society became the overriding principle on which the Church's relations with the regime were based. As far as the faithful were concerned, the Church shared with them solidarity in the face of a totalitarian power and a common language capable of overcoming the phenomenon of conceptual embezzlement. This subtle combination remained unchanged during the period between July 1980 and December 1981 discussed in this chapter.

As in 1970 and in 1976, the mass strikes in 1980 were triggered off by price increases.[2] The decision was taken on 1 July and announced the following day during a television interview with a deputy director of Poland's food-distribution co-operatives. The increases of between 30 and 100 per cent on good quality beef, pork and poultry other than chicken were to be introduced gradually by local authorities as and when they saw fit. Although the increases affected only 2 per cent of the meat on the market, which was transferred to the so-called 'commercial' shops where products were sold at much higher prices than in normal stores, the rise in meat prices, for the third time since 1970, was clearly political in intent. It was meant to affirm the Government's capacity to make difficult decisions and stick by them in the face of social opposition. Introduction of the price increases was met by an immediate reaction from the workers. On 2 July strikes broke out in the Ursus tractor plant near Warsaw and the vehicle plant factory in Tczew near Gdańsk.[3] They later spread throughout the country, setting the stage for the growth of a massive strike movement which rocked the very foundation of the Polish regime.

The official media made no mention of the strikes. The first authentic source of information was a communiqué issued by the Social Self-Defence Committee (KOR) on 2 July.[4] The Committee from then on served as a principal source of information. It collected and spread the news of the strikes in various parts of the country, thus allowing the workers to realize that they were part of a much wider national movement. It also provided vital tactical and legal advice bypassing the Party-controlled trade unions. This was the result of the bond forged between members of the working class and the intelligentsia after the events of June 1976.

During the first two weeks of the strikes the workers' demands were almost entirely economic and included: the restoration of old prices; a wage rise to compensate for the rise in the cost of living; a restructuring of work norms; special compensation for difficult work; family allowances on a par with those of the militia and the armed forces. At that stage the workers were prepared to accept the Government's policy provided that their own economic interests did not suffer. Most negotiating was conducted locally without direct participation by State or Party officials. The strength and sudden spread of the strike movement evidently took the authorities by surprise, and they reacted in a hesitant and confused way. By the end of the first week in July, the price increases were progressively rescinded and in some cases, in an attempt to avert strikes, management granted wage increases to non-strikers. On 9 July however, the PUWP First Secretary, Edward Gierek, in a speech to the Central Committee, reintroduced the price increases and declared that 'any broader increases in salaries would not be acceptable'. This clearly expressed intransigence by the Party, together with delayed reaction by some local Party officials who tried to intimidate the strikers, resulted in the workers' greater mobilization and political awareness.

On 16 July, the train drivers at Lublin blocked the four main railway lines that connect Poland with the Soviet Union. They were joined by other railway staff and dairy and bakery workers. Their demands were not only economic in nature but also for the first time included political ones; the right to strike; immunity for strikers and new elections to trade-union chapters. The workers also demanded direct talks with a Government delegation. For the regime, the Lublin strike presented the most serious challenge so far, not only was a strike taking place in a sensitive communication area close to the Soviet border, but it affected important communication lines with the Soviet Union. In addition the strikers' demands were overtly political. An emergency meeting of the Party's Political Bureau held on 17 July decided to send a special commission headed by one of its members and a Deputy Prime Minister, Mieczysław Jagielski, to negotiate with the workers and a communiqué was issued appealing to patriotic sentiments and calling for a return to work. Significantly the communiqué also referred to 'anxiety among friends'. This explicit reference to possible Soviet intervention would from then on be repeated throughout the Polish crisis and the spectre of such action would determine the role played by the Catholic Church. It is important to remember that while Mieczysław Jagielski was conducting negotiations with the strikers, the first arrests were being made in Lublin. Among the five people detained, four were Catholic opposition activists and one a member of the dissent group, Movement for the Defence of Human and Civil Rights (ROPCO). It turned out that this group, attached to the unofficial Catholic journal *Spotkania*, had been active in co-ordinating strike movements in the Lublin area.

Although the Lublin strike was settled after four days when the workers accepted a compromise pay offer, it signalled the beginning of a new stage in the protest movement. As July wore on, the Lublin demands began to be repeated elsewhere. More importantly, however, the experience of industrial action led to *ad hoc* organizations by the workers and the election of autonomous committees for their representation. This further transformed the strike movement into a political act.

By 14 August, when 17,000 workers of the Lenin Shipyard in Gdańsk began their protest, some 157 strikes of various duration had taken place throughout the country. The immediate cause of the Gdańsk strike[5] was the dismissal of Anna Walentynowicz, a crane operator and a veteran activist of the dissident Free Trade Union of the Coast. Early in the morning, when the first meeting of workers began, Lech Wałęsa,[6] having climbed over the twelve-foot perimeter fence, assumed the leadership of the strike. By midday the strikers had drawn up an eight-point list of demands which included: reinstatement of Walentynowicz, Wałęsa and another worker; erection of a memorial to victims of the December 1970 workers' revolt;[7] pay increases of 2,000 zlotys; family supplements equal to those of militia and security service employees; earlier retirement and better food supplies, including the abolition of the 'commercial' Pewex shops; publication of the strikers' demands in the media and the creation of a free trade-union movement. The strike committee elected by the meeting began talks with the management which were attended by the Party's provincial first secretary Tadeusz Fiszbach, and relayed by loudspeakers to the workers. Although by the end of the day, the first three demands were met by the authorities, the strike spread fairly rapidly to encompass other plants in Gdańsk and the conurbation of Gadńsk-Gdynia-Sopot). On 16 August, representatives of twenty-one striking crews from the coastal area decided to set up the Inter-Factory Strike Committee, which drew up twenty-one demands which consistently remained their negotiating position.[8]

The hierarchy of the Roman Catholic Church appears to have been taken by surprise at the strength and rapid spread of the workers' protest. The communiqué of the Plenary Conference of the Episcopate which met between June 27 and 28 made no mention of the workers' unrest. While conspicuously avoiding involvement in the current situation, possibly in order not to exacerbate the unrest, they nevertheless stated that Catholics felt more responsible than ever for the country's fate. The bishops also wanted to avoid saying anything that could jeopardize the outcome of delicate negotiations with the regime which included several issues vital for the present and future work of the Church, such as the question of its legal status, authorization for a lay Catholic organization, access to mass media and an internal circulation permit for the Polish edition of *L'Osservatore Romano.* More importantly, however, they feared the fall of state authority and a subsequent outside intervention.

Cardinal Wyszyński speaking on 15 August in Czestochowa to a crowd of 150,000 pilgrims also made no direct mention of the strikes but devoted major parts of his sermon to the victory of the Pitsudki Army over the Red Army in 1920 (known as the miracle on the Vistula River). 'God had helped the Fatherland at the time when its freedom was under threat!' 'Bread is the property of the whole nation', he said, adding that Poles this year had been asking for their bread in a tactful and dignified way. A sermon of this content at this time revealed a great deal about the philosophy of the Polish Church. Thoughts about freedom and sovereignty were expressed here in a manner which to many seemed abstract for a time when the workers were demanding concrete freedoms for themselves, society and the Church and when the gates of the Gdańsk shipyard were decorated with religious symbols, the Inter-Factory Strike Committee having placed a crucifix next to the statue of Lenin in their meeting hall.

In Gdańsk, however, the 71-year-old Bishop Lech Kaczmarek, who had witnessed the previous riots in 1970 and 1976, began on 16 August private mediations with the local party and civic leaders. To help maintain peace the bishop suggested that the Church's pastoral care should be allowed for the strikers. When both sides agreed to his proposal, he authorized three priests, including Father Henryk Jankowski, the priest of Wałęsa's parish of St. Brigid to say masses for the workers. In the morning of 17 August the first open air mass was celebrated inside the Lenin Shipyard. Attended by some 4,000 strikers with another 2,000 people outside the gates, the ceremony became a daily part of the strikers' lives. After the mass, Father Jankowski blessed a large wooden cross made by the yard carpenters which was dug into the ground outside Gate No. 2 as a memorial for workers killed in December 1970. Bishop Kaczmarek meanwhile continued to act as unofficial intermediary between local authorities and strikers and visited the shipyard.

Later on that same day Cardinal Wyszyński delivered another sermon—this time at the Marian Shrine at Wambierzyce in Lower Silesia.

At this moment when our country is filled with torment and unrest, we cannot be indifferent to what is worrying the nation, the State, our families, and those workers who are striving for social, moral, economic and cultural rights. These are values required for the normal development of the nation . . . I want to remind you of what this country needs so that calm and reason might reign here: in the first place we must work honestly, with a sense of responsibility and conscientiousness; secondly, we should not squander, we should not waste, but economize, because let us bear in mind that we are a nation still on our way to prosperity; thirdly, we must borrow less but also export less, and on the other hand, better satisfy all the needs of the people, that is their moral, social, religious, cultural and economic needs.[9]

Although this time the Cardinal went slightly further in acknowledging the unrest, his pronouncement was not, however, an expression of unrestricted solidarity with the workers. It mattered little at that stage since selected extracts of his sermon were broadcast (without precedent in People's Poland) by Warsaw Television only on 20 August (excluding references to unrest and freedom of expression) and at that time all communication links were cut.[10]

On 20 August the Pope, for the first time since the beginning of the strike movement, appealed to his weekly general audience to pray for 'my Poland'. The papal reaction came only after the return to Rome of his private secretary Monsignor Stanisław Dziwisz, who was in Poland for a week ostensibly on holiday. On the same day John Paul II sent a personal message to Wyszyński (a fact revealed three days later) in which he said: 'I am with my country and countrymen throughout your ordeal, with all my heart and in all my prayers . . . I pray that, once again, the Episcopate with the Primate as its head . . . may be able to aid the nation in its struggle for daily bread, social justice, and the safeguarding of its inviolable right to its own way of life and achievement . . .[11]

The following day, Bishop Kaczmarek went to Warsaw to brief Cardinal Wyszyński and the Secretary of the Episcopal Conference, Bishop Bronisław Dąbrowski on the situation. He told them that contrary to Government propaganda the Inter-Factory Strike Committee was the authentic representative of the striking workers and that order as well as determination prevailed in striking enterprises and in Gdańsk. It is interesting to note that the press office of the Episcopate felt it necessary in order to put the record straight, to issue a 'note' on the meeting. Such was the degree of alarm and uncertainty about the outcome of the situation among the Episcopate. The 'note' confirmed that Kaczmarek had met the strikers' committee the previous week 'during which he expressed his understanding for the strikers who are striving to improve their lot both in material terms and with regard to gaining respect for their human rights'. However, it noted that he had also appealed to them to act in a wise and prudent manner'. He called their attention to the fact that prolonged strikes and possible disturbances or the shedding of brotherly blood are contrary to the good of society. After his return to Gdańsk on 23 August, Kaczmarek on the same day issued a proclamation in connection with the events on the coast:

> I have always understood and understand today your troubles, sufferings and endeavours. You have the right to raise your voice in matters which cause you pain. This position I have expressed many times in my talks with the authorities. Everything has to take place in an atmosphere of reflection, dignity, mutual understanding and without hatred...
>
> Begin negotiations with the authorities through your elected delegates. Do this in peace and dignity, demanding the fulfilment of all your postulates with understanding and without hatred...[12]

In the Gdańsk shipyard meanwhile negotiations began on 23 August between the Inter-Factory Strike Committee, now consisting of some 800 delegates, and the second Government Commission (after the collapse of negotiations with the first Commission), headed by Mieczysław Jagielski. At the same time another Government Commission headed by a member of the Party's Political Bureau and a Deputy Prime Minister, Kazimierz Barcikowski, had, a day earlier, started negotiations with the Inter-Factory Strike Committee at the Warski Shipyard in Szczecin.[13] The negotiations in Gdańsk which were broadcast on the local radio[14] made little progress; the apparent sticking point was the workers' first demand—independent trade unions. Jagielski returned to Warsaw in the evening to report to the Party leadership. On 24 August the Central Committee met and gave its cautious approval for further negotiations. The meeting also resulted in a major reshuffle of the Party and Government leadership. Although Edward Gierek was able to hold on to his position, six of his most important allies were ousted from the Political Bureau.[15] In his closing speech to the plenum of the Central Committee, Gierek spoke humbly and self-critically about 'our own errors, inconsistencies, delays and hesitations' and proposed new procedures for electing trade-union officials by secret ballot, without limitation on the number of candidates, but he rejected the workers' demand for free trade unions.[16]

The same evening Gierek suffered a nervous breakdown. To the surprise of his entourage he asked Stanisław Kania, Secretary of the Central Committee responsible for security, armed forces and Church-State relations[17] to fetch the Polish Primate, Wyszyński, who went to see Gierek in his residence and found him panic-stricken and confused. For more than an hour he listened to Gierek's explanations and supplications. His main message was that the workers were demanding something impossible, there would be chaos and bloodshed and inevitably Soviet intervention. He implored Wyszyński's help in calming the situation. The Primate, recalling the warning he had given when they met in January 1975, unequivocally stated that he and the Episcopate supported the workers. At the same time he assured Gierek that the Church would do everything possible to plead for restraint in the settlement of the conflict.[18] The workers were impressed neither by Gierek's concessions nor by the changes in Poland's political leadership. They remained committed to accept nothing short of new independent trade unions. During the fateful weekend of 23-4 August a new element entered the situation in Gdańsk. Tadeusz Mazowiecki, editor of the Catholic periodical *Więź*, and a prominent figure in the Catholic Intelligentsia Club in Warsaw organized, at the invitation of the Inter-Factory Strike Committee, a group of intellectuals to act as advisers to the Committee.[19] The team consisted of Mazowiecki; Dr Bohdan Cywiński, historian and editor-in-chief of the Catholic monthly *Znak*; Andrzej Wielowieyski, writer and secretary of the Warsaw Catholic Intelligentsia Club; Dr Bronisław Geremek, historian and political scientist; Dr Tadeusz Kowalik, economist and former editor-in-chief of *Życie Gospodarcze* (Economic Life); Dr Jadwiga Staniskis, sociologist and Dr Waldemar Kuczyński, economist. The latter three had been particularly active in the Flying University.[20] All the team played a vital role in negotiating details with the Government Commission's experts behind closed doors, while the public negotiating sessions between the strikers and the Commission were conducted in front of television cameras from the world's press and broadcast to the strikers on the local State-controlled radio station.[21]

As the delicate and tense negotiations continued in Gdańsk and Szczecin, on 26 August Cardinal Wyszyński delivered a sermon at the monastery of Jasna Góra.[22] He appealed for 'calm, balance, prudence, wisdom and responsibility for the whole Polish Nation'. He continued:

> The better we perform our daily duties, the more assured we can be that help will come. What is more, the more aware we are of our responsibility for the Nation in performing our daily duties, the more justified or substantiated our rights will be, and in the name of those rights we can advance demands. But not otherwise! . . .
>
> The responsibility, then is joint. Why? Because the guilt is also joint. No one is without sin, no one is without guilt. It can manifest itself in various forms. It can be guilt for violating the personal rights of man, which implies a moral and social deformation of man. It can be guilt for not defending our rights, to which we are entitled as we fulfil our duties. This could be the result of a lack of social awareness, a certain passivity and insensitivity to the common weal, social weal, the good of the family, Nation and State . . .
>
> Let us remember how difficult it was to regain our independence after 125 years of subjugation. And as we devoted much time to domestic arguments and disputes, so a great danger threatened us and our independence . . . Today we often complain about the inefficiency of various social and vocational institutions. One branch of work blames another. We know how to enumerate adverse effects of work and management, we know how to talk about various unsuccessful undertakings. We know how to condemn them and how to devolve the responsibility for them on to other vocational groups. But let us think, how do we ourselves perform our work? What is our contribution to social life and the national economy? True enough, there may be

stumbling blocks everywhere. I looked at the fields on my way from Warsaw today. Some of them have been reaped and ploughed. In other, the grain was still standing in shocks or even unreaped. Sure enough, this may be the effect of the weather in that area; nevertheless, diligence and honesty in work do play a part. We know that where there is no honest work even the best economic system will fail while debts and loans multiply . . .

Although man has the right to rest, although sometimes— when he has no other means—he has the right to make his stand also by refraining from work, yet we know that the argument is very costly. The cost of this argument runs in billions, which burden the whole nation, the family and each individual . . .

I think that sometimes one should refrain from too many demands and claims, just so that peace and order may prevail in Poland; this is hard, especially as demands can be justified and they usually are sound; but there never is a situation where it would be possible to fulfil all the demands at once, right away, today. Their implementation must be gradual. And that is why we must talk: we shall first satisfy those demands which have priority, and then others. This is the law of everyday life . . .

Scientists, who deal with issues of international rights, speak of the so-called equilibrium in Europe . . . this equilibrium . . . was disturbed two centuries ago, when Poland was partitioned. It was then that Europe's adversities, perpetual wars and unrest began. Restoration of Poland and a group of Slavic nations to their proper place, restoration of their freedom, became the beginning of a renewal and consolidation of political equilibrium. And this is a profound truth . . .

In order to fulfil our tasks we have to have national, moral, social, cultural and economic sovereignty! . . . And though today there is no full sovereignty between nations linked in various treaties and blocs, there are, after all limits to these treaties, limits of the responsibility for one's own nation, for its rights and for the right to sovereignty . . .

In this powerful and much misunderstood sermon, Wyszyński quite clearly put the whole weight of his prestige into the balance to bring the Government and the workers together. The misunderstanding of the Primate's intention was accelerated by the fact that only carefully selected excerpts were broadcast on the Polish radio that evening and relayed by the Polish Press Agency.[23] A summary of the sermon even appeared the following day, an event without precedent in People's Poland, on the front page of the Party Central Committee's daily newspaper *Trybuna Ludu*. This itself underscored the gravity of the situation.

Wyszyński obviously believed in warnings of possible bloodshed, chaos and military intervention, and as in the past expounded the traditional teaching of the Church on the sanctity of human life, self-examination and professional ethics. The sermon also contained the principle which had guided him throughout the past thirty-two years as Primate; the interest of the nation is paramount. Here he was consistent with the teaching of the Church as well as the demands and expectations of Polish nationalism.

The workers, however, were bitterly disappointed. To them, Wyszyński appeared to be hesitant and vacillating. His intervention was inopportune to say the least. If the sermon was an appeal to go back to work, it made no impact on the strikers. They were determined to carry on until their case was won.

Because of the negative reactions to the Primate's sermon the Main Council of the Episcopal Conference, meeting in an emergency session that afternoon, issued a lengthy communiqué.[24] In it the bishops expressed 'gratitude both to the workers and their committees, and to the authorities for having managed to avoid upsetting public order. This is proof of civil and political maturity.' The bishops emphatically reminded the authorities that internal peace could not be achieved without full civic freedom, honest information about present and past events and a frank dialogue with the authorities about society, just wages and private ownership of land. Most importantly however, they also gave unequivocal backing to the workers' demands for independent trade unions. Quoting the Second Vatican Council they said: 'Among the fundamental rights of the individual must be numbered the right of workers to form themselves into associations which truly represent them and are able to co-operate in organizing economic life properly, and the right to play their part in the activities of such associations without risk of reprisal.'

This was what the strikers wanted. Extracts from the communiqué were printed on the front page of the national daily newspapers on 29 August and published in the Strike Information Bulletin in the Lenin Shipyard on 30 August.

The communiqué was important for at least one other reason. It contained the thoughts and attitudes of the bishops as a collective body as against Wyszyński's sermon, where he was speaking for himself. Thus a certain 'division of labour' seemed to have emerged within the Polish Episcopate at times when matters were particularly delicate. This pattern would become particularly obvious after the declaration of martial law. It served as a useful device to give more room for manœuvre to the Primate who was personally involved in direct and complex negotiations with the State authorities.

As the strikes in Gdańsk dragged on and the Soviet press agency Tass published a commentary expressing fears about subversive antisocialist elements operating in the Polish coastal region, during the night of 27-8 August Cardinal Wyszyński sent Dr Romuald Kukołowicz, a sociologist, former assistant professor at the Catholic University of Lublin to the Party's Political Bureau as his personal representative.[25] Dr Kukołowicz brought with him an offer to mediate between the Government Commission and the Inter-Factory Strike Committee. The Political Bureau agreed. In the morning Kukołowicz, together with another of the Primate's representatives, the distinguished sociologist of religion and professor at the Catholic Academy in Warsaw Andrzej Święcicki, flew to Gdańsk.

The results justified the means. On 30 August the Szczecin agreement was signed and the following day Lech Wałęsa, wearing a rosary around his neck, signed the Gdańsk agreement using an outsize pen adorned with a portrait of the Pope (a souvenir of the papal visit in 1979).[26]

Both the agreements contained demands made by the Church on a number of previous occasions: access to the State-controlled media and a limitation of censorship. While the Szczecin agreement in paragraph 13 merely stated that 'It has been ascertained that the dialogue between the Roman Catholic Church and the State is developing favourably. Wider access to the mass media will be made possible',[27] the Gdańsk agreement was much more detailed and explicit:

> Concerning Point 3, which reads: 'To respect the freedom of speech, print and publication guaranteed in the Constitution

of the Polish People's Republic, and by the same token not to apply repressive measures against independent publications and to give access to the mass media to representatives of all religious denominations', it has been agreed that:

(1) The Government will submit to the Sejm within three months a draft bill on the control of the press, publications and performances, based on the following principles: censorship should protect the interest of the State. This means protection of State and industrial secrets, the scope of which will be defined by law, of matters concerning security of the State and its important international interests, protection of religious feelings and the feelings of non-believers, and prevention of the distribution of morally harmful materials. The draft bill would also include provision for appeal against the decisions of the organs for the control of the press, publications and performances to the Chief Administrative Court. This law will also be introduced by amending the code of administrative procedure.

(2) The use of the mass media by religious denominations within the scope of their religious activity will be realized upon settling the substantive and organizational problems between State organs and the interested religious denominations. The Government will ensure radio broadcasting of the Sunday Mass, within the framework of a detailed agreement with the Episcopate.

(3) The activity of the radio and television, as well as press and publishing enterprises, should serve the expression of different ideas, views and judgements. It should be subjected to public control.

(4) The press, like the citizens and their organizations, should have access to public documents, especially administrative ones relating to socio-economic plans, etc., issued by the Government and its subordinate administrative organs. Exemptions from the principle of openness of the activity of the administration will be specified in the bill in accordance with Point 1.

After the signing of the Gdańsk and Szczecin agreements the Church found itself in a relatively novel position, in which the most important problems for the religious institution had been discussed and/or solved by other social groups without direct participation of Church officials.

Until then both the position and the functions of the Church in Poland had been exclusively defined in terms of its relationship with the Party and the State. While making its complaints and demands public through periodic pastoral letters and statements, the Church had always addressed them directly to the authorities. It had never appealed to society either to approve its actions or to support them publicly. No social group had ever undertaken to argue on behalf of the Church or to defend its interests in dealing with the Government. The reason for this was simply that no public group capable of fulfilling those functions had ever existed in Poland's political life. This situation suddenly changed during the summer of 1980. For the first time the Church was not the sole representative of the interests of the whole nation in dealings with the Party. For the first time the workers represented the nation's interests and because of an unchanged awareness of the identity of Polishness and Catholicism, spoke out for the rights of the Church. In contrast with the workers' upheavals of 1970 and 1976, the Church was now faced with formidable competition in the form of a cohesive, well-organized, disciplined and mature workforce. If this situation were to last, it could weaken the role and position of the Church.

The Roman Catholic hierarchy recognized the prospect of its declining influence and Cardinal Wyszyński moved quickly to ascertain the Church's central position. In a letter sent on 2 September to all parish priests,[28] he commended the workers for their courage during the strikes and fully acknowledged that the primary aims of their actions were the lofty issues of 'social justice and freedom' and the right to organize free trade unions. This letter certainly gave further encouragement to a great many of the local clergy, who had in the past discreetly supported various dissenting groups. To those among them who were ambivalent about the workers' movement it pointed out the direction they should take in the new and unprecedented situation. On 7 September the newly constituted sixteen-member Founding Committee of the Independent Self-Governing Trade Union, led by Wałęsa, travelled to Warsaw for a private but well publicized meeting with the Primate. Wyszyński offered a Mass in his private chapel during which he commended Wałęsa for his display of truly Christian virtues at a time of hard trial. It was followed by a communal breakfast for the whole group in which other Church dignitaries participated, including

THE TRIUMPH OF SOLIDARITY

the Secretary of the Episcopal Conference, Bishop Bronisław Dąbrowski, the person most directly involved in the day-to-day aspects of Church-State relations. During the breakfast both sides were able to ascertain their respective positions and clear up any misunderstandings. The meeting was also important on other counts. On the one hand, the newly founded trade union was able to overtly obtain public recognition from the head of the powerful Church, as well as a boost for the prestige of Wałęsa as a strike leader and chief director of the organization. On the other hand, the Cardinal by identifying himself publicly with the union was able to restore his image, tarnished as a result of his cautious pronouncements during the strikes.

The regime also lent a helping hand to the re-assertion of the Church's position. In early September, during the session of the Sejm the Prime Minister, Józef Pińkowski, expressed the Government's appreciation to the Church for its 'consideration and patriotic care for the country'. Similar in essence was the action of the Catholic laity in providing legal, organizational and technical advice to those planning to set up the new trade-union structures. The first and most influential of these advisory centres was set up at the Catholic Intelligentsia Club in Warsaw on 9 September.

In spite of the atmosphere of euphoria, few ordinary people had realized that Poland was treading an unknown and dangerous path. During the night between 5-6 September Edward Gierek was ousted and replaced as First Secretary by Stanisław Kania.[29] His departure was an attempt to relieve the Party of some of the responsibility for the maladministration of the previous ten years and a convenient moment to start to patch up its shattered image. However, during the following months as the Party continued its routine, and no longer credible, course of sacking national and provincial officials, the new trade union began to consolidate its organization. The talk of renewal, however genuine, had been heard before so many times that it was no longer believed. As the Party's prestige began to plummet, so did the membership figures.[30] Its claim to the leading role in the nation, never particularly convincing, now was only legitimate in terms of membership of the socialist commonwealth and the direct security zone of a world socialist power, the Soviet Union. The Party apparat began to show signs of demoralization and corrosion as a result of the inconsequent and indecisive policies of the country's leadership. Then, when the job security of the middle and lower apparat began to be threatened, it fought back in an uncoordinated way, quite often using provocation in order to secure its members' very livelihood. The ruling elite attempted to change its legitimacy from that based on its claim to be the *avant garde* of the working class, to a new one based on a social contract, thus implying the existence of two sides with different interests. This shift in the philosophy of power produced further confusion among both Party and Government administrators and as it was not followed by any change in the formal political structure, resulted in a series of deep political crises. Poland was in the midst of a revolution, a dangerously unbalanced process—even more so in this case as nobody really knew its direction. Solidarity epitomized the consciousness of the Polish people, a collective state of mind that ironically after thirty-five years of socialist construction assumed the structure of the Independent Self-Governing Trade Union. It was therefore not surprising that the union formula would prove too tight to encompass and reflect in action this state of mind.

In September 1980, however, as the Pope spoke on Poland's moral right to independence, sovereignty and self-determination, and unexpectedly on 12 September sent a message to all the signatories to the Helsinki Final Act reminding them about the implementation of its provisions, the Church and State in Poland seemed to have reached an unwritten agreement on the need for a 'controlled change'. This involved an assurance on the regime's part that it would fulfil the agreements of the summer of 1980 and persuade the Russians to accept this package. On the other hand, the Church agreed to restrain Solidarity from making overtly political demands which could undermine this process and disquiet the Soviet Union. Thus in the ensuing months of conflict between the regime and Solidarity, the Church assumed the role of mediator and shock-absorber. Moreover, it used its stabilizing impact on Solidarity as a bargaining counter with the regime to resolve at least some of the most important issues that had dominated Church-State relations in the past. This unique role gave the leadership of the Roman Catholic hierarchy direct access to formal political structures and placed the Church at the very apex of the institutional framework of Polish politics. The triumph of Solidarity also became the triumph of the Church.

The first success for the Church following the August strikes was the transmission on 21 September of a Sunday Mass from the Church of the Holy Cross in Warsaw. The date and place were symbolic. The Sunday was the traditional Media Sunday during which, in the past, the bishops had demanded access to the mass media. The Church of the Holy Cross was the place where, in October 1979, one of the longest and more successful hunger strikes took place. The hour-long live broadcast, which from then on became a regular transmission each Sunday, was not only a partial fulfilment of the August agreements and a major concession by the authorities which had a tremendous psychological impact on the nation, but also an acknowledgement of the Church's position during the summer strikes.

Another development in Church-State relations was the restitution of the Joint Episcopal-Government Commission on 24 September, after thirteen years of inactivity.[31] Cardinal Franciszek Macharski of Kraków, Bishop Lech Kaczmarek, Archbishop Jerzy Stroba of Poznań, the Secretary of the Episcopal Conference Bishop Bronisław Dąbrowski and his deputy Father Alojzy Orszulik represented the Church. The Government delegation, led by Deputy Prime Minister Kazimierz Barcikowski, also included the Minister for Religious Affairs Jerzy Kuberski, his deputy Alexander Merker and Witold Litski, Deputy Chairman of the Sejm Foreign Affairs Committee. The communiqué issued at the end of the meeting spoke of a unanimity of view that its work 'should be conducive to the development of co-operation and normalization of relations between Church and State with a view to the development of the Motherland and the unity of all citizens'. Although this gave a certain feeling of *déjà vu*, the composition of the Commission indicated formal contacts at the highest level ever.[32]

As the political situation in Poland began to deteriorate after Solidarity's first nationwide warning strike on 3 October in protest at the lack of progress in fulfilment of the summer agreements, the Catholic hierarchy held a series of important meetings in order to influence the situation. The first such meeting took place on 7 October between Bishop Dąbrowski and members of the former Strike Committee in Szczecin, during which the implementation of the agreements was discussed. On 15-16 October the Episcopal Conference met in Warsaw to discuss the country's economic, social and political problems. In a communiqué issued afterwards they gave full support to those demands of the workers which were just and emphasized that the stabilization of life in Poland depended on the fulfilment of the social agreements which were accepted by both the authorities and society during the summer unrest. In a clear reference to the lack of progress with the registration of Solidarity,[33] they stressed that the renewal of society should be based on the right to form free trade unions and the right to strike. In addition they stated that it was the right and duty of citizens to contribute to the progress of their community. Interestingly, addressing themselves to the radical elements which had then begun to influence Solidarity, the bishops warned that careful consideration should be given to Poland's geopolitical position in Europe before any 'unwise' action was taken. On 19 October Cardinal Wyszyński met the Presidium of the Warsaw branch of Solidarity, with its chairman Zbigniew Bujak. During the meeting he gave unequivocal backing to the union, saying 'I am with you'. This was followed by a working meeting with Bishop Dąbrowski, during which he enquired whether the Social Self-Defence Committee 'KOR' was playing an organizing role within Solidarity. Bujak explained that its role was 'inspirational' and that Solidarity owed much to the Committee: 'without them there will be no free trade unions'. This small incident amply illustrates the Church's mistrust of any other influence on the new trade unions.[34]

The most important event however, was a meeting on 21 October between Cardinal Wyszyński and Stanisław Kania. The formal communiqué of these talks gives some indication of the importance of the meeting. The two leaders

> discussed matters which are of great significance for the internal peace and development of the country. A common view was expressed that constructive co-operation between Church and State serves the interest of the nation well, and that is why it will be continued in the name of Poland's well-being and its security.

Significantly, this, the first meeting between Wyszyński and Kania, followed a two-day conference of the Foreign Ministers of the Warsaw Treaty Organization, which ended in Warsaw on 20 October and took place on the eve of the Warsaw court hearing on Solidarity's application for registration. The following day, 22 October, Bishop Dąbrowski met Solidarity's delegation which included Wałęsa. On 23 October Cardinal Wyszyński, accompanied by Dąbrowski, left for Rome to attend the closing sessions of the Synod of Bishops.

THE TRIUMPH OF SOLIDARITY

On 24 October Lech Wałęsa and the Solidarity delegation presented themselves in the Warsaw district court to hear the court's acceptance of the Solidarity statutes and the registration of the union. Wałęsa had previously submitted to the court a separate statement acknowledging the union's allegiance to the Constitution of the Polish People's Republic, which in article 3 stipulates the leading role of the Polish United Workers Party. In addition he submitted, as an appendix to the statutes, the Gdańsk Agreement which in paragraph 1, section 2, in addition to stating that the new union will adhere to the principles defined in the Constitution, also explicitly recognizes the leading role of the Party in the State. There was no ambiguity on the part of Solidarity on these points and the Solidarity delegation, as well as hundreds of their supporters gathered outside the court, expected a straightforward registration.

However, the presiding judge, Zdzisław Kościelniak, after a four-hour hearing announced the court's decision to register Solidarity as an Independent Self-Governing Trade Union, but modified its statutes. He ordered the insertion of a clause repeating that Solidarity recognized the socialist system, Poland's alliances and the leading role of the Party. He also substituted the section on the right to strike and inserted another clause that strikes could not contradict the legal regulations in force.[35]

The court's ruling was not only an example of extreme provocation but an act of political folly. The judge's task was to accept or reject the statutes not to amend them. But instead he adopted a broad interpretation of his prerogatives in registering the union by claiming that the court's duties were not restricted solely to the examination of the formal aspects of registration but must also involve the content of the statutes as the basis for defining the character of the union.[36] This quite clearly implied political rather than legal considerations. The judgement was therefore made under political pressure. The court's action destroyed any belief the workers of the then eight-million strong union might have had in the goodwill of the authorities and their suspicions and bitterness were increased. Wałęsa described the ruling as a 'violation of the freedom and independence of trade unions', which ran contrary to official declarations on the renewal of public life. The union, he said, would ignore the arbitrary changes written into its statute without its consent or indeed consultation, 'We shall never agree with it.'

The issue may seem a pure formality, but it was important to Solidarity in its determination to remain independent. In an atmosphere in which the new unions were yet to organize and consolidate and in the light of past experience, when the gains obtained in the 1956 and 1970 crises were gradually withdrawn as soon as the Party felt strong enough, Solidarity feared that an explicit recognition of the Party in the union's statutes might be used as an argument to place the new trade union under Party control again. The opposition within Solidarity to explicit recognition of the Party's leading role in the statutes was very strong. The court's action not only increased resentment but also hardened the union's position towards the authorities— against the conciliatory line of Lech Wałęsa. In the aftermath of the court's ruling many advisers, who had been sent to Solidarity chapters in various parts of the country by local bishops, had to give way to more radical people. This undoubtedly must have had an impact on the radicalization of the union in subsequent weeks and months.

Solidarity's response to the court's ruling was unequivocal. It simply demanded a retraction of the judge's decision. In addition it also presented the Government with other demands: access to the media, settlement of outstanding pay disputes, better distribution of consumer goods to the shops, an end to repressions and, significantly for the future, recognition of the farmers' rights to form their own union.[37] The temperature in Poland was again running dangerously high.

There was also increasing evidence that Poland's neighbours were beginning to feel more and more uneasy about the situation. On 28 October the GDR and, two days later, Czechoslovakia effectively closed their borders to travellers from Poland and on 29 October Stanisław Kania and Józef Pińkowski unexpectedly flew to Moscow for talks with Soviet leaders. Although the Soviet media remained silent on the situation in Poland, it is significant that the Czechoslovak and East German press unleashed a barrage of accusations against Solidarity and Lech Wałęsa personally.

Meanwhile the meeting of the Synod of Bishops in Rome gave the Pope and Cardinal Wyszyński an opportunity to deliberate at length on the deteriorating situation in Poland. The Cardinal stayed there for two weeks, during which he had a series of talks with the Pontiff. Some of these were attended by the Secretary of the Episcopal Conference, Bishop Bronisław Dąbrowski, and Cardinal Władysław Rubin,

THE TRIUMPH OF SOLIDARITY

Prefect of the Congregation for Eastern Churches, as well as the three other Polish representatives at the Synod, Cardinal Franciszek Macharski of Kraków and Bishops Józef Rozwadowski of Łódź and Wilhelm Pluta of Gorzów. In addition three other bishops (Kazimierz Majdanski of Szczecin, Julian Groblicki, auxiliary of Kraków and Mirosław Kołodziejczyk, auxiliary of Częstochowa) travelled specially from Poland to attend some of the meetings. What happened during these meetings will probably never be known, but the subsequent actions of their participants suggest that the 'Polish conclave' in the Vatican decided that in the short run as well as the long run, the Church must follow a strategy of mediation and compromise rather than a more defiant line and in this they backed Wyszyński's approach. Additional indication of such a conclusion is found in the fact that when the news of Kania and Pińkowski's unexpected departure for Moscow reached the Vatican on 29 October, an official there let it be known that both the Pope and Wyszyński were 'ready to act if their mediation becomes necessary'.

The crisis over the registration of Solidarity ended on 10 November when the Supreme Court overturned the lower court's ruling and accepted the proposal made originally by Solidarity to attach as appendices to its statutes points 1-7 of the Gdańsk Agreement and partial texts of Conventions 87 and 98 of the International Labour Organization.[38] The Supreme Court's decision was also a political one. A discreet private deal was therefore struck with Solidarity on one of its five demands, albeit the most important. However the other four were left on the table to be used as bargaining points in future months.

The registration of Solidarity only temporarily defused the increasingly difficult situation. Cardinal Wyszyński, who returned from Rome on 8 November[39] cautioned Lech Wałęsa during the victory celebrations on 10 November to 'refrain from temptations to engage in political activity' and to 'concentrate on occupational and social tasks', as well as on 'defending workers' rights'. He also appealed for 'patience' and 'understanding' and warned the workers against pushing their demands beyond the limits of the State's capacity to deliver. 'Even the best organized State cannot give what it does not have.' The tone of these remarks and circumstances in which they were made appeared strange then,[40] but perhaps Wyszyński was already aware of the impending storm gathering outside the Polish borders. At that time, however, apart from a series of hastily arranged Soviet bloc meetings there was little overt evidence of military activities from Poland's Eastern European allies. The registration of Solidarity did not bring social peace to Poland. The damage to the credibility of the authorities was so substantial and the militancy of various Solidarity chapters so high that it required all the skills and tact of the combined forces of reason to avert the country sliding into chaos. The Church continued its mediating role but at this time the Pope also became overtly involved in the situation. On 13 November in a private audience he unexpectedly received Jerzy Ozdowski, a member of the Polish Council of State, a Catholic deputy of the Znak parliamentary circle and the Professor of Economics at the Catholic University of Lublin. At first there seemed nothing particularly unusual about this meeting. However, seven days later Ozdowski was appointed a Deputy Prime Minister with special responsibility for family and social affairs. It was in fact Cardinal Wyszyński's idea, put forward during his October meeting with Stanisław Kania, that one way of restoring public confidence in the Government was to appoint a Catholic deputy to a leading Government position. It took a month of careful negotiations for his suggestion to materialize. Ozdowski's appointment, made after prior consultations between the Church and State authorities at the highest level,[41] was a significant development in Polish politics. For the first time in the history of People's Poland (or any other socialist country), a representative of a Catholic group was given an executive position in the Government. The symbolic as well as political significance of this appointment was inescapable. Equally significant was the bargaining process that brought about this direct input of Catholic opinion into the executive branch.

Just as tension began to subside in Poland after the successful resolution of several strikes that had occurred around the time of the 'registration affair', there was increasing alarm abroad about the possibility of imminent military intervention of Warsaw Pact forces. First warnings of signals for a 'Czechoslovak-type' invasion of Poland emerged on 26 November from Yugoslavia. Milika Sundić, a leading commentator, whose pronouncements reflected the views of the Yugoslav leadership, let it be known that both the GDR and Czechoslovakia were giving signals for solving the ferment in Poland 'in the same manner as that which was used in Czechoslovakia in 1968'.[42] Ominous hints were repeated in Moscow, East Berlin and Prague during the next few days, but that the situation was serious became clear when on 2 December the GDR closed its border area with Poland to Western military attachés. The US State Department announced that 'several' Warsaw Pact countries had put their forces on alert. The military build-up was accompanied by a flurry of high-level political and military meetings between Eastern European leaders, underlying their growing concern about the situation in Poland. On 4 December Józef Klasa, the head of the Polish United Workers' Party Central Committee's Department for Press, Radio and Television, confirmed the hypothetical possibility of Soviet military intervention. Such a move, he said, could occur only if and when 'socialism becomes endangered' that is 'only if authority slips into the hands of anti-socialist elements. Polish Communists would then have the right and duty to ask for assistance from the Soviet Union and from other countries.' Although he quickly affirmed that no immediate prospect of such a development existed in Poland, his statement only encouraged world-wide nervousness. On the same day all the Polish newspapers printed an appeal to the nation from the Party's Central Committee,[43] issued during the night, which began: 'Compatriots! the future of the nation and the country is at stake.' On 5 December leaders of the seven Warsaw Pact countries held an unexpected meeting in Moscow, which was only announced to the world that evening when the participants were already on the way home. Although the statement issued at its conclusion amounted to a vote of confidence in Kania's government, Poland was assured that it could count on the 'fraternal solidarity and support' of its allies. The Moscow meeting gave Poland a breathing space but did not reduce the preparations for military action. These preparations entered their most menacing phase during the next few days. There was a call-up in the Baltic republic and the Ukraine that involved the requisition of civilian vehicles. In the Baltic Sea there were, unusually, many military ship movements and on 7 December several Soviet divisions moved out of Kalinigrad and camped on the Polish border in tents. On the same day in a hastily summoned press briefing the White House announced that 'preparations for possible Soviet intervention in Poland appear to have been completed'.

Whether all this amounted, as Neal Ascherson suggests, to a 'two-track policy of negotiations and military preparation at the same time'[44] is a matter for conjecture. It seems hardly convincing that such elaborate preparations on military and political levels would have taken place merely to bring the Poles 'to their senses' and around the negotiating table. If that were the intention it failed, as it did not bring an end to various workers', students' and peasants' protests taking place in the very same week, (let alone in subsequent weeks and months), during which the preparations for intervention appear to have been completed. The more likely explanation is that the actual invasion orders were issued and then withdrawn. The tacit opinion among Catholic Church leaders in Poland was and remains that there existed a plan for the division of Poland between the Soviet Union and the German Democratic Republic. Under this plan Silesia and Western Pomerania would be placed under East German supervision and the rest of Poland under Soviet supervision. An indication that there was a plan to use East German troops in a December 1980 invasion was contained in a message from six Polish generals and 200 staff officers, sent at the beginning of December to the PUWP Central Committee, saying that any incursion by East German forces would be regarded as an act of war, which they would resist.[45]

On 8 December just as the Poles were beginning to draw comfort from the outcome of the Warsaw Pact meeting in Moscow, the Soviet news agency, Tass, issued a report from its Warsaw correspondent (subsequently broadcast on Radio Moscow's home service and English-language world service) that counter-revolutionaries were seeking to de-stabilise Poland. To support this allegation, the correspondent gave an example of an electronics factory in Kielce, where Solidarity supporters dismissed the manager and disarmed the factory guards, and added that those who opposed them had since been missing. There was not a grain of truth in this. But coming only a few days after the Moscow meeting, which expressed confidence that Polish Communists would be able to settle their internal crisis, the Tass report contradicted the Moscow statement. Furthermore it was reminiscent of the war of nerves conducted by the Soviet media in 1968 on the eve of the invasion of Czechoslovakia, when the Russians accused the Czechoslovak leadership of losing control to the counter-revolutionary forces.

On the same day the Pope, who watched the mounting tension with apprehension, briefed regularly not only by Vatican officials but also

THE TRIUMPH OF SOLIDARITY

by Cardinal Wyszyński by telex or telephone from Warsaw, departed from the text of his Angelus address and asked Catholics everywhere 'to invoke the protection of the Virgin Mary over Poland my country'. Later in the afternoon he again departed from the official text and said: 'I cannot help but speak as a son of Poland of my beloved homeland. Alarming news is being broadcast. We all hope it will not turn out to be true.'

The Pope's actions were, however, not restricted to pleas and prayers. As the Soviet and East German tanks massed on the Polish border he sent a letter to President Brezhnev assuring him that 'Poland will help itself' and of continuous Church assistance in the mediation process. This was an unprecedented step. But quite clearly the Pope, after consultations with Cardinal Wyszyński and his Vatican advisers, felt that in order to avoid major national and international tragedy he himself should appeal to the Soviet leader for restraint.

The papal letter, its content and the time of its sending has been the subject of wild speculation by the media, as well as individuals. An elaborate scenario of the consequences of this letter in connection with the subsequent assassination attempt on the Pope's life, has been constructed on the basis of 'informed leaks' from members of the Vatican curia. Claims that the letter was in the Pope's own handwriting, and in Russian, and that it contained a threat that should the Russians move against Poland the Pope would leave the Vatican and return to Poland to stand shoulder to shoulder with his people, have become part of journalistic folklore. The Vatican Press Office itself is at fault for at first denying the existence of such a letter when it came to the notice of journalists,[46] and an un-named Vatican official for leaking it to US Senator Alfons D'Amato.[47] The matter was and continues to be too important to be treated in a half-hearted way. However, a basic lack of information could only result, as in this case, in bizarre suggestions that the head of the Roman Catholic Church would return to Poland in the event of an invasion. Even if the Pope wanted to do this, which is most unlikely, one can assume that curia officials would not permit him to leave the Vatican. This suggestion is in the best tradition of a Hollywood melodrama and not in keeping with the effective and highly structured bureaucracy at the Vatican.

The truth of the matter is that a letter from the Pope was sent to President Brezhnev. This fact was confirmed by Cardinal Wyszyński in his address to the Senate of the Academy of Theology in Warsaw in March 1981. The Cardinal's remark, although presented in rather a convoluted way, nevertheless was clear as to this fact. The context in which the remark was made, with clear reference to Poland's first constitution of 1791 and the country's new-found vitality achieved by its own efforts after a period of stagnation, gives a clear indication as to the content of the papal communication. The letter was most probably delivered by Cardinal Franz König of Vienna, who had in the past often been involved in secret Vatican diplomacy with the Soviet Union and other East European regimes and who is well respected in Moscow. The letter gave Leonid Brezhnev not only a re-assurance of the Polish Church's continuing role as a moderator but, since such a guarantee came from such a high level, it indicated not only the intensification of this role, but also provided the best proof of its possible success. In a situation where the Party and Solidarity were at loggerheads, the Church's offer of mediation was the best option possible and preferable to the use of force. The Pope's letter was probably the factor that changed Brezhnev's mind and precipitated the withdrawal of the invasion order, but the Soviet troops stayed in their temporary tents around the Polish borders throughout most of the winter months.

Brezhnev did not have to wait long for the Church's assurance to be put into practice. On 12 December the Episcopal Conference issued a communiqué after its two-day meeting. It gave a direct and powerful endorsement to the regime's policy of renewal which 'gives much hope', and warned against any actions that might be regarded as adversely affecting the well-being of the nation.[48]

> Action must not be taken which could drive our fatherland into danger of losing its freedom or its existence as a sovereign state. The efforts of all Poles should be directed to strengthening the already initiated process of renewal and to creating conditions for implementing the social agreement between the authorities and society . . .
> A determined will is needed to counteract all attempts to slow down the process of national renewal, to stir up differences within society and to exploit the existing difficulties for purposes alien to the well-being of the nation and the State. Our country chiefly needs internal peace in order to stabilize social life in

an atmosphere of mutual trust, which is in the process of being reconstructed at present.

The need for social peace was amplified in a special pastoral letter 'To the Polish Nation', read in all the churches on 14 December. Confirming once again the Church's overriding concern about the security of the country, the letter which in its tone and content was similar to the Central Committee's 'Appeal' of 3 December, declared, that 'our nation is now facing a period of yet another historical test, yet another experience, yet another shock. This is, at the same time, yet another test of national and social maturity'. The letter went on to remind Poles that 'the fate of the fatherland depends on every citizen and the whole society . . . The Church teaches us that love for the fatherland is our duty and a virtue. Christ is our example. Although he came to save the entire world, he nevertheless by the will of God lived in a political system.'

Asserting the urgent need to 'restore stability as well as normal conditions in the social, economic, and political life of the country', the letter emphasized that to achieve this goal

> each social group and every individual . . . must contribute their share in common effort. Everyone should examine his conscience in search of the causes of the current drama. Yet it is not enough to recognize the source of neglect of the national interest. Action is needed to bring about an improvement. No declaration about past mistakes, even if it can explain the reason for the current *malaise*, is sufficient. Nor is this the time for mutual accusations. At the moment we must unite all efforts to ensure the survival of the State and the sovereign existence of the fatherland.

The letter also contained what can only be seen as a rationale for Poland's membership of the Warsaw Pact; 'it is common for countries to belong to blocs and to be linked by international alliances'.

These two important statements by the bishops which were disseminated by the Polish mass media, went further than any before in support of the regime and amply underlined the seriousness of the situation. Furthermore, on the day the bishops' communiqué was published, the deputy secretary of the Episcopal Conference, Father Alojzy Orszulik, in an informal interview with Western correspondents, criticized some statements by individuals associated with dissident groups on the nature of political changes in Poland, as well as on Polish-Soviet relations. He referred specifically to recent pronouncements by one of the leaders of the Social Self-defence Committee 'KOR', Jacek Kuroń, calling them 'irresponsible' and criticized them 'for stirring up nervousness among Poland's neighbours'. Orszulik's remarks, which were subsequently denied by him, nevertheless became the subject of a strong letter of protest from KOR and lay Catholics sent to Cardinal Wyszyński on 20 December. Whatever the actual expressions used by Orszulik, this incident nevertheless illustrates the extent of the Church's nervousness at that time, both about the external repercussions of KOR's pronouncements, which had for some time been criticized in the Soviet and Eastern European press, and its influence on Solidarity. A potential open rift, however, was averted when on 4 January 1982 Cardinal Wyszyński had a meeting with a delegation from the Warsaw branch of Solidarity, which included two prominent members of KOR, Adam Michnik and Henryk Wujec. During the meeting he explained that Orszulik's words had been misinterpreted and had led to regrettable and misleading comments.

Some of the reasons for the anxiety amongst Poland's neighbours in December 1980 were the commemorative ceremonies in Gdańsk (16 December), Gdynia and Szczecin (17 December) for the workers killed in 1970. In the event all passed without any disturbances or confrontations. The most impressive ceremony was that in Gdańsk in which State, Party and Church dignitaries participated shoulder to shoulder with the leadership of Solidarity and several hundred thousand workers from all over Poland. Lech Wałęsa, in his speech echoing the bishops' pronouncements, made a forceful plea for reconciliation and prudence. Central to the celebrations was a Mass during which a telegram from the Pope was read. The liturgical framework for that occasion gave assurance of its peaceful and dignified course. It was also a suitable method of disciplining large crowds. This pattern was observed on similar commemorative occasions during 1981, for example in Poznań (28 June) and Lublin (14 July). It appears that the political influence of the Church on such occasions was seen by the regime as the lesser evil when contrasted with the danger of demonstrations of political opposition.

In the middle of January 1981 Lech Wałęsa, with a delegation of fourteen Solidarity representatives, went to Rome. It was Wałęsa's first trip overseas and although he arrived there at the invitation of the three biggest Italian trade unions he declared, somewhat to the consternation of Luciano Lama, the Communist secretary general of the General Confederation of Italian Workers, 'I have come to visit the Pope. There are very important reasons for my visit'.[49] The Pope received the Solidarity delegation on 15 January. The audience began with a 25-minute private meeting between the Pontiff and Wałęsa and later continued in a public ceremony for the remaining members of the delegation, Church dignitaries and Polish Government representatives. During the ceremony the Pope stressed that he supported the right of working men and women to 'associate freely' and in what can only be seen as a reference to his own private undertakings, added that he had been saying as much to 'all people of good will as discreetly as possible'. He praised the courage, maturity and moderation of the Polish workers and commended the way Poles have sought solutions to their problems through dialogue and without violence. There did not exist, he said, 'because there *must* not exist, a contradiction between such a social initiative by workers and the structures of a system which looks on human labour as fundamental to State and social life'. After stating that the events of the summer of 1980 had not been directed against anyone particular, the Pontiff stressed: 'The activity of trade unions does not have a political character, it must be the instrument for action by anyone, by any political party, so as to concentrate in an exclusively and entirely autonomous manner on the great social benefit of human labour and of the working people'. The Pope also expressed his joy at the formal registration of Solidarity two months previously, and significantly for the future, mentioned the aspirations of the Polish farmers to form their own trade union. In reply Wałęsa, speaking without notes, said: 'We are not and never will be a political group. Politics does not interest us. What concerns us are the rights of man, the rights of society, and the rights of faith . . . People must help their neighbour, their fellow men. This we have learned from you, Holy Father.' On the last day of their week-long visit the delegation attended Mass in the Pontiff's private chapel, followed by a communal breakfast. This gesture, the warmest reception the Pope can offer a visitor, is usually reserved for close friends or heads of state.

Throughout January 1981 Poland witnessed a sudden rush of conflicts arising from a number of grievances that might have been defused if they had been handled in time. One source of a number of brief strikes in many parts of the country was the Government's announcement that the serious economic crisis made it impossible to fulfil the undertaking in the Gdańsk agreement on work-free Saturdays. Students in Łódź University began their strike and occupation of university premises in support of the registration of an Independent Students' Union and greater academic freedom,[50] a strike which spread to other institutions of higher education. Also the peasants accelerated their actions for the registration of a trade union for individual farmers, with sit-in protests in Rzeszów and Ustrzyki Dolne. But perhaps one of the most potentially dangerous disputes took place in the province of Bielsko Biała close to the Czechoslovak border. The strike, which began on 26 January, spread rapidly and paralysed the province for eleven days and involved Solidarity members in some 120 plants. They demanded the resignation of the provincial governor and his two deputies, accusing them of corruption, illicit financial dealings and administrative mismanagement of the local government. The issue was potentially explosive as the strikers appeared to be challenging the regime's personal policy at a high level. For Solidarity the strike also represented a direct challenge. It was staged on a local issue and without the approval of the National Co-ordinating Commission in Gdańsk, who wanted to discourage local branches from striking against provincial governments. As one Solidarity official put it: 'We want to stop this anti-corruption strike; otherwise, the whole country would have to go on strike'.

When all efforts failed to find a way out of what was clearly an embarrassing situation for both the central State authorities and Solidarity, Lech Wałęsa suggested that the Episcopate should be asked for help in order to break the deadlock. After a series of high-level talks involving Cardinal Wyszyński and Government officials, Bishop Bronislaw Dąbrowski, accompanied by two other bishops as representatives of the Primate, arrived during the night of 5–6 February in Bielsko Biała. The next morning Solidarity and the Government Commission reached an agreement, which Dąbrowski signed as a guarantor of the fulfilment of the obligations undertaken by both the workers and the Government. During a thanksgiving Mass celebrated at the conclusion of the negotiations he spoke of the interest taken in the conflict by the

Pope, 'who telephoned several times' to find out about the progress of the talks.

The Church's direct involvement in the settlement of the Bielsko Biała dispute contributed to its already high prestige as an institution trusted and respected equally by the authorities and the population. One wonders, however, what effect it would have had on the entire political system if the Church's involvement at such a high level had been repeated. But after the Bielsko Biała settlement the Church refused to act as a mediator in subsequent industrial disputes. The reason for the Church's unwillingness to mediate was the regime's refusal to register the trade union of private farmers, a class which was the Church's main and most loyal constituency and one to which, above, all, the Catholic hierarchy felt bound.

In the autumn of 1980 four main centres of peasant trade unionism emerged in various parts of Poland: Peasants' Solidarity; Rural Solidarity; Peasants' Trade Union of the Dobrzyń Region; and the most important Trade Union of Individual Farmers. The fragmentation of the movement, as well as the differing political complexions of these groups, allowed the authorities successfully to resist applications for registration as a trade union. Their argument was based on the grounds that since farmers work on their own land, being neither salaried employees nor employers, they do not meet the conditions required by law to form a trade union. Since the main purpose of a trade union is to prevent conflicts between employers and employees, there was no point in trade-union status for an organization whose membership is so obviously self-employed. Behind this argument lay a fear that the legalization of a peasants' trade union would substantially undermine the position of the United Peasants' Party, the PUWP's long and trusted ally, which supposedly represented the farmers' interests. The farmers, on the other hand, argued that since the peasants' material reward depends on the work they do rather than on ownership, even if the size of the property is undoubtedly a factor, the primary criterion to be adopted should be the relations between farmers and the State administration. This is mainly because the farmers' dependence on the administration is so all-embracing that it is difficult to conceive of a peasant farmer as being totally his own master. The argument on both sides was obviously a political one. When on 30 December 1980 the Supreme Court adjourned its hearing on the farmers' application, a group of peasants began on 2 January 1981 to stage a sit-in strike in Rzeszów. By 12 January the protest had developed into the nucleus of an all-Poland Rural Solidarity strike aimed at winning the registration of the farmers' union, and it continued for seven weeks.[51]

Both Solidarity and the Church supported the farmers' demands. In a sermon on 2 February, Cardinal Wyszyński stated: 'Further delay in giving the rural population the right to organize itself independently seems not only unreasonable but a violation of the basic rights of those who produce food for the nation'. Nevertheless, in its ruling on 10 February the Supreme Court rejected the peasants' application for registration but simultaneously announced that there was no legal impediment to the farmers forming an association. On the same day the Main Council of the Episcopate issued an angry statement: 'The existence of labour organizations for farmers is, according to Pope John XXIII's teachings expounded in his encyclical *Mater et Magistra*, an absolute necessity'. Dr Romuald Kukołowicz again rushed to Rzeszów to help, together with Wałęsa, to negotiate a settlement.

The protest in Rzeszów ended on 18 February, a week after the election of General Wojciech Jaruzelski as Prime Minister and his appeal for a ninety-day moratorium on strikes. The agreement between the Government Commission and the strike committee acting in the name of the national founding committee of the Private Farmers' Union did not provide for the recognition of the union, but in accepting the signatures of its founders the authorities recognized the organization in fact, if not yet in law. The farmers agreed to shelve the issue, hoping for a possible compromise solution. Nevertheless the agreement heralded radical changes in Poland's agricultural policy and the status of private farmers, whose co-operation was vital for the new government of General Jaruzelski. It included a guarantee of land ownership (to be incorporated into the constitution), improved supplies and investment outlays in agriculture, better prices and old age and disability pensions.

The question of registration, however, remained and dominated the discussions during the first national congress of what was to become the Independent Self-Governing Trade Union of Private Farmers' Solidarity, also known as Rural Solidarity. The congress was held in Poznań between 8-9 March and merged the four farmers' organizations into a single union. After the congress the Primate received a group

THE TRIUMPH OF SOLIDARITY

of delegates on 10 March and again assured them of his support. Three days later the Episcopal Conference issued a communiqué giving full support to the new free trade union:

The eyes of all honest citizens are on the Polish countryside with sympathy and trust. We are full of respect and admiration for the work of the farmers, who with such determination defend their land and their rights. Our farmers must have the same rights as other workers to form trade unions that would serve their interests and at the same time promote the economic development of the entire country. We have high hopes for the Independent Self-Governing Trade Union of Private Farmers. The Union will relieve tension and restore trust in the authorities and above all will have a positive effect on the increase in production. The Church will continue to support the efforts of the Polish farmer in his patriotic and social service to the nation.

The issue of Private Farmers' Solidarity was brought to a head by the Bydgoszcz incident on 19 March. Six Solidarity delegates, including Dr Romuald Kukołowicz, were invited to attend a meeting of the Provincial People's Council to discuss farmers' grievances. But the meeting was suddenly adjourned before the delegates had a chance to speak. While some members of the Council left the chamber others remained and tried to continue the discussion, but were asked to leave by the head of the Council. Later the local prosecutor arrived and told the Solidarity delegates that they would be ejected if they did not leave. While the delegates were asking for a little extra time to complete the discussion the militia moved in and removed them with totally unnecessary brutality, making a special point of beating up Jan Rulewski, the chairman of the Provincial Chapter of Solidarity as well as several others, three of whom subsequently required hospital treatment. The beatings were the first to be politically instigated since the emergence of the union and were therefore regarded as an attack on the union itself. There is little doubt that the action was a deliberate provocation staged by Party hardliners to undermine the positions of Kania and in particular Jaruzelski, who only a month before had called for a ninety-day strike-free period and had succeeded in getting Solidarity's co-operation. There followed ten days of desperate tension and intense negotiations, during which the 'Soyuz 81' manœuvres of

the Warsaw Pact taking place in Poland, the Soviet Union, Czechoslovakia and the GDR were 'extended indefinitely' without explanation. The spectre of military intervention re-emerged once again.
The Church became fully involved in the delicate negotiations. In addition to Kukołowicz, the auxilliary Bishop of Gniezo Jan Michalski was also involved in negotiations with Solidarity in Bydgoszcz while the Primate, Bishop Dąbrowski and Father Orszulik took part in various meetings with the authorities in Warsaw. The tension increased further when on 24 March the National Co-ordinating Commission of Solidarity issued a call for a four-hour national warning strike for the 27 March, unless those responsible for the Bydgoszcz incident were brought to justice and the Government entered into serious negotiations. It is difficult to imagine how the first of these demands could have been met since the chain of command of those responsible for the incident most probably ran to the top of the Ministry of the Interior and the group of hardliners in the Political Bureau opposed to Kania and Jaruzelski. To bring to justice individual members of the militia responsible for the beatings would have opened a 'Pandora's box' and undermined the credibility of the entire oppressive apparatus. This seemed impossible even for Kania to accept.

Nevertheless, on 25 March Solidarity's National Co-ordinating Commission, during talks with the Government delegation headed by Deputy Prime Minister Mieczysław Rakowski, laid down five conditions for the resolution of the crisis: punishment for those responsible for the incident; permission for the peasants to form their own union; security for union members and the right to reply through the media to criticism; the annulment of the Government strike pay directive; and the closure of all pending cases against people arrested for political opposition to Government policies between 1976 and 1980, 'even if in the light of existing laws their activities constituted offences'. It is not surprising that with such demands the talks broke down. The Primate wrote in his notebook 'The situation in the country is dangerous. There is a desperate atmosphere building up'.[52]

On 26 March Cardinal Wyszyński, who by now was seriously ill, received the Prime Minister General Wojciech Jaruzelski. Their meeting lasted for three and a half hours. The press communiqué issued after the meeting indicates the range of topics discussed which included: the elimination of strikes and social tensions, food shortages, delays in the spring sowing season, response to the 'current expectations' of individual peasants and full and objective investigation of the Bydgoszcz events. However, according to the Cardinal's own account[53] most of the time was spent on arguing the Bydgoszcz events and the peasant's case. During their discussion General Jaruzelski gave the Primate assurance that a way for the recognition of the peasants' trade union would be found and asked for Solidarity to be restrained from continuing with its demand for investigation into who was responsible for the Bydgoszcz events. He also outlined to Wyszyński the grim scenarios of the consequences if the general strike planned for 31 March went ahead.

The Church now intensified its pressure on Wałęsa and hung all its hopes on a settlement during the next round of talks on 27 March. Poland was paralysed by a four-hour national strike on that day— the first such protest in a Communist country. The talks between Solidarity and the Government, which lasted well into the night, did not, however, 'bring the expected settlement'.[54] nor did the next round on 28 March which lasted only two and a half hours. The 'tragic news'[55] was communicated to the Primate by the Government's representative in the late afternoon and shortly afterwards Lech Wałęsa and the National Co-ordinating Commission of Solidarity were called to the Cardinal's residence, where Wyszyński delivered an unequivocal warning to them.[56]

> From my talks I see that the situation is becoming increasingly complicated not only internally but also externally. We talk among ourselves as Poles, citizens of this land, responsible for it not only jointly but also individually ... If it were through negligence on my part, for whatever reason or as a result of irresponsible moves, that even one Pole should die, I would never forgive myself. This is what I think. I think that everyone of you gentlemen think so too ... Pondering on the situation I ask myself: Is it right to fulfil today's demands, however just, at the cost of endangering our freedom, our territorial integrity? Is it better to achieve some today and for the rest say: 'Gentlemen, we will return to this matter later.'

Throughout his speech he emphasized that a clear distinction should be made between economic, institutional and administrative demands.

He suggested that institutional demands concerning the activities and organization of Solidarity should be given priority. But he advised very strongly against raising demands concerning individuals and warned of the consequences of a general strike.

> I am not a melodramatic person but I insist—the situation is dangerous. Therefore I think that if we stretch the point in submitting our demands, we could later very much regret the consequences that we bring on Poland.

On the same day Pope John Paul II appealed for compromise in the spirit of Gdańsk and called for Poland to be allowed to solve its own problems without outside interference. The East European media, as in December 1980, now intensified their campaign against Solidarity asking the Polish leadership to take a harder line against the 'anarchy and lawlessness' spreading in Poland. During the night 28-9 March the airspace over Poland was closed to commercial traffic for five hours between 10.30 p.m. and 3.30 a.m. in what appeared at that time to be preparations for outside intervention. In fact Polish army communication equipment was placed and tested at strategic points throughout the country. The next day the Central Committee met in an emergency session. In a heated debate during which Kazimierz Barcikowski, the moderate who negotiated the Szczecin agreement, told his colleagues that political ambitions were coming to dominate Solidarity and that Poland was facing 'creeping counter-revolution', the group of hardliners, Stefan Olszowski, Tadeusz Grabski and Roman Ney, tendered their resignations from the Political Bureau. Wisely in the circumstances, in order not to produce a fifth column, these were refused and the existing Political Bureau was given a new vote of confidence. By now the Soviet press agency, Tass, which had remained remarkably silent until this point, had published a terrifying report, ostensibly written by the agency's correspondent in Warsaw, of how Solidarity was launching a *putsch* by setting up roadblocks, destroying road signs, occupying telephone exchanges and intimidating police and security members.

It was clear that the planned general strike for 31 March must be prevented at any cost. During the night of 29-30 March a Government emissary was sent to the Primate with information that in the event of the general strike not being called off by midnight on 30 March, the Council of State would proclaim martial law. To prove the point he brought with him a poster with the proclamation already printed on it.[57] But Wałęsa and Rakowski had already roughed out a formula. Several more hours of talks on 30 March produced an agreement and the general strike was called off. The agreement fell short of expectations but Solidarity was promised an investigation into the Bydgoszcz incident and punishment for those responsible. As for recognition of the peasants' trade union, the Government declared that it would not question the legality of the organization and that the union could act as if it had legal status pending a final decision on registration. But there was no mention in the agreement of the other demands put forward by Solidarity and some members of the delegation let it be known publically that they felt distinctly unhappy about the agreement and the cancellation of the general strike, for which elaborate preparations were well-advanced in factories, offices and other places of work. Wałęsa was publicly accused of a sell-out and several resignations from Solidarity's National Commission followed. Only a handful of people, however, knew how high the stakes were at that time.

On 2 April Cardinal Wyszński received the Presidium of the Independent Self-governing Trade Union of Private Farmers Solidarity in a special audience, during which he delivered a long address which gives an interesting and unique insight into the Church's philosophy and strategy regarding the farmers as a social group and its own role in Polish society:

> A human being is a social person—*persona socialis*—this means that he possesses a social nature, social disposition, social competence, social expectations and social needs. This is the basis of Catholic social philosophy and social teaching. Everything arises from this. All authority must state and accept this. It is not the authority's duty to confirm this since the attributes of a human being need no confirmation . . . There are doctrines and social systems which do not take this into account and maintain that all rights are granted by the State. This is not the case! A human being does not require the grant of rights which are his fundamental rights as a person; these rights cannot be questioned, he simply possesses them.

He went on to explain that the questioning of these fundamental rights results in alienation and distortion of the social system, as well as social and political life. This was the case with Poland. The emergence of workers' Solidarity was a natural and logical development arising from the rights of man. The same rights also apply to private farmers. The argument for their trade union, the Primate said, was reinforced by the fact that the farmers are also owners of small particles of the native soil for which they are socially responsible, the soil which is not only used by the farmer and his family but also feeds the nation. Consideration of the peasants' important assignments and responsibilities should give them special social protection and the right to form their own trade union.

The Cardinal stressed that the present geopolitical situation requires Poland to be a highly populated country. The Germans had only wanted our land, not us. 'If the soil is covered by grass even the strongest storms won't move it. When it is bare it is easy to conquer it'. He deplored the building of large towns and their attraction of young people away from the country. 'This policy is a crime.' There was urgent need to halt the process and populate the countryside. 'I have an instruction for you, beloved, do not allow the land to be snatched from you.'

The last part of his address he devoted to Solidarity:

> Solidarity's biggest achievement is that it is based on social and occupational foundations, which are already in existence and which have brought people together. It has authority, so we can say that besides the authority of the Party there is also social authority in Poland . . . I continuously explain to Lech Wałęsa: In a few months you have achieved so much that even the most efficient political machine would not have achieved . . . You must now tighten your organization, strengthen yourself, create union administration, train people to achieve these goals, give them education in politics, social ethics, agricultural policies . . . The time will come sooner or later when socio-economic demands will not be the only ones achieved by this massive movement of industrial Solidarity and the Solidarity of the Trade Union of Individual Farmers. This you will certain achieve!

The battle for official recognition of the peasants' union was not over yet. A few more conflicts ensued before an agreement was reached between yet another Government Commission and striking farmers in Bydgoszcz on 17 April,[58] paving the way for the formal registration of the union on 10 May.[59] The Church and the peasants thus won the battle over Eastern Europe's first free trade union of private farmers, in spite of the Party First Secretary's claim that the union was harbouring in its midst people 'who make no secret of their anti-socialist intentions and, one has to say it, their counter-revolutionary intentions'.[60] The victory was impressive and the Cardinal could rightly tell the Pope during their telephone conversation on 3 May, 'After securing the trade-union rights for individual peasants there has emerged a huge social base for the Church's activity—industry and countryside'.[61]

It appears that at that time the regime was willing to allow the Church to wield this unprecedented political influence as long as the hierarchy was able to exert its authority and continue its moderating influence on Solidarity, the farmers' trade union and the youth.[62] The Catholic hierarchy saw a continuous threat to Polish independence and regarded its preservation as paramount in its actions. Consequently it consciously allowed itself to be used by the regime and extended a helping hand to the Party on the road to 'socialist renewal'. The Church thus filled the power vacuum left by a Party increasingly demoralized and torn between hard-line factions and the so-called 'horizontal movement' of rank-and-file members demanding greater democratization in Party and national life.[63] The Church could remain in this precarious role as long as its own leadership remained unchanged, the chain of consequent commands in both Warsaw and Rome uninterrupted and the Party in disarray.

From the beginning of May, however, Cardinal Wyszyński's health began to deteriorate rapidly to the extent that he could no longer say his daily mass. By now he also realized and accepted that his end was near. Though he remained actively involved in Church and State affairs, receiving visitors, commenting on reports and memoranda, and signing documents, the day-to-day running of affairs became the responsibility of Bishop Bronisław Dąbrowski in consultation with Cardinal Franciszek Macharski. Wyszyński, who had been the Primate of Poland for thirty-three years, must have pondered on the question of his successor. He had offered his resignation twice, in 1977 and 1980, but on both occasions his request was turned down, first by Paul VI and later by John Paul II, who himself as the Cardinal Archbishop of Kraków would have been his most likely successor. After Cardinal Wojtyła's election to the papacy the obvious candidate to succeed Wyszyński became Bishop Bronisław Dąbrowski. However, in 1981 he was already in his sixties, his health had been causing some problems and he was too closely involved with the day-to-day running of Church-State affairs to distance himself and become an adjudicator like Wyszyński. Also the Church's position in Poland had changed dramatically for the better during the previous nine months as it gained unprecedented direct access to the very centre of power and was able not only to influence policies but also to make a direct contribution to the decision-making process. From a reading of the Cardinal's notes it is clear that he did not anticipate subsequent events, and that he probably thought that a younger man should take over after him, someone whom he had personally trained and trusted and a person whom he knew would continue his policies essentially and expand his religious and nationalist philosophy. The appointment of his successor was the Pope's prerogative but in the special circumstances of Poland and the Polish Pope his suggestion was not only appropriate but necessary. On 11 May Monsignor Stanisław Dziwsz, the Pope's private secretary, called on Cardinal Wyszyński and collected a private letter for the Pope. Subsequent developments suggest that this letter probably contained Wyszyński's suggestion for his successor, someone whom he thought able to continue his work and had the most intimate experience of his own handling of the formidable problem of Church-State relations.

Two days later on 13 May an assassination attempt was made on the Pope's life. There was a unanimous feeling of revulsion and horror throughout Poland at the attempt on the life of a Pope who, to quote the official mass media, was 'the champion of universal values, symbol of good and humanity, servant to mankind and ultimately a Pole loved by all Poles'. As in all moments of national importance the bells began to toll in the Polish churches and the faithful flocked for special Masses. All public entertainment was cancelled, radio and television programmes were rescheduled and the Party's First Secretary, Stanisław Kania, Chairman of the Council of State, Henryk Jabłoński, and Prime Minister General Wojciech Jaruzelski sent a joint telegram wishing the Pope a speedy recovery. The shooting in St. Peter's Square aroused a clearly noticeable feeling of sudden general despondency among the Poles, a symptom of general uncertainty of the solution to the seemingly increasingly insurmountable political, social and economic, as well as every-day problems facing ordinary people. The queues for practically all daily requirements, which were already rationed, were getting longer in spite of Solidarity. The standard of living had visibly declined and the continuous social strife slowly began to sober up the initial intoxication with the newly found freedoms. The Government sidestepped and put off fundamental and necessary economic reforms. Solidarity's demands were bouncing off a rubber wall. Both sides, the regime and Solidarity, wasted their resources on 'secondary theatres of war'. No one knew how the renewal process should continue.[64]

'The power lies on the street, but no-one picks it up' was a current saying in Warsaw in the spring of 1981. And now the living symbol of Poland, its greatest son, John Paul II, lay critically ill in hospital.

On 28 May Cardinal Wyszyński died from abdominal cancer at the age of 79.[65] His death not only marked the end of an era in the history of the Roman Catholic Church in Poland, but occurring as it did at a particularly difficult time it undoubtedly had adverse repercussions on the delicate internal situation. With the departure of Wyszyński and the Pope being seriously ill, the essential and effective leadership of the Polish Church had lapsed for a while. The State authorities ordered a four-day national mourning period, during which all entertainment was suspended in a tribute to a former adversary and a man who had become a myth in his own lifetime. A joint statement signed by Stanisław Kania, Henryk Jabłoński and General Wojciech Jaruzelski, as well as by the leaders of the United Peasants' Party and Democratic Party, paid fulsome tribute to the Cardinal. They praised his patriotism and pledged the authorities to persevere in efforts to improve relations between the State and Church. The message said the Cardinal had understood the 'historical process and civic responsibility' and had thus proved to be 'a great statesman, a man of great moral authority recognized by the nation'. He had by his 'thoughts and work' created a pattern of co-operation between the Church and socialist states.

The Primate's funeral ceremony was attended by an official Party and State delegation which included the Chairman of the Council of State, Henryk Jabłoński, the Speaker of the Sejm, Stanisław Gucwa, two deputy Prime Ministers Jerzy Ozdowski and Mieczysław Rakowski, Foreign Minister Józef Czyrek as well as Kazimierz Barcikowski, member of the Political Bureau. The funeral was broadcast live by the State radio and television for more than five hours. Both the level of the delegation and the broadcast was unprecedented and an unthinkable occurrence in any other Communist country. The climax of the ceremony was a requiem Mass attended by 250,000 people and celebrated by the Pope's personal envoy, Vatican Secretary of State Cardinal Agostino Casaroli, on Warsaw's Victory Square exactly where the Pope celebrated his first papal Mass in Poland on 2 June 1979. As on that occasion, a wooden cross forty-three feet tall dominated the square. One could not help but wonder how dramatically the situation in Poland had changed since then. Beside the Party and State dignitaries stood the National Co-ordinating Commission of Solidarity with Lech Wałęsa and the Presidium of Rural Solidarity, together with a host of other dignataries from home and abroad. Casaroli, the architect and the executioner of former Vatican *Ostpolitik* who not only read the liturgical texts but also delivered his sermon in Polish, extolled Wyszyński as a 'man of an indestructable hope nourished by faith in the virtue of his people', a man who had only 'two great passions in his life: the Church and Poland'. A special message from the Pope, who was convalescing and who had wanted to come to Warsaw, was read by Cardinal Macharski. Apart from praise for the late Primate it also significantly contained a plea to extend the period of national mourning to thirty days which should be 'a period of special prayers, peace and reflection'. The latter was a direct attempt by the Pope to prevent further confrontations between the regime and Solidarity before the approaching Party congress in July. The Primate's body was buried in the crypt under St. John's Cathedral and at the end of the ceremony Cardinal John Krol of Philadelphia read his last will and testament.[66]

The Pope's plea for thirty days of national mourning was broken on 4 June when Solidarity's National Co-ordinating Commission decided, despite an appeal by the auxiliary bishop of Gniezno, Jan Michalski, to call a two-hour warning strike a week later in protest against the authorities' failure to punish those responsible for the Bydgoszcz incident in March. As Mieczysław Rakowski conferred with bishop Bronisław Dąbrowski late that night it was becoming apparent that the Church's moderating influence was diminishing day by day after the death of Wyszyński. The strike was eventually suspended on 9 June after a direct appeal to Solidarity's National Co-ordinating Commission by the Main Council of the Episcopal Conference, which was conferring with the Pope in Rome.

By this time Poland's Warsaw Pact allies had again begun voicing their alarm at the situation. Their main concern was the forthcoming Congress of the PUWP due to start on 14 July and which they viewed with considerable apprehension. On 5 June 1981 the Soviet leaders sent a letter to the Central Committee of the PUWP,[67] the text of which was made public five days later when the Central Committee was meeting in an emergency session. The letter expressed great anxiety over the 'mortal' danger to socialism in Poland and Polish independence, represented by 'counter-revolutionary forces', which the PUWP leadership had failed to bring under control. It singled out Stanisław Kania and Wojciech Jaruzelski for their poor performance and policy of concessions and compromises. The Soviet leaders voiced severe criticism and obvious concern over the preparation for the Extraordinary Ninth PUWP Congress, the tone of which was being set 'to an increasing degree by forces hostile to Socialism'. The letter accused the PUWP leadership of allowing open opportunists to be elected as delegates to the congress and said that 'possibility cannot be excluded that an attempt might be made at the congress itself to defeat decisively the Marxist-Leninist forces of the Party in order to liquidate it'.

The letter was verging on an ultimatum and was similar in language and tone to that sent by five Warsaw Pact leaders in June 1968 prior to the invasion of Czechoslovakia. It left Kania and his supporters dumbfounded. In the absence of Bishop Bronislaw Dąbrowski, who together with Cardinal Macharski and Archbishop Stroba was in Rome for consultation with the Pope, Dr Romuald Kukołowicz was called on 5 June to the building of the Central Committee and made familiar with the contents of the letter from Moscow. The Party leadership apparently confessed the hopelessness of their situation and sought his advice. The complexity of developments in Poland was tellingly illustrated in the request from Polish Communists to the Roman Catholic Church for help out of the apparently hopeless situation after the threatening letter from their Soviet comrades. However, it was clear that there was no easy answer for the Church either. In the event those Polish bishops who were in Rome issued an appeal on 5 June reiterating the Pope's request for thirty days of national mourning.

In spite of the criticism of Kania expressed in the Moscow letter, he managed to survive an explosive meeting of the PUWP Central Committee where he was openly challenged by hardliners.

The Primate's seat in Warsaw remained vacant for a surprisingly long time considering the difficult situation in Poland. It was expected that the Pope would announce Wyszyński's successor after the thirty-day period of national mourning. But there was no announcement on 28 June. The normal procedure for appointing Catholic hierarchy is to present, after wide consultations with local clergy and lay groups, a list of three names for the Pope's consideration. Surprisingly in the case of the Polish Primate no such consultations took place and the envelope delivered to the Pope contained only one name, that of bishop Józef Glemp of Olsztyn. [68] He had been recommended by Wyszyński whose private secretary and chaplain he had been for twelve years. The fact that the Pope hesitated for six weeks before appointing Glemp indicates that his candidature was not particularly favoured by the Pontiff. It had to be pointed out to him that, with the approaching Party congress due to begin on 14 July, Poland could not be left any longer without a Primate, and on 7 July the Pope announced Glemp's appointment.

The appointment of the new Primate was warmly welcomed by Party and State authorities. Stanisław Kania, Henryk Jabłonski and General Jaruzelski sent a congratulatory message wishing Archbishop Glemp success 'in the service of the Church and the nation' and, expressing their firm conviction that he would 'continue the task of his great predecessor', they admitted that Poland sorely needed such a 'unifying force' at the present difficult time: 'In fulfilling this important mission and developing the values that serve the internal peace and the well-being of the nation, the authorities of People's Poland fully appreciate the responsible role of the Church and its Primate and will do so in the future.'[69] There could hardly have been a more explicit admission of the Party and State leadership's heavy reliance on the good offices of the Church as a key factor in maintaining social peace and order in the country.

The new Primate quickly settled to his duties. Only two days after his appointment he presented his archiepiscopal and primatial credentials to the cathedral chapter in Gniezno and later the same day in Warsaw, thus formally taking control of the archdiocese. Unlike his predecessor, who did not easily mix with people and shunned publicity, Archbishop

Glemp began his duties by delivering sermons, travelling, appearing on television and granting interviews in which he stressed that he intended to continue Wyszyński's policies of 'dialogue and co-operation' with both the authorities and Solidarity. While admitting that his work as a Primate was not of a political, but primarily of a pastoral, nature, he nevertheless stressed that in order to fulfil his duty properly a Church leader should not 'remain above social issues'. In his interview for the Warsaw daily newspaper, *Życie Warszawy*,[70] he stated that social peace was an important prerequisite for the continuation of the process of renewal begun in the summer of 1980 and offered the Church's 'indirect influence' on society to prevent people from being motivated by 'private ambitions' rather than common interests. As for the main legacy left by Wyszyński to his successor, Glemp mentioned two principal signals, to 'look at the changing times and to listen to what is happening in the nation'.

The authorities were also eager to establish direct contact with the new Primate. On 11 July Archbishop Glemp met General Jaruzelski in the office of the Council of Ministers for over an hour, during which they discussed 'the most important problems of the country including the ways of preserving social peace, the continuation of the process of renewal, ways of avoiding the occurrence of crises, as well as the main problems concerning Church-State relations.' The meeting between the new head of the Catholic Church in Poland and the Polish Prime Minister, only three days before the Party Congress, was not only of considerable practical value but even more importantly it served a symbolic purpose. It was as much for internal as external consumption. Its aim was to reassure domestic and external adversaries of the Church's unchanged support for the regime prior to the congress, the consequences of which were highly unpredictable.

On 11 July, perhaps with the same aim in mind, the Pope sent a letter to Cardinal Macharski addressed 'to all Polish archbishops, bishops and the faithful'. The text of the letter or its summary appeared in almost all Polish newspapers including the Party's Central Committee daily *Trybuna Ludu*.[71] Recalling Wyszyński's contribution to the people of Poland and the entire Polish nation, the Pope again underlined the 'internationally respected conviction that the Poles have full rights to determine the destiny of their nation'. 'Let the difficult work of renewal which is desired by millions of people of good will in spite of particular or even fundamental differences among them, be continued with full respect for human rights and the rights for the nation.'

The Ninth Extraordinary Congress of the PUWP, much feared by Poland's Eastern European allies, opened in Warsaw on 14 July. It soon became clear that the congress delegates were not unaffected by the general climate of democratization of life in Poland. The congress, which normally is a stage-managed and formal affair with the Party leaders treading well-worn and uncontroversial paths, became a platform for genuine expression of the rank-and-file feelings.[72] For the first time a secret ballot was used for the election of the Central Committee, Central Revision Commission and the Central Party Central Commission, as well as in electing the Party's First Secretary and the Political Bureau. The result was that the personal and social composition of all these bodies changed beyond recognition. During the unprecedentedly free debates during the proceedings of the Congress the delegates were, however, surprisingly reticent about the Party's relations with the Catholic Church. In his speech outlining the Government's programme the Prime Minister Jaruzelski pledged to continue the dialogue, saying: 'We value the constructive relationship with the Episcopate which is based on mutual understanding and respect. Talks with the new Primate encourage us to believe that the co-operation of past years will be continued and strengthened.'[73] But only two other speakers mentioned the role of the Church in Poland at all. Zbigniew Ciechan listed the Catholic tradition as one of the national features specific to the country on which the Polish model of socialism must be based.[74] Edward Skrzypczak suggested that openess and dialogue with a whole gamut of social forces should also include trade unions and the Church.[75]

However neither the Party Congress nor its leadership's promises of the continuation of the process of renewal managed to defuse the increasingly tense and desperate situation in Poland. How could the leading role of the Party be reconciled with the fact that the Party was mistrusted by a great majority of the population? The Party appeared to have been tolerated in order to satisfy the Russians that it remained in some sort of control. Throughout the summer of 1982 acute shortages not only of essential goods but of practically everything, became a source both of strikes and a new form of protest, hunger marches. The situation was further exacerbated by the regime's continuous denial of media access to Solidarity to prevent the latter from explaining its position on vital issues publicly. The authorities' response was that it would never relinquish control of the mass media, which was not only an important vehicle for expressing public opinion but also for shaping it. At the same time, divisions within Solidarity itself were adding to its problems, as regional branches were taking the initiative in carrying out protest actions, and these were becoming increasingly difficult for Solidarity's national leadership to control.

The Church's continuous appeals for all protest actions to be suspended had had increasingly scant effect. Nevertheless, the new Primate persevered in his mediation efforts. On 11 August he received Solidarity officials with Lech Wałęsa and the following day he met Stanisław Kania at the latter's own request. In a joint statement after their meeting the two leaders stated that 'in view of the social tensions, strikes and demonstrations and the country's currently very difficult economic situation, all patriots and social groups have the task of saving Poland'. On 13 August the Episcopal Conference warned against attempts to use the growing tension in order to fight political battles, and against hatred and vindictiveness. Archbishop Glemp made himself still clearer in a sermon in Częstochowa on 26 August in which he complained about the increasing polarization within society and blamed it on both sides: while each side was blaming the other and claiming innocence for itself, while reciprocal accusations continued to increase tensions, 'poverty is knocking on our door'. But he left no doubt that the Church was supporting Solidarity's demands for access to the media. It was enough, he said, to turn on the radio to hear accusations levelled at the unions, while the unions, deprived of such access to the media, were pushed into the self-defence of counter-accusations and abusive words. In the sermon he also appealed for a moratorium of thirty days of peace and work without conflicts.

His appeal was aimed to coincide with the first part of the First National Congress of Solidarity, due to begin in Gdańsk on 5 September. As the congress delegates began to arrive on 5 September, in what must be considered an act of extreme provocation the Soviet Union began a nine-day massive naval and military exercise in the Baltic, with more than sixty ships and 25,000 troops, involving landings on the shores of Latvia and Lithuania.[76] At the same time the Czechoslovak Party daily newspaper *Rude Pravo* charged that Solidarity

133

was finishing preparations to seize power in Poland, saying 'there is not the least doubt that counter-revolution has raised its head high in Poland'. On the eve of the congress Stanisław Kania warned that the Party would use all constitutional means at its disposal to defend socialism and hinted for the first time that the authorities would declare a state of emergency if necessary. Meanwhile 896 Solidarity delegates, representing 9,484,000 members, unimpressed by the pressures surrounding their historic meeting, began their deliberations.

The Catholic Church was much in evidence during the opening of the congress. Its proceedings were inaugurated by a Mass concelebrated by Archbishop Józef Glemp and two bishops of Gdańsk, Lech Kaczmarek and Kazimierz Kluz. During his sermon,[77] the Primate reminded the audience that while the primary task of Solidarity was to defend the interests of the workers it also had 'an obligation to serve' society and Poland. Expanding on the meaning of 'serving', he said that it would require the 'elimination of the mistakes that have developed in our society and still linger here, impeding movement towards renewal and morality'. The historical role of the congress, the Primate told the delegates, was in 'shaping conditions for the working population as well as the future of our country'.

The Church's symbolic presence was clearly marked by a cross hung prominently at the front of the debating hall, next to the national emblem, just above the podium. There were also many references to the Church and religion in speeches by various delegates, and the official report by the National Co-ordinating Commission of Solidarity emphasized that the movement had enjoyed constant support from the Church in various activities. This link between the Church and Solidarity was also emphasized by the Pope, who said on 6 September to a group of pilgrims from Poland that 'we must connect' the Solidarity congress and the strikes at Gdańsk a year before that led to the union's formation with the 'events of the Second World War'. The great number of deaths in that war, he said 'confirms our desire to live as a nation that has its own culture and its individuality. Respect of this right of our nation to independence is a condition for world peace.'

The fact that the Church's moderating influence was fading became particularly noticeable when the delegates adopted a message 'To the Working People of Eastern Europe'.[78] The defiant character of the statement, openly challenging to both Polish and other Communist establishments and addressed to the workers of Albania, Bulgaria, Czechoslovakia, the GDR, Romania, Hungary and all peoples of the Soviet Union offered 'support [to] all of you who have decided to take the difficult path and fight for free trade unions'. Also the programmatic declaration adopted on the last day of the congress contained politically explosive suggestions which the delegates considered as 'the most important national needs'.[79] These included free elections to the Sejm and peoples' councils and the implementation of economic reforms through both the creation of authentic self-management bodies and the abolition of the party *nomenclatura* in appointments (the system under which appointments to a wide range of posts in the State and society can only be filled by people approved by the Party).

The reaction from Poland's neighbours was predictable and Solidarity was accused not only of seeking power but also of interference in other countries' internal affairs.[80] On 11 September, the Central Committee of the Soviet Communist Party sent another letter to the Central Committee of the PUWP,[81] which referred to Solidarity's congress as 'disgusting provocation' and called on the 'PUWP leadership and the Polish Government immediately' to take 'determined and radical steps'. Although the letter stopped short of actually demanding that the second part of Solidarity's congress (due to take place between 26 September and 7 October) should be cancelled, it firmly set the limits of Soviet tolerance.

On 15 September Pope John Paul II published his encyclical *Laborem Exercens*,[82] devoted to the dignity of human labour. The timing of its publication was not accidental. The encyclical defended the rights of workers to organize into unions, but at the same time dealt with their responsibilities and role in social and economic life, emphasizing that they cannot serve individual or group interests but must take into consideration the restriction of existing economic circumstances. It is the task of trade unions, it said, to work for the common good and to seek to repair what is defective in the system of possessing and managing the means of production. Trade unions should not, however, acquire the attributes of political parties struggling for power nor maintain excessively close links with such parties, lest they become their instruments.

The encyclical thus reiterated the Church's view on Solidarity's role in Polish society, a view expressed implicitly and explicitly by the

Polish Catholic hierarchy many times in the past. This view, however desirable, was not entirely realistic in the circumstances in which the country found itself in the last quarter of 1981. The problem for Poland now was not whether Solidarity and representatives of other social groups would become directly involved in exercising political authority, but to what extent the Party would be willing to admit others to a genuine power-sharing arrangement. As Deputy Prime Minister Mieczysław Rakowski admitted in September 'the political and social situation has changed so much that the Communists simply cannot rule by themselves'.[83] From the end of September high-ranking members of the Party establishment as well as Government officials, including the Prime Minister General Jaruzelski, began to advance the idea of a new Front of National Unity. Various suggestions[84] were put forward for a new form of 'grand coalition' of Communists and Catholics: a tripartite alliance of Party, Church and Solidarity as a Front of National Accord; or a Government of National Unity, either as an advisory council only with the direct involvement of the Church or with a Church-inspired Christian-Democratic party, in which the political goals of Solidarity could also be incorporated and controlled. The suggestion, however attractive, was nevertheless full of insurmountable difficulties. The first and perhaps the most important question concerned the role of the Party, a demoralized and dwindling body, in the possible new arrangements. Any change in the Leninist concept of the Party's leading role in Polish society, even if it were offered for negotiation by the Polish Communists, would certainly never have been acceptable to the Soviet Union or its Eastern European allies. Perhaps there was agreement amongst the Party leadership on the broadening of the political platform but not on sharing power. The Party was adamant on keeping its right to control the principal nerve of political and social life. For Solidarity any direct involvement in a formal power-sharing arrangement would not have been acceptable, since it saw its role as one of controlling, not governing. Attempts to draw the union into formal collaboration were perceived by Solidarity as a trap designed to deprive it of effective influence on the day-to-day running of the country. The Episcopate on the other hand, while remaining silent on the question of national coalition, indicated at least in the initial stages of the discussion that it might be prepared to put the weight of its authority behind the Party's efforts to create some form of national union. The Church's attitude was dictated partly by its desire to act as a stabilizing factor in the interests of social peace and partly by its willingness to exchange concessions. However, it appears that the most the Church could agree would be to support certain individuals enjoying its confidence rather than to participate directly in government. Thus on all fronts the idea was meeting considerable difficulties, but nevertheless the search for a possible formula continued. On 13 October, Polish Foreign Minister Józef Czyrek held private talks in Rome with the Vatican's Secretary of State Cardinal Agostino Casaroli and immediately afterwards was received by Pope John Paul II in his summer residence, Castel Gandolfo. The Pope, who normally does not receive official visitors there, spent two hours with Czyrek, the longest papal audience on record. Archbishop Glemp conferred with the Pope several times during his stay in Rome between 16 and 21 October, but the consensus that emerged from these meetings was that the Church, despite its political role, should not become directly or permanently involved in Polish politics. On his return from Rome on 21 October, the Primate, after his talks with Wałęsa, met General Jaruzelski, who by then had also become the Party's First Secretary after the resignation of Stanisław Kania on 18 October. Although they stressed the need 'to continue the co-operation between the Church and the State, for the sake of well-understood national interests, internal peace and the successful implementation of the renewal process, as well as for the sake of Poland's security and international prestige', there was no progress on the formation of a Front of National Accord. There now followed on 4 November an unprecedented meeting between Archbishop Glemp, General Jaruzelski and Lech Wałęsa. This certainly was a symbolic landmark in Polish politics, an explicit reminder of the institutional divisions within the country and a recognition of the equal or at least comparable status of the Church, Party and Solidarity in determining the future evolution of Poland's political life. Symbolism apart, however, the meeting (according to the communiqué issued afterwards) served merely as an 'exchange of views on ways of overcoming the crisis . . . and on the possibility of forming a Front of National Accord that could serve as a permanent forum for dialogue and consultations among political and social forces on the basis of Poland's constitutional principles'. But, since the three leaders had not been able to reach agreement on any significant issue, the meeting appears to have been counter-productive in the long run. To the Soviet and East European critics of the Polish regime, as well as to the hardliners inside the Party leadership, the meeting became evidence that the Party's leading role was compromised too far. By the end of November there were further signs that the Jaruzelski regime had begun to panic under increasing external and internal pressure. The despatch on 24 November, of military task forces to some two thousand major centres throughout Poland, ostensibly to co-ordinate preparations for contingency plans for the winter, was in fact a step towards gradual militarization and a test of the army's efficiency for its future role. This move further aroused the already deep mistrust of the authorities, who no longer hid the fact that they would resort to the use of force unless Solidarity accepted solutions to the Polish crisis on the regime's terms. The era of negotiations was fast coming to an end.

On 26 November the Episcopal Conference issued a communiqué which drew a grim picture of the situation in Poland. 'The country is faced with the threat of civil war and loss of all gains so far achieved', it said, and warned that there was no other way of overcoming the crisis unless all Poles, individuals and organizations united in their endeavours. The bishops strongly criticized the authorities for hampering the process of bridge-building between the Government and the people. They warned that no understanding or reconciliation would be possible if there were no freedom of expression. 'The television and press should not use half-truths, for this leads to deceitfulness and arouses people's anger . . . At such a difficult time all sides should make responsible use of their words'. The Episcopate urged: 'all prejudices and interest groups now have to be subordinated to the common good', and emphasized that only through negotiations between all sides concerned could the future of the country be protected.

By now, however, it had become clear that the regime wished to include in the much heralded Front of National Accord some organizations that did not appear to have any major significance in politics or any discernible public support. This substantially changed the nature and possible impact of the institution, which was originally to be composed of groups that commanded the respect and recognition of the whole of society. By implication this would have reduced the Front to representatives of the Polish United Workers' Party, Solidarity, the Church and the other two political parties, the United Peasant Party and the Democratic Party. Even now the Episcopate urged some form of national accord on crucial issues in Poland's public life. On 27 November the Episcopal Conference issued a communiqué declaring:

> Such a national accord should be achieved through both the specific solution of separate problems and the establishment of new and indispensable structures that would make it possible to concentrate the efforts of all citizens on improving the situation and would ensure that mistakes would not be repeated in the future.

The communiqué, warning that the nation could face a 'frantic struggle', called for unity, peace and reconciliation and reaffirmed the Primate's readiness to act as mediator.

The following day, however, the Party's Central Committee directed the PUWP parliamentary group to introduce, during the next session of the Sejm due to take place on 15-16 December, legislation giving the Government extraordinary powers including the right to ban strikes. For Solidarity the Central Committee's instruction amounted to 'an attempt to eliminate the workers' and civil rights that had been achieved in the 1980 agreements'. For the union this call effectively ruled out any chance of national accord. On 3 December, Solidarity used the only effective threat available and stated that the acceptance by the Sejm of the Party's recommendation would provoke a 24-hour general strike throughout Poland. Furthermore, any attempt to implement such legislation would result in a general strike of unlimited duration. On 5 December Archbishop Glemp again met Lech Wałęsa in a desperate effort to calm the rising tension. Whatever the prospects for a cooling off that emerged from that meeting, their realization was effectively emasculated by a call on 6 December from the Warsaw branch of Solidarity for co-ordinated protest rallies across Poland on 17 December, in protest against the regime's intentions to solve the conflicts by force.

On 7 December in what appears to have been a last-ditch attempt to head off a collision between the regime and Solidarity, the Primate took the unprecedented step of directly intervening in Poland's politics[85] and sent four separate but related letters to all deputies to the

Sejm, to Prime Minister General Wojciech Jaruzelski, to the Chairman of Solidarity's National Co-ordinating Commission Lech Wałęsa and to the Independent Students' Union.

In the letter to the deputies to the Sejm,[86] which was written on behalf of the entire Episcopate, the Primate appealed to them to refrain from passing the recently proposed legislation giving the Government extraordinary powers in dealing with social problems: 'In the interest of the workers and the country, the Church, which has shared the fate of our fatherland for over one thousand years, warns the Sejm . . . that taking such a decision may lead to tragic consequences for the future of our country . . .' In justifying the Church's opposition to the proposed legislation, Glemp both criticized its possible implications for the country's public life and questioned its usefulness at the present time. Such a law, he argued would make it possible to restrict civil rights (including the right to strike) and could undermine the unity of the nation. He was also sceptical about the effectiveness of such legislation in quelling social unrest.

> Internal peace, mutual understanding, and the need to avoid conflicts are now of the utmost importance. The Church is anxious and worried that adoption of this law might upset internal peace, destroy the communications that have been maintained with so much difficulty and give rise to serious social conflicts . . .

In this context the Primate drew the deputies' attention to two important facts, namely, that 'the country at present is not threatened by any large industrial strikes' and that 'the unions, among them Solidarity, have been opposed to any wildcat strikes'. In view of those facts, the Archbishop said, 'to adopt an exceptional law prohibiting, through administrative means, the right to protest would . . . poison the atmosphere . . . expose the trade unions against their will to pressures from below in favour of a general strike . . . and could provoke a general strike, the extent and consequences of which cannot be foreseen . . .'.

The Primate's private letter to General Jaruzelski (never published) contained a call for the continuation of the trilateral talks on ways of finding solutions to the current crisis, which had begun with the meeting on 4 November but which, despite expressly stated desires for further such consultation, had not in fact been followed up.

In his letter to Lech Wałęsa, Archbishop Glemp again stressed the need for dialogue between Solidarity and the regime.[87] Decrying the manifestations of hatred in Poland's public life the Primate said that:

> The Catholic Church has, from the beginning, looked with sympathy at the renewal that has been undertaken by the union represented by you. The great accomplishments that have been achieved up to now must not be destroyed by any imprudence, such as confrontation. There is a need for a dialogue, which, while difficult until now, is not fruitless. I trust that the style of dialogue that was shown during the meeting on 4 November will provide a model for further talks and will involve other social groups. In this trio of institutional forces the Church wishes to serve the partners—the authorities and the trade union movement—to serve with its experience, evangelical considerations and human charity...

Finally, in the letter to the Independent Student Union,[88] the Primate appealed to the Union to end protest at universities and colleges, for the sake of preserving the accomplishments achieved by the union in defending justice and freedom for science and research.

The four letters from Archbishop Glemp together amounted to yet another appeal for dialogue and consultations. In his intervention he showed no partisan preference in the shaping of politics within the system. Instead the main motivation behind his action was his insistent belief in the need to find ways of accommodation among the various groups and institutions. The lines of confrontation, however, appear to have been firmly drawn up and the authorities were determined to have a show-down with Solidarity. Glemp's intervention had no effect.

On 11 and 12 December, Solidarity's National Co-ordinating Commission met in the Lenin Shipyard in Gdańsk to consider the union's deteriorating relations with the authorities and the mounting criticism from the Soviet Union and other East European countries. After a heated debate the Commission decided, despite objections from their Church advisers, to call a referendum by 15 January 1982, on public confidence in the Government.[89] As the 107 members of the Commission concluded their meeting, they realized that the

THE TRIUMPH OF SOLIDARITY

telephone and telex lines had been cut off. Poland was already under martial law.

Notes

1. It should be remembered that since 1976 the Church was not alone in vocalizing the social and political aspirations of the population. The range of groups and organizations included: the Confederation for an Independent Poland; Farmers' Self-Defence Committees; Centre for People's Thought; Polish League for Independence, Young Poland Movement; Students' Solidarity Committees and the Independent Publishing house (NOWA), to name a few. For details see *Dissent in Poland, 1976-77*, London, Association of Polish Students and Graduates in Exile, 1977; P. Raina, *Political Opposition in Poland, 1954-1977*, London, Arlington Books, 1978; and Raina, *Independent Social Movements in Poland*, op. cit.
2. The following is partially based on my 'Poland in 1980: the breaking of the system?', in Szajkowski (ed.), *Documents in Communist Affairs—1981*, op. cit., pp. 3-10.
3. For detailed chronology of the strikes in the summer of 1980 see: Anna Sabbat and Roman Stefanowski (compilers), *Poland: A Chronology of Events, July-November 1980*, Radio Free Europe, RAD Background Report/91, March 1981; *The Strikes in Poland; August 1980*, Munich, Radio Free Europe Research, 1980. Detailed account of the strikes in Gdańsk and Warsaw voivodships, as well as their appraisal is given in *Who's Who, What's What in Solidarność*, a book issued at the time of its First Congress in Gdańsk in September 1981 (no place or date of the publication given).
4. For complete text see Raina, *Independent Social Movements in Poland*, pp. 437-9.
5. It is not my intention to analyse in detail the evolution of the Gdańsk strike. For an excellent account see Neal Ascherson, *The Polish August*, Harmondsworth, Penguin, 1982 (second edition); and also Denis McShane, *Solidarity: Poland's Independent Trade Union*, Nottingham, Spokesman, 1981. Detailed chronology of the strikes in August was published by the *samizdat* publication *Robotnik* (The Worker). For its English translation see Szajkowski (ed.), *Documents in Communist Affairs—1981*, pp. 201-9. See also *The Strikes in Poland*.
6. Unlike Walentynowicz, Wałęsa had not been employed at the shipyard since 1976. Born to a peasant family on 29 September 1943 in the village of Popowo near the town of Lipno in northern Poland, after completing his secondary education as an electrician, Wałęsa moved to Gdańsk. His involvement in the trade-union movement began in 1968 when he agitated for a boycott of a workers' meeting organized by the authorities to condemn the student protests in March 1968. In December 1970 he was a member of the strike committee of the Gdańsk shipyards and represented strikers at a meeting with Edward Gierek on 25 January 1971. When the unrest subsided, he was chosen as a delegate to the local works council, but was dismissed from his job on 30 April 1976 after making a fiery speech to a meeting of the official union. Following this, he found a job with the Association of Building Machinery Repair Works (ZREMB) as a vehicle-repair electrician

and continued his extracurricular activities. His passionate defence of workers' rights brought him into contact with the publishers of the bi-weekly *samizdat* publication *Robotnik* (The Worker), which supported any initiatives aimed at the defence of workers' interests. Through them he came into contact with democratic opposition circles, in particular the Social Self-Defence Committee, KOR. He also became a member of the Founding Committee of the Free Trade Unions of the Baltic Coast and, together with sixty-three other free trade-union activists from all over Poland, signed the Charter of Workers' Rights. In December 1978 he was arrested after a memorial ceremony for workers killed in the Gdańsk riots of 1970. He was tried, sentenced to a 5,000 złotys fine for allegedly disturbing the peace, and again dismissed from work on 31 January 1979. Subsequently he managed to find employment at the Elektromontaz plant in Gdańsk but was dismissed yet again in January 1980 after taking part in another commemorative ceremony. He was one of a five-man 'workers' commission' set up to fight these dismissals and resist further harassment by management and the militia. He became a member of the editorial board of *Robotnik Wybrzeża* (The Worker of the Coast), a *samizdat* publication published by the Founding Committee of the Free Trade Unions of the Coast in 1979. He was frequently detained or hauled in for questioning by security officials. Since 1976 he reckons that he has been arrested about a hundred times. The best account of Wałęsa's role in the Gdańsk strike and subsequent events is undoubtedly *The Book of Lech Wałęsa*, Harmondsworth, Penguin, 1981.

7. This according to Ascherson (*The Polish August*, p. 147) was a particular obsession of Wałęsa.
8. For complete text see Solidarność, *Strike Information Bulletin, Gdańsk Shipyard. No. 2.* For an English translation of the complete text of the Bulletin see Szajkowski (ed.), *Documents in Communist Affairs—1981*, pp. 160-5.
9. *The Strikes in Poland*, pp. 133-4.
10. Also on 20 August the Primate's remarks were broadcast by the Polish Section of the Vatican radio, which is received in Poland. The Polish Press Agency PAP reported excerpts from the sermon in its English bulletin on 22 August.
11. For complete text see: Szajkowski (ed.), *Documents in Communist Affairs —1981*, p. 160. Similar messages were sent to Cardinal Franciszek Macharski of Kraków and Bishop Stefan Bareła of Częstochowa.
12. The proclamation was accompanied by the following instructions: 'The proclamation should be read during all Masses on Sunday 24 August 1980. In the event of the strike being ended the proclamation should be read nevertheless, as information'.
13. The strike at the Warski Shipyard in Szczecin began on 18 August and the Inter-factory Strike Committee issued, on 19 August thirty-three demands similar to those in Gdańsk, though the final agreement contains only twenty-nine points. In Szczecin the Church was much less in evidence than in Gdańsk. The main gates of the Warski Shipyard, like those of the Lenin Shipyard, bore a picture of the Black Madonna of Częstochowa and there was a cross, but the railings did not become the open air altar for offerings, which had been the case in Gdańsk. A suggestion that Mass should be held inside the yard on Sunday was accepted only after a long debate

among the workers, and then on the grounds that it would not be compulsory.
14. For transcript see *The Strikes in Poland*, pp. 349-64. It is interesting to note that in his reply to the two demands, point-by-point, Jagielski ignored point 3, which asked for respect of the constitutional guarantee of press freedom and for access to the media for all religious denominations.
15. Four were members of the Political Bureau: Edward Babiuch (Prime Minister); Jerzy Łukaszewicz (Central Committee's Secretary responsible for propaganda); Jan Szydlak (Chairman of the Central Trade Union Council); and Tadeusz Wrzaszczyk (Deputy Prime Minister and Chairman of the Planning Commission). Two others were alternate members: Tadeusz Pyka (who headed the first Commission for negotiations in Gdańsk); and Zdzisław Żandarowski (Central Committee Secretary). In addition eleven changes were made in the Government. Apart from the replacement of Babiuch as the Prime Minister by Józef Pińkowski, the changes also included the dismissal of all the Deputy Prime Ministers, as well as the Ministers of Foreign Affairs, Finance, Machine Industry, the Chairman of the Planning Commission, the Chairman of the State Price Committee, the Chairman of the Radio and Television Committee and the Director of the Main Statistical Office. In all, this constituted one of the most complete leadership changes in the post-war history of Eastern Europe.
16. For complete text see Szajkowski (ed.), *Documents in Communist Affairs— 1981*, pp. 166-9.
17. For biography of Stanisław Kania see: *Communist Affairs: Documents and Analysis*, vol. 1, no. 2 (April 1982), pp. 584-6.
18. The following is based on Raina, *Independent Social Movements in Poland*, pp. 524-5. Since the publication of this account I have been able to confirm its authenticity.
19. Mazowiecki together with the historian and political scientist Dr Bronisław Gieremek, went to Gdańsk on 22 August to deliver an appeal signed by sixty-four intellectuals in support of the strikers and their demands, and thus established direct contact with the workers. This intervention turned out to be crucial in the development of the strike and subsequently in the politics of Solidarity.
20. A team of experts led by the writer Andrzej Kijowski was also accepted, but with less enthusiasm, by the Inter-Factory Strike Committee in Szczecin. However, due to substantial differences between them and the leadership of the strike, the experts left Szczecin before the signing of the agreement.
21. The best account of these private talks has been given by Jadwiga Staniszkis. In her article 'The Evolution of Forms of Working-Class Protest in Poland: Sociological Reflections on the Gdańsk-Szczecin Case, August 1980', published in *Soviet Studies*, vol. XXXIII, no. 2, pp. 204-31, she wrote: 'During the first meeting of the working party, a peculiar, semi-relaxed atmosphere, gentle and even ironic, prevailed. One reason was that experts on both sides . . . were more or less members of the same Warsaw millieu. The Government experts were rather critical but basically loyal professionals; we were more openly critical, but still acceptable within the framework of Gierek's "window-dressing" liberalization. If it had only been a matter of our political attitudes, we could very easily have changed places. This atmosphere made negotiations easier: the element of mutual trust already existed,

THE TRIUMPH OF SOLIDARITY

and leaks from both sides helped things to move more smoothly. And the surreal nature of our joint situation made bargains more possible. It created a curious detachment from the real context in which we were talking ... But on the other hand, this climate dangerously increased our mutual loyalty to each other as we bargained. It was one of the main reasons why, in order to keep the negotiations going, the workers were not informed about crucial details and choices established by the working party. We ended this first meeting in an optimistic mood'.

22. For complete text see Szajkowski (ed.), *Documents in Communist Affairs —1981*, pp. 174-81.
23. On 27 August the Episcopate's Press Office issued the following communiqué: 'With regard to the broadcasting on Polish radio and television and the publication in the press of the Primate of Poland's homily, delivered by Cardinal Wyszyński during the central celebrations dedicated to Our Lady of Częstochowa, the Press Office of the Polish Episcopate is instructed to declare that the text broadcast and published is not complete, is not authorized, and that the author's consent to its dissemination in the Polish media was not requested.'
24. For complete text see: Szajkowski (ed.), *Documents in Communist Affairs —1981*, pp. 182-3.
25. Kukołowicz has since 1972 belonged to a group of the Primate's private advisers. He was sent by Wyszyński to the Lenin Shipyard as early as 21 August, after the Primate's meeting with Bishop Kaczmarek. From then on he seldom left Wałęsa's side. On 6 September he was appointed by Cardinal Wyszyński as his special delegate to the Inter-Factory Strike Committee in Gdańsk and on 17 September after the creation of the National Commission of Solidarity he became Wyszyński's envoy to that body as well as his personal representative to Wałęsa.
26. For the complete texts of both agreements see Szajkowski (ed.), *Documents in Communist Affairs—1981*, pp. 184-98.
27. This point was subject to much tougher negotiations in Szczecin than in Gdańsk. Barcikowski objected to the inclusion in the agreement of references to the Church's access to mass media, insisting that the Government could not impose something which the Church had not directly requested. The strikers then broke off the talks and sent two representatives to the local bishop to get his confirmation.
28. The full text of the letter also appeared on the front page of the Catholic weekly *Tygodnik Powszechny*, on 14 September 1980.
29. At the same time in another reshuffle of the Political Bureau, Kazimierz Barcikowski, and the First Secretary of the provincial committee in Katowice Andrzej Żabiński were appointed its full members. The ranks of the PUWP Secretariat were swelled by the inclusion of Tadeusz Grabski, Zdzisław Kurowski and Jerzy Wojtecki.
30. On 22 February 1981 the Central Control Commission of the PUWP announced that during the last three months of 1980 the names of 50,875 members and 11,004 candidate members had been removed from the Party's register, mostly at their own request. It is estimated that by October 1981 the PUWP's membership, which had been some three million in February 1980, was halved. For detailed figures on the decline of PUWP membership consult the Chronology of Events section of *Communist Affairs: Documents and Analysis*, vols. 1 and 2.

31. The announcement of the restoration of the Joint Commission was made by Prime Minsiter Józef Pińkowski in the Sejm on 5 September. Set up in November 1956 the Commission was convened at irregular intervals only seven times between 1956 and 1967: 8 December 1956; 14 March 1960; 25 May 1960; 11 July 1961; 27 May 1963; November 1965; 20 January 1967. The Government's side was represented by the PUWP Central Committee's Secretary in charge of Church matters, Jerzy Morawski (1956–60) and since 1960 Zenon Kliszko. The Church was represented by Bishop Zygmunt Choromański, secretary of the Episcopal Conference and the Bishop of Łódź Michał Klepacz.
32. Two further sessions of the Commission were held in 1980; 20–1 November, and 8 December. At the December meeting agreement was reached on the building of two new seminaries, in Szczecin and Koszalin, in addition two working parties were created; one on the problems related to seminaries, the other to study the growth of alcoholism. During the fourth meeting of the Commission on 10 January 1981 three further working parties were established: for legal matters; for religious publications; and for educational matters. (For list of members of the working parties see Radio Free Europe Research, Munich, *Polish Situation Report*, 30 January 1981.) The fifth meeting of the Commission took place on 2 March 1981. The issues discussed included the Church's access to the media, changes in the law on censorship, especially with regard to religious publications, the law controlling Church property, pastoral work in hospitals and prisons, and the organization of the Catholic University of Lublin. Subsequent to the meeting an agreement was reached in April 1981 between the Episcopate and the Ministry of Education on the re-establishment of the Department of Social Sciences (abolished in 1952) at the Catholic University of Lublin, to consist of three sections: sociology, psychology and education.
33. Solidarity statutes were submitted for registration to the Warsaw District Court on 24 September and subsequently the court sent a communication listing its complaints about the statutes. In the main the court's objections related to three aspects: the claim to operate nationally, Solidarity's ban on Party members and managers holding union office, and its attitude to the Party's 'leading role'.
34. It should be recalled that the Gdańsk agreement contained a demand for the release of political prisoners including fourteen members of KOR who were imprisoned on 20 August. They were all released within a few days after the signing of the agreement. Jacek Kuroń immediately upon his release on 1 September was appointed one of Wałęsa's chief advisers. During the next weeks other members of KOR also became advisers to Solidarity not only in Gdańsk but also in other branches. In fact the group of experts advising the leadership of Solidarity consisted of the three groups: a group created by the Primate of Poland and led by Dr Romuald Kukołowicz; a team from the Catholic Intelligentsia Club headed by Tadeusz Mazowiecki; and a group of KOR members.
35. For the complete text of the Solidarity Statutes and insertions made by Judge Kościelniak see Szajkowski (ed.), *Documents in Communist Affairs —1981*, pp. 275–89.
36. Radio Warsaw, 24 October 1980.
37. It is worth recalling that by now there existed an Independent Self-Governing

Peasant's Union in Zbrosza Duża. It emerged on 29 October 1980 from the former Farmers' Self-Defence Committee.
38. See Szajkowski (ed.), *Documents in Communist Affairs—1981*, pp. 286-9.
39. It is significant that on 9 November an announcement was made that the Polish radio would extend its religious broadcasting and transmit Mass on other holidays: New Year's Day, Easter Monday, Corpus Christi, All Saints' Day and the first and second days of Christmas.
40. Wyszyński's remarks to Wałęsa were broadcast by Radio Warsaw on 16 November after the transmission of Sunday Mass.
41. On the night before Ozdowski's appointment was made public Bishop Bronisław Dąbrowski held a meeting with the Catholic deputies in the parliament building which was also attended by the Party's First Secretary Stanisław Kania.
42. Radio Zagreb, 26 November 1980.
43. For complete text see Szajkowski (ed.), *Documents in Communist Affairs —1981*, pp. 304-5.
44. Ascherson, *The Polish August*, p. 216.
45. *Guardian*, 4 December 1980.
46. According to Senator D'Amoto's spokesman, Mike Heatherway, the Senator 'was told by a member of the Vatican curia during his visit to Italy in the summer of 1981 that a communication was sent to the Kremlin from the Vatican by the Pope, who had stated that he would be with his people in the event of Soviet invasion'. Substantially the same remark is repeated by Ascherson on p. 223 but according to him it was made during the Pope's meeting with the deputy director of the Soviet Communist Party Central Committee's Foreign Department, Vladim Zagladin. The Vatican's press spokesman Father Romeo Pancieroli had, however, on 17 December 1980 denied that such a meeting ever took place. Painstaking research at the Vatican had nevertheless revealed that although Zagladin's name does not appear in the alphabetical record of persons received by the Pope, his name is listed under the heading 'visitors USSR', with a pointer 'see 17 December'. This apparently refers to Father Pancieroli's verbal statement 'it does not seem that Mr Zagladin was received in the Vatican'. The denial, is, however, well short of being categorical and does not preclude the possibility that the meeting might have taken place outside the Vatican. Further investigation has revealed that Zagladin, who attended on 6-7 December the Congress of the San Marino Communist Party, arrived in Rome on 9 December. During his stay in Rome he requested a meeting with the Pontiff. According to some sources, during the meeting, which was primarily concerned with the Roman Catholic Church in the Soviet Union, the subject of Poland was also discussed. It also appears that during the meeting he delivered President Brezhnev's reply to the Pope's letter.
47. The Joint Church–Government Commission meeting on 8 December also issued an appeal for national unity regardless of philosophies and political differences to enable the country to emerge from the crisis then taking place.
48. During the meeting the Primate asked the union representatives to provide him with a list of those being detained for political reasons in a bid to intercede on their behalf. He also assured them of the Church's full support,

offering his services as a mediator between Solidarity and the authorities should this be required.

49. The visit was viewed with considerable concern both in Moscow and Warsaw. On 29 December, four days after his hurried trip to Moscow, the Polish Foreign Minister Józef Czyrek, met Wałęsa for more than two hours. During the meeting, which dealt primarily with Wałęsa's visit to Italy, Czyrek asked him to refrain from making any statements which might irritate the Soviet Union.

50. The registration was only one of forty-nine demands put forward by the students. During the strike students received special pastoral care. According to *Religion in Communist Lands* (vol. 9, nos. 3-4, Autumn 1981, pp. 155-6), 'every day Masses were said with the majority of students participating. A special "room for prayer" was designed in each university building where students gathered to pray together. Religious literature, Bibles and Catholic papers were distributed, and a number of religious films were shown and discussions organized. Every Saturday all the chaplains met the students' representatives to discuss the current situation and to draw up plans of action for the following days. On 2 February Bishop J. Rozwadowski, the ordinary of Łódź diocese, issued a special pastoral letter to the people of Łódź asking them to pray for a speedy solution to the conflict. On the day after the settlement was reached on 18 February, Solemn Masses were said in many of the university buildings and other colleges. On 8 March, Bishop J. Rozwadowski himself celebrated a Thanksgiving Mass for the students, professors and people of Łódź'. The Łódź agreement signed between the students and Government commission is the most comprehensive, penetrating and interesting of the 651 agreements signed during the first nine months of the Solidarity period. For its complete text see *Communist Affairs: Documents and Analysis*, vol. 1, no. 1 (January 1982), pp. 219-33.

51. Throughout the strikes in Rzeszów the farmers openly displayed their association with the Church. Timothy Garton Ash, one of the few Western correspondents who managed to get to Rzeszów, published the following account of the scene in *The Times* on 22 January 1981: 'When the workers occupied the Lenin shipyard in Gdańsk last August, they kept their bust of Lenin in their assembly hall. Lenin now stands with his face to the wall and a broken nose. Here in Rzeszów, peasants demanding the national registration of the rural counterpart to Solidarity . . . have replaced him with an altar. Behind the altar the assembly hall of the former state trade-union headquarters in this traditional centre of peasant radicalism is decorated with pictures of the Pope and the Black Madonna of Jasna Góra, papal and national flags, and a six foot cardboard copy of the Gdańsk monument to the workers killed . . . in December 1970. On this extraordinary stage a priest administers daily the sacrament to the 300 farmers and workers who have been occupying the building . . . "Be not downcast", the priest admonishes them. "The whole nation is behind you. The disturbance to the economy caused by your strike is nothing compared to the damage it has suffered under the Communists since 1945. Right will prevail." At the side of the stage another priest hears the strikers' confessions even though there can be few sins to confess within these walls. The discipline of the farmers occupying the building is perfect. Alcohol is strictly forbidden. One lives by tea alone. Even the use of a swear word is punished by a 2 złoty fine . . .

THE TRIUMPH OF SOLIDARITY

An excellent public address system, the "strike radio station", broadcasts regular communiqués from Solidarity branches all over Poland, new summaries, lectures about agricultural law in Sweden, and a strangely moving poem—an appeal to Mary, Queen of Poland—written and recited by a peasant. Such is the security organized by the strike committee that a visitor's identity is checked five times between the entrance and the first floor office . . . Their revolutionary demands . . . [include] not merely . . . the registration of Rural Solidarity but they are seeking the return of land requisitioned by the state for cooperative farms, the right to buy, sell and inherit private land without restriction, and free elections to key posts in local government. It all adds up to a programme for a peaceful revolution in the Polish countryside . . .'

52. Bronisław Piasecki, *Ostatnie dni Prymasa Tysiąclecia* (The last days of the Primate of the Millenium), Rome, Dom Polski Jana Pawła II, 1982, p. 29.
53. Op. cit., p. 148.
54. Op. cit., p. 32.
55. Ibid.
56. Ibid.
57. At a press conference on 2 April 1981 Solidarity's press spokesman Janusz Onyszkiewicz told the journalists that during the negotiations the Government raised several times the possibility of declaring a state of emergency. 'It was made clear that a general strike would have meant a total confrontation including some bloodshed'. It was understood that the army might have been called out and that outside intervention was also possible. 'This time it looked as if it were not a bluff' and the union's negotiators 'felt tremendous pressure and responsibility, because it was said that there was no option'.
58. For complete text see *Communist Affairs: Documents and Analysis*, vol. 1, no. 1, pp. 269-73.
59. For details see Radio Free Europe Research, *Polish Situation Reports 7 and 8*, 24 April and 8 May respectively.
60. This rather ill-advised and probably later much regretted remark was made by Stanisław Kania at a joint conference of the provincial first secretaries of the Polish United Workers' Party and provincial chairmen of the United Peasant's Party on 10 January 1981. By April, however, the situation had visibly changed and on 1 April the official Polish Press Agency issued a communique in which the Government positively assessed the endeavours of the Church over this issue and expressed its gratitude to the Pope, Cardinal Wyszyński and the entire Episcopate for helping to defuse the conflict. Also on 7 April during an unprecedented joint meeting of the Sejm's Monitoring Commission for the Implementation of Social Accords and the Presidium of the Independent Self-governing Trade Union of Private Farmers 'Solidarity', the Primate's personal envoy Dr Romuald Kukołowicz addressed the Commission and acknowledged that Cardinal Wyszyński himself played a prominent role in helping to bring about the union. After the registration, a delegation of Rural Solidarity with the Chairman of its Presidium, Jan Kułaj, which participated in the congress of the Italian Union of Workers (UIL), was on 17 June 1981 received in a private audience by Pope John Paul II. The audience with the Pontiff who was recovering from the assassination attempt on his life and who at that time held no audiences and

received no official visitors was a symbolic recognition of the union as well as evidence of the importance he attached to the creation and registration of the union.

61. Piasecki, *Ostatnie dni Prymasa Tysiąclecia*, p. 57. During April and May 1981 other significant concessions were granted by the regime in response to the Church's long-standing demands. On 15 April the Ministry of Education issued a Memorandum which revoked its earlier prohibition banning children in State-organized summer camps from attending church on Sundays. The Ministry of Health and Social Security gave similar instructions concerning pastoral work in hospitals including the right to celebrate Masses on the premises. Yet another Government instruction officially removed State supervision over religious instruction and declared cathechization of children and young people to be 'an internal matter for the Church'. The Church was free to give instruction in catechetical centres, in private flats and even on schools premises (illegal since 1961). In areas which lacked suitable places the local authorities were enabled to give permission for the construction of a catechical centre. In October, the Ministry of Justice issued regulations giving the Church permission to pursue pastoral work in prisons.

62. Polish youth, like industrial workers and peasants, were not unaffected by changes taking place in Poland. University students (see note 50) and even secondary-school pupils created their own organizations parallel to those sponsored by the regime. An interesting example of both dependence on the Church and its influence was provided by the first national congress of the Independent Students' Union held in Kraków on 2-4 April 1981. During the opening of the congress (interestingly attended by the representatives of the local Soviet and American consulates), a letter from Cardinal Franciszek Macharski was read, in which he, as the host in Kraków welcomed the delegates and presented them as a symbolic gift with a copy of the Pope's UNESCO speech on the role of culture in Poland's independence and the importance of conscience in scientific work. The Cardinal, on 5 April, officiated at a concelebrated Mass attended by many of the Congress participants.

63. For discussion of the 'horizontal movement' see Ascherson, *The Polish August*, pp. 200-74 especially.

64. It is interesting to recall that on 21 May 1981 the GDR party daily newspaper, *Neues Deutschland*, published the first highly critical comment on the Church in Poland. Reflecting presumably not only its own view, the newspaper claimed, 'Apparently life is now determined more by Solidarity and the priests than by the appropriate powers. The crisis in the country is running ever deeper although this is being ignored by those who are currently in power'.

65. For the text of his farewell message to the Main Council of the Polish Episcopate see Appendix 2.

66. Cardinal Wyszyński left two testaments. The first dated 23 April 1969 was superseded by a second one dated 15 August 1969. In the second document Wyszyński expressed his deep gratitude to the Holy See for the 'respect and love' that successive popes had shown for the Church in Poland and for him personally in the many years he had served the Church there in accordance with 'its situation and needs'. The Primate had always enjoyed the 'full understanding' of the Vatican in his complex tasks and had never been

'reprimanded or judged critically' in his work; the Polish Church had always been fully trusted by the Holy See, although the popes were not always in a position to 'fulfill all its demands'. The Cardinal said that he had drawn attention to this fact in his will because of various Polish attempts to 'distort the proper picture' of the relations of the Episcopate with the Vatican; 'a whole library of political publications' had been written to that end by the Church adversaries. Stating that he always understood his mission as an imperative to defend the Church against 'atheism, social hatred, and laxity', Wyszyński expressed his 'warm wish' that the nation would remain faithful to the obligations that had been made at Our Lady's shrine of Jasna Góra during the millenial celebrations of 1966. The Cardinal declared his deep esteem and love for his fatherland and his conviction of the 'importance of social changes'. Recalling his own lifelong endeavours to 'serve the working masses unselfishly', chiefly through cultural and educational work 'in the spirit of the papal encyclical letters', Wyszyński stated that, in his opinion, this work was still far from complete in Poland, 'despite the social and political changes'. 'After the overthrowing of the slavery of capitalism, the workers found themselves in totalitarian-collective slavery, and now they are threatened as much, like whole of humanity, by the slavery of technocracy'. He expressed his trust that what he called the 'healthy spirit of human personality' would win in the end 'in the struggle for the dignity and freedom of mankind'. With reference to the treatment he was himself accorded by the regime in the past, especially during the years 1953-6 when he was put under house arrest and prevented from performing his functions, the Primate displayed magnanimity toward his persecutors in stating that he had never felt hatred towards his countrymen, 'exercising power on behalf of the State. Being aware of all wrongs done to me, I forgive them from my heart for all the calumnies with which they have honoured me'. The Cardinal appointed two auxiliary bishops of Warsaw and his closest associates, Jerzy Modzelewski and Bronisław Dąbrowski, the executors of his testament. Expressing deep love for his immediate family, he asked his two sisters to take care of his father, and to understand his decision to leave all his personal possessions and papers to the Church. For excerpts from both of Wyszyński's testaments see Piasecki, *Ostatnie dni Prymasa Tysiąclecia*, pp. 169-73.
67. The Soviet media published the letter only on 12 June. For its complete text see *Communist Affairs: Documents and Analysis*, vol. 1, no. 1, pp. 297-300.
68. Józef Glemp was born on 28 December 1929 in Inowrocław (Central Poland) to a peasant family. During the Second World War he worked as a farmhand in his native area. After leaving the Jan Kasprowicz Secondary School in 1950, he studied Polish language and literature in Warsaw and Toruń before entering a seminary in Gniezno. He was ordained in 1956 and subsequently served for two years as a parish priest. Between 1958 and 1964 he studied at the Lateran and Gregorian Universities in Rome, graduating with a double doctorate in Canon law, and in civil law, and subsequently became an advocate to the Sacred Roman Rota. His stay in Rome coincided with the Second Vatican Council (1962-5). Returning to Poland in 1964 he began work in the Metropolitan Curia in Gniezno. In 1967 he was transferred to the Primate's office in Warsaw and soon

became Wyszyński's secretary and his chaplain. In this capacity he repeatedly accompanied the Primate on his frequent journeys to Rome. Glemp lectured on Roman and Canon law at Warsaw's Catholic Theological Academy and published a number of scholarly studies. He was also secretary of the Episcopate's commission on Polish institutes in Rome and a member of its commission on the revision of the Canon law, as well as a legal adviser to the Primate's secretariat. Over the years Glemp became one of Wyszyński's most trusted aides. He was consecrated Bishop of Warmia (with his seat in Olsztyn) in March 1979. During the two years of his work there Glemp won general support and admiration for his talents as an able administrator and skilful negotiator. The 1980 summer strikes on the Baltic coast made his assignment even more difficult and delicate, especially since the city of Elbląg, one of the earliest centres of workers' unrest, was part of his diocese, and he included the study of those 'social phenomena' in the agenda of a forthcoming diocesan synod, with the aim of 'properly defining the local Church's stand' on the problem and working out appropriate pastoral approaches to it. On the national level, Glemp took part, as an acknowledged legal expert, in the work of the Joint Church-State Commission studying the future agreement on the Church's legal status in Poland. His international assignments included a visit to Paris in September 1980 that helped to establish official relations between the two countries' episcopates. He also paid frequent visits to Rome. He was also the president of the Polish Commission for Justice and Peace. Glemp is the eightieth Metropolitan Archbishop of Gniezno, the twelfth Metropolitan Archbishop of Warsaw, and the fifty-sixth Primate of Poland.

69. Radio Warsaw, 7 July 1981.
70. *Życie Warszawy*, 10 July 1981.
71. *Trybuna Ludu*, 13 July 1981.
72. For an analysis of the Congress see Bogdan Szajkowski, 'Democracy without Centralism? The Ninth Extraordinary Congress of the PUWP', *Communist Affairs: Documents and Analysis*, vol. 1, no. 2 (April 1982), pp. 522-7.
73. *Trybuna Ludu*, 21-2 July 1981.
74. *Gazeta Poznańska*, 16 July 1981.
75. *Gazeta Poznańska*, 21-2 July 1981.
76. *The Times*, 4 September 1981.
77. For its complete text see *I Krajowy Zjazd Delegatów NSZZ Solidarność, I tura, 5-10, IX, 1981* (The First National Congress of the Delegates of the Independent Self-governing Trade Union Solidarity, First stage, 5-10 September, 1981), Solidarity's Press Office, Gdańsk, 1981, pp. 53-4.
78. For complete text see *Communist Affairs: Documents and Analysis*, vol. 1, no. 2 (April 1982), p. 538.
79. See the Declaration of the First Congress in *I Krajowy Zjazd Delegatów NSZZ Solidarność, I tura, 5-10, IX, 1981*, p. 16.
80. *Eastern Media Coverage of Solidarity's Congress: The First Session*, Radio Free Europe Research, Munich, Background Report 274, 24 September 1981.
81. For complete text see *Communist Affairs: Documents and Analysis*, vol. 1, no. 2 (April 1982), pp. 541-2.
82. *Laborem Exercens*, London, Catholic Truth Society, 1981.
83. 'Poland: Co-operation or Confrontation. Interview with Mieczysław Rakow-

ski by Monty Johnstone', *Marxism Today* (October 1981), p. 10.. Such was also the view of Professor Jerzy Wiatr, the director of the PUWP Central Committee Institute of Marxism-Leninism, who in his lecture to the Kraków Marxist Discussion Club 'Kuźnica', suggested the power sharing scenario as the most likely way out of the Polish crisis. Notes from this unprecedented lecture have been published in the Kraków provincial Party daily newspaper *Gazeta Krakowska*. For complete text see *Communist Affairs: Documents and Analysis*, vol. 1, no. 3 (July 1982), pp. 679-88.
84. For detailed discussion see *Poland's National Unity Front: A Genuine Coalition or Party Appendage?* Radio Free Europe Research, Munich, Background Report 304, 3 November 1981.
85. Although it is, of course, true that in the past the Church had frequently made known its views on social and political issues confronting Polish society, particularly at times of profound crises, such interventions were made either as public appeals for calm or through pastoral letters. Only in 1976 did the Episcopate send a formal letter to the Sejm protesting against changes in the constitution, but even then that protest was not formally made public.
86. The full text of the letter was given by Agence France Presse on 8 December 1981.
87. For the text of the letter see *Życie Warszawy*, 12-13 December 1981.
88. As quoted by Graham Bradley in *Washington Post*, 9 December 1981.
89. The proposed referendum was to include the following four questions: 1. Are you in favour of expressing a vote of no-confidence in the Government of General Wojciech Jaruzelski? 2. Would you favour a provisional government and free elections? 3. Are you in favour of Solidarity and the provisional government guaranteeing the Soviet Union's military interests? 4. Can the PUWP be the instrument of such guarantees in the name of the entire society?

4 Tribulations under Martial Law: 1981-1983

Around 1 a.m. on Sunday morning, 13 December, the Pope was woken up to receive a telephone call from the Polish ambassador to Italy, Emil Wojtaszek. He was told that General Jaruzelski had found it necessary to introduce 'temporary emergency measures' which would be limited. The ambassador also assured the Pontiff that in the new situation the Church would be expected to play a key role in attempts at mediation to eliminate the 'temporary measures' as soon as possible. With the telex and telephone links between the Vatican and the Primate's residence in Warsaw cut, the Pope could not communicate directly with the Church in Poland in order to ascertain the situation.

That night the majority of Poland's population had retired without realizing that the country was under military rule. Even the sudden cessation, at 11.45 p.m., of the broadcast by Polish television of an Italian comedy film (at the point where the hero was just about to murder a soldier) was interpreted as typical Polish inefficiency. The announcer simply said that the film would have to be continued another day, as the station was closing down. At three minutes to midnight, in a remarkable feat of technological co-ordination, every one of Poland's 3,439,700 private telephones went dead, but few people took this as a sinister development. Erratic communications were part of daily life. One of the first visible signs of the martial law was the ransacking of Solidarity offices in Warsaw at midnight by the anti-riot police, the ZOMO. By this time also a systematic and well co-ordinated action of mass arrest was underway of prominent Solidarity members and other reformists of all complexions.

The round-up continued throughout the night. The ZOMO and militia units had at their disposal the Security Police computer at Gdynia, providing them with the last-known address of every Pole both at home and abroad. They were able to lift around four thousand people that night with a minimum of commotion. Most members of the Solidarity National Co-ordinating Commission were rounded up from their beds at their Gdańsk hotel around 2 a.m. Lech Wałęsa was taken from his home and put on a plane bound for Warsaw. By first light Poland resembled a huge concentration camp with armed personnel carriers and army and police patrols on the streets of all major towns.

Contrary to subsequent reports Archbishop Glemp had no prior knowledge of the declaration of martial law. The Primate was surprised to learn shortly before 5 a.m. on Sunday morning that a high-level delegation, including a member of the Political Bureau, Kazimierz Barcikowski, and the Minister for Religious Affairs, Jerzy Kuberski, was at the gates to his residence at Miodowa Street in Warsaw. They were admitted to the reception room and during a meeting which lasted three minutes simply announced that General Jaruzelski would broadcast the declaration of martial law at 6 a.m. He was told that he would be able to move freely throughout the country and if he needed to use the telephone, one would be available in the office of the Council of Ministers a mile and a half away from his residence. The Primate's only response was 'Thank you gentlemen' and the delegation departed. That morning as Poland was waking up to the signs of military rule, the Primate went to Częstochowa to address youth groups gathered there the previous day, and to pray to the Black Madonna.

General Jaruzelski addressed the nation on radio and television at 6 a.m.[1] Announcing the formation of the Military Council for National Salvation (Wojskowa Rada Ocalenia Narodowego—WRON) he also said that the Council of State had introduced a state of war[2] throughout the country from midnight, 12 December. He stressed that he was speaking as a soldier and the head of government but he did not even mention the Party of which he was also the leader. In effect the Polish army had stepped in to fill a political vacuum left by the vanishing authority of the PUWP. Significantly, the General in his address also reaffirmed the regime's commitment to the 'idea of national accord' and emphasized that 'there is no going back to the erroneous methods and practices before August 1980 . . . All important reforms will be continued . . . this also applies to economic reforms'. It was this explicit assurance of continuation of the policy of reform that to a greater extent determined the Church's attitude to the military regime.

The declaration of martial law had all the standard ingredients of a military coup.[3] It involved the banning of all trade-union activity,

TRIBULATIONS UNDER MARTIAL LAW: 1981-1983

the appointment of military plenipotentiaries in Government ministries, provinces, towns and even factories 'to ensure the execution of orders of the WRON', dawn to dusk curfew, mass interment, a ban on public gatherings as well as on the wearing of specific uniforms and badges, limitation on the freedom of movement of the population, strict censorship of mail and telecommunications and the closure of Poland's borders. The Military Council thus equipped itself with all the draconian measures normally required in war time. It was quite clear that these measures were not 'temporary emergency measures'. Most Poles were dazed and listened to the General's broadcast in hostile silence and with utter incomprehension. Poland was at war, but with whom? By moving on Saturday night the military had struck when most workers were at home, making organized resistance all but impossible. It was the unity of the workers, striking inside the factories, which gave Solidarity its immense power. Union officials still free had to concede that they were caught totally by surprise by the military takeover which had been planned months in advance and executed with precision.[4] The Polish military had in effect carried out an internal invasion. The army daily newspaper *Żołnierz Wolności* (Soldier of Freedom), Solidarity's most consistent and vehement critic, declared on 13 December 'a sort of liberation has today taken place'. It would be naive to think that the imposition of martial law could have happened without the full knowledge and support of the Soviet Union. It was not coincidental that the Commander in Chief of the Warsaw Pact forces Marshal Viktor Kulikov arrived in Warsaw on 11 December and stayed there for a week, though his visit was never officially confirmed.

For the Church, the declaration of martial law was a particularly severe and unexpected blow. The Primate's mediating efforts seemed to have born no results and the ideas which underpinned Solidarity and were complimentary to Catholic thought and practice were now almost in ruins. Although Jaruzelski in his address recognized 'the Church's patriotic attitude' and 'religious services' were specifically exempted from the ban on public meetings, the Church could not have been expected to support the military junta. At the same time the Primate knew that outright opposition would only result in considerable loss of life which the Church could not support either.

The first pronouncement on the situation came from the Pope, who, speaking in Polish during his traditional Sunday Angelus said:

> The events of the last few hours require me to turn my attention once again to the cause of our homeland and to call for prayer. I remind you of what I said in September. Polish blood cannot be spilled because too much has already been spilled especially during the War. Everything must be done to build the future of our homeland peacefully. I entrust Poland and all my countrymen to the Virgin Mary who has been given to us for our defence.

The Pope was aware that his words would be heard by many Poles listening to the Vatican radio, one of the few remaining links that Poland had at that time with the outside world.

The Pope's message was echoed later in the day by Archbishop Glemp who after his return from Częstochowa, speaking in the evening in the Jesuit church of Mary the Patroness of Warsaw, in the Old Town of the city, said:

> Martial law found us astounded on Sunday morning.... A believer in Christ ought first of all to ask God, who is the God of peace . . . God's answer is to remember the Commandments and the teachings of Jesus Christ. Blessed are those who starve and thirst for justice. Blessed are the charitable. Blessed are those who introduce peace. Blessed are those who suffer martyrdom for justice. Such is God's answer. But such an answer does not satisfy many people. They will say: This is unrealistic; this means a retreat from achievements; this is an admission of defeat. It is possible to interpret the worlds of Jesus Christ in many ways. But he really said these words and that is why, for the one who loves God with all his heart and all his soul, those words constitute the ultimate authority. A representative of the Church cannot teach different things to those stated in the Gospel. It is necessary that with his teachings he should illuminate the new reality. In our country the new reality is martial law . . . The authority ceases to be an authority of dialogue between citizens . . . and becomes an authority equipped with the means of summary coercion and demanding obedience. Opposition to the decisions of authority under martial law could cause violent coercion, including bloodshed because the authority has the armed forces at its disposal. We can be indignant, shout about the injustice of such a state of

things, protest against the infringement of civil rights and human rights. However, this may not yield the expected results, the authority under martial law is not an authority of dialogue . . . The Church wants to put itself in the place of every man and understand him. That is why it felt pain at the severance of the dialogue, which had been started with such difficulty, and at the switch to the path of force in the form of martial law. This cannot happen without the infringement of basic rights. It carries with it, in many instances, the trampling of human dignity, arrests of innocent people, contempt for men of culture and science, anxiety in many families. The representatives of the Church will continually demand, as much as they are allowed, the release of citizens who have been detained without justification. . . The Church wants to defend each human life and therefore, in this state of martial law it will call for peace, wherever possible, it will call for an end to violence, for the prevention of fratricidal struggle. . .

There is nothing of greater value than human life. That is why I, myself, will call for reason even if that means that I become the target of insults. I shall plead, even if I have to plead on my knees: Do not start a fight of Pole against Pole. Do not give your lives away, brother workers, because the price of human life will be very low. Every head, every pair of hands will be essential to the reconstruction of Poland which will come, which must come, after the end of the state of martial law. . .

The Primate's sermon, delivered in the uncertain state of shock immediately following the imposition of military rule, was based on the longstanding tradition and aspiration of the Church to act as a custodian of the country's moral and national destiny. He neither approved nor legitimized the imposition of martial law, but merely implied the acceptance of a *fait accompli*. He took stock of the situation and kept his and the hierarchy's options open for further action. At the same time Archbishop Glemp and his advisers were persuaded by several important assurances and explanations given by Jaruzelski. Perhaps one of the most significant of these was that the military coup staged in order to prevent another coup planned for 15 December by Stefan Olszowski and a group of hardliners, who had direct support from Moscow. Jaruzelski assured the Primate that he took the initiative in order to save Poland and to forestall the emergence of a regime dependent ideologically and politically on the Soviet ruling group. At the same time he repeatedly reaffirmed to Glemp his intention to continue the reform programme and that a trade-union movement along the lines of Solidarity, and incorporating its main ideas would be reestablished once the country returned to normal life. There was an explicit warning in these assurances that should the WRON not succeed in stabilizing the situation Soviet military intervention would take place and the real catastrophe would then begin. The Church clearly preferred a solution within Poland and the Primate's pronouncements were meant as much for internal as external consumption. There is little doubt that his sermon on the evening of 13 December was instrumental in calming the situation and in avoiding large-scale bloodshed. Needless to say the homily was deliberately exploited by the authorities. Carefully selected excerpts from it, read by an announcer, were repeatedly broadcast throughout Sunday evening and Monday, in between Jaruzelski's speech and Chopin martial music, by the single television and radio channel transmitting from special emergency military studios. Similarly selective were reports of the sermon in the eighteen Party newspapers allowed to publish in the country.

While the Church allowed its authority to be exploited, a little-publicized 'crisis team' set up by the Primate headed by Stanisław Stomma, the Emeritus Professor of Law at the Jagiellonian University of Kraków was in constant touch with the military authorities negotiating for the release of detainees, information on their whereabouts and access to internment camps.[5] Also on 13 December the Primate set up a group of lay Catholics and priests in order to collect and deliver food parcels, warm clothing and medicines to internment camps, and care for the internees' families. Cardinal Macharski negotiated the regime's permission for the group's activity with General Kiszczak. Thus during the first days of martial law the Church was able to make a limited but effective contribution to alleviate some of the suffering.

The unknown factor in a now complex situation was Solidarity's response. A solidarity Committee comprised of little or virtually unknown trade unionists hastily assembled in the Lenin Shipyard on 13 December and issued a communiqué late that day calling for a general strike in response to Jaruzelski's declaration: 'Our answer to violence is a general strike,' said the one page document, 'we state that we are forced and provoked into staging it.' The communiqué demanded the release of those interned and the cancellation of the state of martial law. 'When these conditions are fulfilled we may undertake talks in order to find a platform of agreement', the communiqué said. It also asked the workers to maintain discipline and peace, to respect State property and to avoid unnecessary fighting with the security forces. 'Our weapons are calmness, honour and organization in the factories. Our hope is the unity and solidarity of all the working people of Poland.' But this call did not get outside Gdańsk. The key to Jaruzelski's strategy was to isolate and thereby neutralize every group and deprive them of any information except their own decrees and propaganda gains. This was achieved with ruthless ingenuity and considerable effectiveness. Almost every possible forum for ordinary people was banned or obliterated. By Monday 14 December, most of Solidarity's leadership was in custody. Even the 'shadow' leaders, appointed for just such an emergency, were under arrest too; or holding out inside factories and mines totally cut off from any information about what was going on outside. Although a number of strikes broke out in various parts of the country[6] the security services, including the notorious ZOMO units, were able to break the resistance, dealing with the country region by region. After ending strikes in one region the units simply moved on to another zone.

In response to the increasing use of force and mass arrests the Main Council of the Polish Episcopate issued a communiqué, after its meeting on 15 December, to be read in all Polish churches on 20 December. The message was unequivocal:

Our suffering is that of the entire nation, terrorized by military force. Many trade-union leaders have been interned . . . strikes are taking place in many factories. The uncertainty and powerlessness of the workers have caused an ever-increasing wave of emotions—bitterness, disgust, extreme hatred and determination. The dramatic determination of the authorities who decided on the proclamation of martial law is a blow to the expectations and hopes of society. . . The moral feelings of society have been deeply hurt as a result of the drastic limitations imposed on civil liberties.

The Church according to its mission always defends human rights and human dignity, which are the basis of social ethics. It defends the nation and the common good. The time will come when we will know the whole truth surrounding the imposition of martial law. In spite of everything, even today there is a place to begin positive action. The Main Council of the Polish Episcopate with a feeling of responsibility for the nation, appeals for peace and restraint over passions and anger, without renouncing the fundamental rights and achievements of the whole society. We are convinced that the nation will not step backward and cannot give up the democratic renewal . . . in the country. . . The Church and society should concentrate on the following two aspects: 1. The freeing of internees. Until their liberation they should have humane conditions in their places of internment (for we know of numerous excesses in that respect: they are being held in unheated cells without glass in the windows). 2. The revival of trade unions and above all Solidarity's statutory activity. This implies that the free activity of the Chairman and the Presidium of the trade union is permitted. Solidarity, defending the working people, is indispensible for the return of social life to its equilibrium. . .

The text of the communiqué was dispatched by messengers to diocesan bishops throughout Poland and from them to the parishes. Then on 17 December as the news reached Warsaw that seven miners at the Wujek colliery in Katowice had been killed and thirty-eight injured during the ZOMO attack,[7] the Primate, under pressure from General Jaruzelski, withdrew the communique. Some priests, however, disobeyed the instruction and read out the bishops' statement.

The first confirmation of bloodshed signalled that in spite of official assurances of normality throughout the country, the crisis was deepening and no one could foresee the way it was likely to develop. The Pope now sent a private appeal to Jaruzelski pleading for the 'cessation of any actions that could lead to the spilling of Polish blood'. On the same day the Polish section of the Vatican Radio pointedly asked for the release of Lech Wałęsa saying that his presence was 'absolutely indispensible for national equilibrium'. Wałęsa who was held in a Government house in Konstancin near Warsaw and who had been visited by

TRIBULATIONS UNDER MARTIAL LAW: 1981-1983

Father Alojzy Orszulik, the deputy secretary of the Episcopal Conference, was expected to deliver a public appeal for calm and restraint. However, before doing so he requested a meeting with the Presidium of Solidarity and Archbishop Glemp. When the authorities vetoed his his request he refused to speak.

The Pope, who was still unable to communicate directly with the Church in Poland and who had received briefings from Western diplomats, decided to send a personal envoy to Poland to ascertain the situation. Archbishop Luigi Poggi accompanied by a Polish-speaking Vatican official, Monsignor Janusz Bolonek, flew to Vienna on 19 December and then took the night express to Warsaw. With them they carried the Pope's personal letter to General Jaruzelski.[8] In it the Pope earnestly appealed for 'an end to . . . acts of bloodshed against Poles' and for a 'return to the peaceful dialogue which since August 1981 has been solving the problems involved in the renewal of society'. 'I appeal to your conscience, General, and to the conscience of all those with whom this decision now lies.' In the postscript the Pope added 'I have sent a copy of this appeal to Lech Wałęsa,[9] leader of Solidarity, and through the Primate of Poland, Archbishop Józef Glemp, to the whole Episcopate, and also a copy to Cardinal F. Macharski. I shall inform representatives of world governments about my intervention'.[10]

In the complex and unclear situation at that time both the Pope and the Polish Primate continued a policy of caution in commenting on the events. On 20 December the Pontiff's Sunday blessing included an appeal for all men of good will to surround Poland with their prayers. But his greetings were shorter than usual. On the same day Archbishop Glemp's letter was read in all churches throughout Poland. The letter pleaded: 'Only self-control and maintainance of calm can save the country and the Church which fulfils her mission in it. We beg you in the name of God not to raise an arm filled with hate against one another. Keep calm, do not drive our country to a still greater disaster.'

With reports of continuing resistance in many parts of the country and increased tension in Silesia where miners in two collieries barricaded themselves in, the Church hierarchy became extremely anxious about the deteriorating situation. So it appears were the military rulers. Polish embassy officials throughout Europe were busy distributing to the media copies of Archbishop Glemp's sermon a day before it was read in Polish churches. Once more the rulers of Poland turned to the Church in an attempt to give their actions legitimacy.

On 21 December Bishop Bronisław Dąbrowski unexpectedly arrived in Rome after a weeks' delay for a hurried one-day visit and was rushed to the Vatican for a meeting with the Pope that began late at night. He was able to give the Pontiff his first full briefing on the crisis in Poland. The next day the Pope spoke of the deadly shadows threatening peace in Poland and prayed 'that Poland, my people, already so tested by wars throughout its tormented history, may be saved from further suffering'. By now it was becoming clear that the possibility of the Church playing a mediating role was extremely limited if it ever existed. The Catholic hierarchy in Poland was becoming increasingly distressed about the level of brutality employed by the authorities and pessimistic about the outcome of their conciliation efforts. The Church's constant demands for an early release of internees had met with no response in spite of calming the public in the week after the introduction of martial law. Letters from the Primate, although always answered, bore no practical results. Although the Church was able to conduct limited pastoral work among those interned and deliver warm clothing, food and medicines, this obviously fell short of society's and the Church's own expectations.

Until about Christmas time the Church believed that its discreet negotiations with the regime could bring about an early end to martial law and negotiations between Solidarity and the junta. It thought that with strikes still continuing the Polish leadership might be increasingly ready to listen to a Church initiative aimed at breaking the deadlock. There was a distinct possibility that the WRON would allow Lech Wałęsa to meet the full Presidium of Solidarity. He repeatedly stated that he could not make any public pronouncements on radio and television about martial law without first discussing it with his Presidium. But around that time the first sign of deep divisions among the military leadership appeared, over the future of Solidarity and over what to do with Wałęsa. The basic dilemma facing the junta was whether to risk allowing Solidarity to regroup in its original form or whether to smash it once and for all. The Church in its negotiations with the military demanded the reinstatement of Solidarity. However, around Christmas time it was becoming increasingly evident that with the division within the ruling group the crisis was deepening and more people were being interned. It seems almost incomprehensible that at the end of 1981 the Church was faced with essentially the same existential question that it had had to face on and off since 1945. Should it retreat from the national stage and give up the expectations of gradual change leading to more pluralistic social and political structures? Should it assume the role it bore in the 1950s, that of a torchbearer for the national conscience? Should it co-operate with the regime without the participation of Solidarity? None of these options appeared acceptable either to the hierarchy or to the great mass of the faithful. However, the middle ground was full of pitfalls, uncertainties, misunderstandings and conflicts. It seems that the Church decided on the only realistic line of action possible: to preserve at all costs whatever could possibly be preserved from the ideas of Solidarity; to continue its role as a spiritual platform to political opposition and to continue to mediate and negotiate with whoever was in power for as long as this could serve its own role as the guiding force of the nation's destiny.

It should also be noted that the Polish hierarchy remained unequivocally opposed to any Western economic sanctions imposed on 23 December by the Reagan administration, on the grounds that such sanctions would impose further hardship on the Polish population and force the regime to increase its dependence on Soviet and Eastern European economic aid. In this context the Episcopate made several representations to Western governments and bishop's conferences for the continuation and intensification of the Western aid programme.

On 26 December Cardinal Franciszek Macharski spoke of 'the present tragedy as the beginning of new hope':

> Martial law does not signify the death of Polish aspirations, it is the baptism of the Polish nation. . . None of us can agree to the use of force, oppression and fabrication as a foundation on which to build good and happiness. None of us can agree to the spilling of one's own and others' blood. None of us can agree to any civil war or world war. . . However, we will continue to defend the truth, good, justice, order, love and loyalty. We will defend every man. . .

On 28 December Archbishop Glemp sent a strongly worded letter to General Jaruzelski[11] protesting at the recently instituted practice of requiring state employees to sign, under threat of dismissal, a pledge of loyalty to the system and renouncing his or her membership of Solidarity.[12] In it the Primate warned that such a practice, while obviously unconstitutional, was reminiscent of the situation that had prevailed in 'certain circles until August 1980' and was contrary to the intentions of Jaruzelski's 'political programme declared on 13 December'. 'I appeal to you therefore to withdraw this memorandum and cancel its implications. I do this in the name of our country and for the sake of continuing renewal.' The Primate returned publicly to the same theme in a sermon delivered in Warsaw on 6 January 1982. He deplored that demands to renounce membership of Solidarity were spreading and reminded the congregation of 'the clear principle also respected by our civil code that statements of intent made under compulsion are invalid. . . Personal honour remains, the preservation of one's dignity and one's full personality.'[13]

On the same day Cardinal Macharski also delivered a sermon in which he condemned martial law as 'a great evil':

> Let us look on our predicament in the light of divine wisdom. Almost every Pole agrees that the imposition of martial law was a great evil. I reiterate these words with even greater force as I speak here, beside the tomb of St. Stanisław, who is the patron saint of moral order and not an order enforced by the sword of violence. It was in the name of St. Stanisław that I preached the right to dialogue . . . (during the past few years) and even here, less than a month ago, I appealed to Solidarity and to every Pole to give up any thought of a confrontation. I will never forget the dozens of sermons I have preached recently in which I tried to show what is the way, our Polish way, towards freedom and justice. True freedom is grounded in God, in truth, in culture and wisdom, it serves the good of the country, such freedom is based on common concern, it is based on rights as well as responsibilities. . .
>
> There are some who will say that this is politics from the altar. I now receive letters which say that I must cease my support of Solidarity, that I must keep away from politics. Is this politics? I remember my predecessors Cardinal Sapieha, the Primate Cardinal Wyszyński, Cardinal Wojtyła, our present Holy Father,

they too were accused of meddling in politics . . . and yet they only served God and the Motherland. And so following in their footsteps I, too, will speak the language of the Gospel, the truth about God and man for people in these difficult times. . . This is not politics. Only recently I received a letter which said: Remember what happened to your predecessor Stanisław, remember what happened to Archbishop Romero of San Salvador. I would like to reply to this that I do indeed remember them, I remember them with great respect. And therefore I emphasize again, the only way out of our predicament is a return to dialogue with the people. . . It must be conducted in an atmosphere free from fear. . . How often we hear people's laments about the so-called 'invitations' to talk under threat of losing one's job. I ask what sort of a dialogue is this? I ask what sort of results can this bring when human conscience is violated? Therefore I beg—note that I do not demand but beg—for a return to dialogue between free and equal partners. . .

But the Church's pleas for the reintatement of Solidarity, also echoed in numerous papal pronouncements[14], and for dialogue with it, were falling on stony ground. There was no real sign apart from rhetoric that the military rulers were prepared to respond positively to these requests.

On 9 January 1982 Archbishop Glemp and General Jaruzelski met in Warsaw for direct talks. The one-sentence communiqué issued after the encounter said that the two men had 'exchanged views on the current situation and expressed intentions related to the normalization of life in Poland.' The meeting was far from successful. There was now a clear indication that Jaruzelski was under pressure from the hardline faction within the regime and was unable to discuss methodically let alone decide on the shape of the junta's policies. The prospects for immediate negotiations with Solidarity were fast fading away.[15] The Church was left with the traditional method of exerting pressure on the authorities through public statements. In his sermon on 17 January the Primate complained 'we cannot see any initiatives' by the authorities while 'there are still more and more people being interned and more people being arrested'.[16] A week later in a pastoral letter the Episcopal Conference demanded:

a return to the normal functioning of the State, the release of all those interned, cessation of all duress on ideological grounds and of dismissals from work for political views or trade-union membership. We make it clear that the right of working people to organize themselves into independent self-governing trade unions and of the youth to form their own associations[17] must be restored in the name of freedom... The understanding of the right to freedom and to respect for freedom by those who govern and are governed gives meaning to social justice. It is only justice that is the foundation of peace. Let us state emphatically that infringements of the right to freedom lead to protest, rebellion, and even civil war. We must return to a form of dialogue between the authorities and society. Dialogue may be difficult, but it is not impossible. Everyone expects that dialogue. We, the bishops, appeal for it.

This was a tough message. Its timing was clearly aimed at influencing the outcome of the session of the Sejm, due to begin on 25 January, the first session since the declaration of martial law. The bishops perhaps hoped that the Polish parliament, which during the previous fifteen months had been the scene of lively and frank debates, could add its voice to the Church's demands. On 24 January, a day before the Sejm's session, Cardinal Macharski in his sermon again spelled out quite clearly the Church's role in the present situation.

A person who feels he has been treated unfairly, should defend himself with the law, including the regulations of labour law. If he does not know how to go about it he should come to me and I will help him, and in doing so I will be giving a helping hand not only to him and his family but also to the whole nation which wants to defend itself against the devastation caused to the victims by the desire for retaliation within them... All of us— we trust all of us—desire that the internees be set free as soon as possible. Before this happens one has to accept the consequences of the fact that they have been interned and not sentenced for crimes, not even suspected of committing crimes... We are saying to our internees: we do remember you. We are praying for you. We are constantly looking for ways of reuniting you with your families as soon as possible and to improve internment conditions immediately...[18]

TRIBULATIONS UNDER MARTIAL LAW: 1981-1983

In the event the Sejm's two-day session, which was convened primarily to invest the ruling military authorities with a semblance of legality by ratifying the emergency decrees announced by the Council of State six weeks earlier, proved to be a disappointment. There was no substantive discussion about any of the fundamental problems facing the country and General Jaruzelski in his speech had to admit that he did not know what to do with Solidarity and merely promised the easing of martial law by the end of February if the situation remained calm. One member of the Sejm, Romuald Bukowski, a non-Party deputy from Gdynia registered a vote against the martial law regulations and six other deputies abstained. The Church now had a clear message; there was no hope for an early end to internment, however intense the pressure. Also Archbishop Glemp returned disappointed from his visit to the internment camp in Białołęka where many of the Solidarity Presidium were held. They appeared to have toughened their attitudes in the six weeks of internment. The Church therefore decided that since the camps were there to stay its immediate goal must be to ensure that conditions in them should become as tolerable as possible.

Even before the Sejm's session Archbishop Glemp, on 21 January 1982, had formally established the Primate's Committee for Help to Internees. Its work was carried out through five sections: the Pastoral Section, which organized pastoral care amongst the internees; the Help to Internees Section, responsible for the delivery of food parcels, clothing and medicines to prisons and camps; the Family Aid Section, which collected information on the needs of families and organized help in the parishes; the Legal Section, which dispensed legal advice, gave aid in drafting petitions to the authorities and procured suitable defence lawyers for trials; and the Information Section, responsible for collecting information on those imprisoned, interned or dismissed from work and their families. The Church hierarchy row also gave formal backing to similar committees in all the dioceses.[19] How extensive the Church's involvement was in the care for the victims of a martial law was best testified in an article in the Party daily newspaper *Trybuna Ludu*[20] which said that by 26 January 1982, 2,000 food parcels had been delivered to internees on behalf of the Church; masses had been said 237 times in the camps and prisons, and representatives of the Episcopate, including Archbishop Glemp, had made seventy-six visits to the 'isolation centres'.

At the same time the bishops issued guidelines to priests on their pastoral work in the difficult and complex conditions of everyday life. The document, subsequently broadcast by the Polish service of Vatican Radio, advised priests to set up permanent legal counselling centres attached to churches to advise on defence in court cases and where someone had lost his job. Priests should know the names and addresses of barristers from their area ready to undertake defence, the document said. Not only those accused but also those interned had the right to appoint a lawyer to act on their behalf.

> People must be informed . . . that despite the imposition of martial law the Labour Code is still binding; it is precisely that Labour Code which requires that dismissal with immediate effect must be justified by objective circumstances. On no account can refusal to sign the said declarations of loyalty be such a justification.
>
> The demand to sign the declarations under threat of being dismissed from work constitutes a form of coercing a person into giving statements, and this is forbidden by law. According to international agreements ratified by the Polish People's Republic, nobody can be discriminated against because of affiliation to a trade union. The refusal to sign the declaration does not lie in the sphere of employees' work duties and it cannot therefore be a basis for breaking a contract of employment. In the Polish People's Republic there is no statute which forbids affiliation to a trade union. Resignation of Solidarity membership can take place on a voluntary basis only and, moreover, it must be submitted to the authorities of the union, whose activities are at the moment suspended.

On 26 February, the bishops issued a communiqué[21] after a two-day meeting of the Episcopal Conference. Significantly the meeting was held after the return from Rome of the Primate, Cardinal Macharski and the Archbishop of Wrocaw, Henryk Gulbinowicz, who during their week-long visit, the first since the declaration of martial law, held extensive talks with the Pope. The communiqué again stressed that dialogue and social accord were the only ways out of the present situation which 'bears the hallmarks of a real moral, social and economic catastrophe'. This accord should be based on truth, justice, freedom and charity. It should contain guarantees for the realization of the justified needs and aspirations of the people and of their participation in public life as well as in the exercise of social control over all aspects of life. It should include the ruling authorities on the one hand and representatives of organized social groups on the other; 'among them the Independent Self-governing Trade Union Solidarity, which has broad social approval, cannot be absent'. The bishops drew up a list of what they considered the most immediate responsibilities of each side. The Government's responsibility—to create a suitable climate—required on the one hand a sincere readiness to listen to the voice of all social groups in free and responsible debate' and on the other hand a guarantee of 'basic civic freedoms which recognize human dignity'. These basic freedoms were: an end to martial law 'as soon as possible', release of detainees, amnesty for those convicted for activities related to martial law, immunity for those still in hiding, job security regardless of union affiliation, freedom of religious life, cultural pluralism, and reactivation of youth organizations. As for the people, they had to be guided by a 'sense of realism in assessing the geo-political situation of the country'. This does not mean either conformism or rejection of the supreme national values. A sense of realism and prudence requires that we do not accept the principle of 'all or nothing'. This required a systematic, persistent and gradual approach 'towards the implementation of our aims'.

The communiqué was undeniably the most forceful and unequivocal appeal for the creation of a 'social accord' so far. Its comparison with the Primate's statements suggested a split within the Polish Episcopate in the Church's attitude towards the military authorities. Although there certainly were differences in emphasis in the pronouncements of various bishops about the regime, these were mainly due to the different circumstances in which they were delivered and to the individual traits of the speakers, rather than to differences in approach. Another problem appears to have been that of semantics and precision of language used. This relates in particular to the sermons and statements delivered by the Primate, whose expressions lent themselves to varying interpretations. However, close analysis of individual and collective statements of the bishops show a pretty consistent and coherent line.

The hierarchy of course needed to be united, especially in the spring of 1982 when there were many indications that the regime was preparing a crackdown on the Church. Local Party zealots embarked on a campaign against parish priests for organizing help for internees and their families, crosses began to be removed from schools and public places and even the cross erected in front of the Wujek colliery to commemorate the death of seven miners was desecrated and broken up. Commentaries in the mass media showed increased hostility, accusing various clergymen of 'irresponsible performances' and 'disloyalty'. There were also arrests and sentencing of priests for anti-martial law sermons. At the beginning of March the Church hierarchy also became aware that the group of hardliners within the Polish leadership led by Stefan Olszowski had prepared a list of priests to be interned or arrested sometime in April.[22] At the same time tapes were being prepared with the help of a technical laboratory in the German Democratic Republic, consisting of edited excerpts from sermons, talks and conversations, constructed in such a way as to suggest that priests were making incriminatory declarations. The hardliners sought to provoke confrontation in order to secure a suitable situation to demonstrate their strength, to keep the initiative in their own hands and to prevent the Jaruzelski group by any means at their disposal from finding a political solution.

In these circumstances the Church refrained from direct criticism of the regime which was becoming increasingly paralysed not only by an internal power struggle but also by sporadic yet massive resistance to martial law. The Church was fully aware that destabilization of the military regime would inevitably result in the hardliners getting an upper hand and a subsequent full crackdown and possible outside intervention. It also feared that a ban might be imposed on its charitable activities which would cut off help to those most in need. Another important consideration was that the Church's gains, so slowly and carefully constructed, would inevitably be lost should Jaruzelski's position become even more precarious. Consequently the Church again found itself, as so often in the past, in the position of walking a tightrope. Wishing to advance the legitimate aspirations of the people and to secure in the long term some of the gains of Solidarity, it had to remain aloof from being drawn into a position of supporting any faction within the leadership of the military regime as well as avoiding overt association with any particular group within the society. This approach, realistically the only available in the circumstances of an overwhelming display of the oppressive apparatus, was nevertheless not without conflicts and lent itself to open criticism, particularly apparent in subsequent months, from some of the faithful who felt let down by the Church's approach. Meanwhile the Church, which could not advocate confrontation leading to further despair and casualties, continuously stressed the necessity for dialogue.

At the same time there was no sign that the regime, despite its commitment to dialogue, was prepared to embark seriously on a road to find an acceptable compromise with the overwhelming majority of Polish society. In February, March and April, the meetings of the Joint Church-Government Commission, which were supposed to be held on a regular monthly basis, did not take place. The dialogue was virtually at a standstill.

To break the deadlock, on 8 April 1982 Archbishop Glemp released for public discussion a ten-point plan on social accord prepared by the Primate's Social Council.[23] The document, entitled 'Theses of the Primate's Social Council in the Matter of Social Accord' (see Appendix III) was envisaged as a platform for negotiations with the authorities.[24] A copy of the 'Theses' was sent to General Jaruzelski and its text circulated through diocesan councils to as wide an audience as possible, using the limited channels of communication available to the Church, since the official Government-controlled mass media did not lend itself to the dissemination and discussion of the document. The 'Theses' should be considered as the most important political and social initiative to emerge in Poland since the declaration of martial law, and while condemning it as an act that dashed the hopes for a genuine reform which could be realized within the framework of the existing system of international alliances, the document suggested ways of ending the state of emergency by way of a common search for mutual understanding between the rulers and the ruled, and a renewed dialogue. Such a dialogue should involve all authentic social forces, in particular Solidarity, the trade union of private farmers, and other organizations representing craftsmen, youth, the academic community, creative arts and culture. The proposed discussion should centre on ways of lifting martial law, the restoration of civil rights, reactivation of suspended trade unions and other organizations, as well as on suggestions for the necessary social and economic reforms. The document stressed that the prerequisite for any agreement negotiated was a declaration of adherence to all social agreements concluded in 1980 and recalled that both Jaruzelski in his speech on 13 December 1981 and the Sejm in its resolution of 25 January 1982 pledged to respect those agreements. The document also listed particularly urgent social demands which were important conditions for internal peace. These included: the lifting of martial law; the release of all internees; an amnesty for both those convicted for 'acts of resistance after the introduction of martial law' and those in hiding for fear of political repression; the return to full employment of people dismissed for their union activities or for their political convictions; no pressure to be applied on anyone to emigrate. As an essential element of the envisaged reconciliation, the 'Theses' singled out the reactivation of Solidarity. Significantly, while crediting the union as an important factor in social, political and economic renewal, the document stated that the union 'also bears a part of the responsibility for the serious crisis which has happened to our country'. Although the union attempted to set its own limits to its activities and to separate itself from the activities of political opposition groups, this was clearly insufficient. It should have defended the idea of a limited social and union programme with more determination and consistency. Therefore it should make an effort to look at its activities and experience critically, and in the future should remain apolitical and opt for a step-by-step approach in working for its goals.

The document warned against any attempts to resort to violence in opposing the military authorities which would lead to a 'vicious circle of terror and oppression', and against fatalism which would allow a passive acceptance of change. In order to initiate changes and to remove the existing barriers separating the rulers from the ruled, the 'Theses' proposed the creation of advisory bodies attached to the Government or the Sejm, composed of people delegated by independent social organizations and groups. What was needed was 'the reorientation of society and the outlining of prospects for the appearance of a new type of civic activity and a democratic direction of change.' 'Self-government in the widest and most profound conception of the word can be the only model of this kind.' As a starting point for self-government, the document suggested elections to local people's councils. In contrast to central elections, necessarily involving political elements, the basic level ones could and should remain free of political considerations and the population should be given the chance to select the council officials from those people known for their honesty, professional and social prestige. Although the elections could not be conducted before martial law was lifted, some preparations could be started earlier and would help create an atmosphere of mutual trust and reconciliation. The proposals included in the 'Theses' went much further and deeper than the attempt at the formation of a Front of National Accord suggested in the autumn of 1981. These, now, were detailed and concrete proposals suggesting an end to the impasse and a way out from the increasingly difficult and dangerous social and political situation. In addition to a clearly defined Church opposition to martial law, something that was welcomed by the majority of the society, the Church also made it explicit that it was prepared to respect the regime's internal and external liabilities on the condition that the authorities truly sought to re-establish social peace by reinstating civil rights and granting the public a greater share in running the country.

The publication of the Council's Theses was also timed for the approaching meeting of the Central Committee scheduled for 22 and 23 April. The plenum devoted to economic matters, however, made no decisions on the resolution of mounting financial, industrial and agricultural difficulties.

On 25 April Archbishop Glemp met General Jaruzelski. At the meeting, according to a subsequent communiqué, they both agreed that the current difficult situation 'requires united effort on the part of the authorities and the community'. In this context they discussed national accord and social agreement and 'stated unanimously that these goals ought to be achieved by means of dialogue in which State-Church relations play a significant role'. But there was no specific agreement on how the dialogue should be conducted. The Church's insistence on the preservation of pluralistic organizational structures was clearly incompatible with the regime's claim that only the Party had the right to shape and organize public activities. At the same time the Church seemed to have facilitated contact between the regime and the three principle leaders of Solidarity (Zbigniew Bujak of Warsaw, Bogdan Lis of Gdańsk and Władysław Frasyniuk of Wrocław), who had been in hiding since the start of martial law.[25] As for the 'Theses', General Jaruzelski let it be known that they were too far-reaching and unrealistic. Nevertheless, there were reports that they had become the 'subject of preliminary discussions in Government circles'.[26]

Perhaps encouraged by this and in order to stimulate further interest in the Church's suggestions, in May 1982 the Council issued another document entitled 'Propositions of the Primate's Social Council on Social and Economic Matters', which was again submitted to the military authorities. The document, divided into two parts, was essentially a more detailed and in-depth analysis of the Council's April 'Theses'. In the first part, headed 'The Broad Social Programme', the Council pointed out that the overriding principle accepted in the formulation of the propositions had been the seeking of solutions which would enable the free and conscious involvement of the population in economic activity. Analysing the shortcomings of the social and economic policies and detailing plans for economic recovery, the document listed the main factors that had caused substantial damage to the Polish economy. In addition to the mistaken investment policy which concentrated on heavy industry to the neglect of housing and consumer goods, the Council pointed to the centralization of the economy combined with the lack of any form of public control over economic decisions, which were quite often taken by people without sound economic knowledge. The socialist economic model developed in Poland was too inflexible to take into account the peculiarities of Polish social structures and to utilize the skills of the Polish people. The Council singled out as one such example the agricultural policy of respective post-war Polish regimes which favoured unproductive individual farmers' plots. This according to the analysis has caused the total collapse of Poland's agriculture. The document therefore emphasized the need for a thorough reform of the economic system—decentralization of the economy and introduction of public control over economic decisions at all levels. It called for a return to productive individual farm structures and privatization of small enterprises. It suggested the abolition of the State monopoly of the wholesaling of agricultural products and called for a restructuring of the price system on agricultural goods in such a way that it would allow a 'free exchange between towns and the countryside'. The Council also indicated that social accord should rejuvenate private and co-operative economic activity particularly in the areas of commerce, handicrafts and the hotel and catering industry. Moreover, it called for limits on and the eventual removal of the 'administration of prices', and more independence for the banking system.

In the second part, under the heading 'Programme for the Way Out of the Crisis', the Council made it clear that no plan of economic reform had any chance of success unless a social accord was reached between the authorities and society. Such an accord was impossible without the lifting of the restrictions imposed by martial law regulations, the prior reinstatement of trade unions, including Solidarity, and other suspended social organizations, and the restoration of suspended laws—in particular the law on the control of the press. Furthermore, the document stipulated that it would be impossible to overcome the crisis without an increase in co-operation with foreign countries 'both in the East and the West'. Above all, the Council stated, the only solution to the present crisis is a political solution which is impossible 'without a real understanding between the authorities and society'.

Although the Council's proposals were accepted by the underground leadership of Solidarity, there appears to have been some considerable apprehension that the continuing activities of the Social Council might have harmful implications for the trade union. Criticism of the Church's involvement now began appearing in the underground publications, and dissenting voices from among the more radical clergy were also openly heard. The main objections were that in becoming directly involved in the process of political bargaining the Church was assuming the role played by Solidarity until the imposition of martial law, and that prolonged bipartite negotiations between the Church and the regime might render Solidarity's presence at the conference table redundant.

But there was more specific criticism voiced against the Council. Father Franciszek Blachnicki, for example, one of the more radical priests with a long association with dissident movements, in his 'Reflections on the Theses', questioned the basic assumption that changes were possible within the present political system of Poland and suggested that 'hope of any changes within the framework of the system . . . is an illusion, a victory for the deceitful propaganda of the system and the beginning of defeat for all liberation movements.' Another radical priest, Father Stanisław Małkowski asked in the underground *Tygodnik Wojenny* (The War Weekly):

> Is the Church strong enough to restrain the enemy's rage and treachery merely by acting on its own and operating within its own ethical constraints? The positive answer to that appears doubtful unless God Himself wished to intervene . . . the *dictum*

of the day for the Church can only be 'endure and pray' . . . until such time when the greater forces of this evil beyond our border shall be defeated, this time, for ever. . . .[27]

Anka Kowalska, a founding member of the Committee for the Defence of Workers (KOR), in her letter to Archbishop Glemp, written from an internment camp[28] voiced the anguish of many by saying:

> The 'Theses' of the Primate's Social Council in effect justify crimes: the imposition of martial law, mass round-ups, lawless and draconian sentences, the killing of workers defending not their mines and steelworks, but their souls and the Polish social consciousness so recently awakened . . . we all turn our eyes and hearts towards the Church. Why does she not raise her voice against those traders peddling human souls? How can the Church suggest instead that this tortured and betrayed society admits to being wicked and behaving improperly, and show understanding for its hangmen who lost their temper? Any concessions then granted would be nothing more but a return of part of our inalienable rights—nobody knows for how long, nobody knows for what price and above all, nobody knows whether it would be for real. . . Who has the right to speak on behalf of those victims about an attempt at reconciliation? I cannot believe that the Church is willing to do so. I cannot believe that without calling black black, and white white, the Church could call for the beginning of a spiritually fatal process of false reconciliation between the naughty criminals and their humble and—for a long time yet to come—bleeding victims. I cannot believe that the Church would want to take the side of falsehood—to be used to this end by politicians.

The discussion on the Church's role conducted in the underground press[29] reflected to a large extent popular impatience with any visible progress in finding a way out of the increasingly depressing situation. Periodic strikes, mass protests on the 13th of every month and other national anniversaries, as well as other forms of resistance, were ample examples of the strength of feeling of a great number of people in Poland, which the Church neither wanted nor could ignore. That the regime always responded to any form of protest with the full use of the oppressive apparatus at its disposal, arrests, heavy sentences, internment, to name just a few, further exacerbated the situation and deepened the crisis. A great many people felt confused as to how they should respond to the situation and tackle everyday dramas and tribulations. Many asked why the Church, which adopted such authoritative positions on problems as complex as divorce and abortion, failed to provide a positive lead in this situation where it was so badly needed. There was undoubtedly a gap emerging between segments of the Polish society and the Church hierarchy; the Primate and the Episcopate faced an increasing dilemma. Were they to take a harder line against the regime in order to improve the nation's confidence and having done so call for moderation, which after all was the only realistic alternative to bring possible results in the long run? One of the fundamental difficulties the Church had to face was that short of being accused by its external and internal enemies of directly meddling in politics and thus undermining the Party, it could never fully reveal the state of the delicate negotiations with the regime and thus make its position clear. The Polish hierarchy, which has always had only a limited access to the mass media inside Poland, has always been reluctant to open itself to the mass media from abroad. Such contact risked accusations of using Western propaganda centres. There is also among the hierarchy a sneaking suspicion and distrust of outsiders who do not really understand the complexities of the Polish situation. Quite often this approach has worked to the Church's advantage. However, it is quite clear that this was not the case in the summer of 1982, when, in addition to the results of the Primate's Social Council's deliberations, the Primate and his immediate inner-circle of clerical and lay advisers had been involved in delicate and complex negotiations to solve some of Poland's outstanding problems. The successful conclusion of these negotiations required, however, substantial co-operation on the part of Western governments, public and private institutions and Churches: in a nutshell, success required international solidarity.

'Solidarity without frontiers' was one of the main themes of the Pope's address to the 68th session of the International Labour Organization delivered in Geneva on 15 June 1982.[30] The problems of work, he emphasized, 'problems that have repercussions in so many spheres of life at all levels, whether individual, family, national or international, share one characteristic, which is at one and the same time a condition and a programme and which I would like to stress before you today: *solidarity*.[31] He then went on to say that the need for man to safeguard the reality of his work and to free it from any ideology in order to bring out once more the true meaning of human effort, 'becomes particularly apparent when one considers the world of work and the solidarity that it calls for in the *international context*. The problem of man at work today must be set against a world-wide background which can no longer be ignored. All the major problems of man in society are new world problems!' More significantly, the central theme of the address stressed:

> This also means that the world-wide common good requires a *new solidarity without frontiers*. In saying that, I do not wish to belittle the importance of the efforts that each nation must make within the limits of its own sovereignty, its own cultural traditions and in accordance with its own needs, to achieve the type of social and economic development which respects the distinctive character of each of its members and of its entire people. Nor must it too readily be supposed that consciousness of solidarity is already sufficiently developed because of the simple fact that we are all aboard this space-ship Earth. On the other hand, we must ensure that nations complement each other in their efforts to develop their own spiritual and material resources, and on the other, we must proclaim the demands by universal solidarity and the structural consequences it implies... All must be prepared to accept the necessary sacrifices, all must co-operate in the establishment of the programmes and agreements through which economic and social policy will become a tangible expression of solidarity, all must help in erecting the appropriate economic, technical, political and financial structures which the establishment of *a new social order of solidarity* indisputably requires.

The Pope thus internationalized the solutions to workers' problems and this quite clearly included the problems of Poland as well. In his speech he emphasized the word 'solidarity' in several contexts. There was also praise for 'constant dialogue... of ever renewed and recurring problems' between government employers and workers. The references to Poland were unmistakable particularly since the seats of the workers' delegation were empty. In contrast to the previous year when the Polish delegation was led by Lech Wałęsa, Poland was now represented by an official from the Ministry of Labour, Wages and Social Affairs, and the Polish ambassador to Switzerland.

The Papal address to the ILO must have been seen as a direct pointer for all those who were busily engaged in considering the Polish hierarchy's 'Memorandum on the Assistance Programme for Private Agriculture and the Private Enterprise Sector' which was circulated with considerable secrecy in June 1982 to several Western episcopal conferences, governments, and individual politicians including President Ronald Reagan, as well as private foundations and international agencies. The Memorandum outlined a unique and ambitious programme to rejuvenate private agriculture,[32] small private enterprises, handicraft-industry, trade and services, pointing out that successive Polish regimes, by concentrating on heavy industrialization, had neglected Poland's private sector economy so that due to chronic under-investment it remained almost entirely unmodernized, which in the case of agriculture led to extremely low productivity. Handicraft, trade and service industries had also suffered in this way and contributed to the general decline of the rural areas.

The suggested Polish Recovery Programme modelled on the European Recovery Programme (the Marshall Plan) which was instituted after the Second World War, aimed at stimulating initiative and motivation, through aiding self-help programmes. The priorities were to overcome the tight supply situation and to increase the productivity of private agriculture by improving the necessary infrastructures. The programme envisaged financial, advisory and practical aid, the latter to include such necessities as seeds, fertilizers, pesticides, transport, storage and food processing equipment, particularly spare parts, veterinary aid and not least the teaching of up-to-date methods. It was left open as to whether the equipment necessary should be imported from the West or whether it would be possible to produce it in Poland.

According to the provisional estimates drawn up by the hierarchy's experts this aid should cover about 10 per cent of the present input in all sectors of the Polish economy. This would involve DM 1,000 million, or about £252 million a year, and in the case of the envisaged five-year programme the total sum required was DM 5,000 million or around £1,260 million.

To administer this programme it was suggested a new organization should be created under the auspices of the Episcopal Conference, to include various professional groups and to be run by the recipients of the programme. The allocation of money and practical aid would be attached to conditions guaranteeing the setting up of a positive development programme. All aid, which would be in the form of credits given directly to the respective enterprises, would have to be repaid at a reasonable rate in order to use the proceeds for the creation of an investment fund.

The financing of the Polish Recovery Programme was to come from various sources in the West. About 25 per cent from Western church funds, another 25 per cent from Western private banks and foundations, companies and professional groups. It was expected that the remaining 50 per cent could be contributed by member states of the European Community and the United States.

It is obvious that the Church felt that since the State and other institutions would be unsuitable for the implementation of such an assistance programme for various reasons, it should take over the responsibility itself, formally regarding the task as part of its Catholic social teaching and seeing a direct link with its pastoral interests. The longer term significance of such a role, while never alluded to, is the re-creation of a legitimate social and even political role for the Polish Church. Such a prospect must have made Jaruzelski and his associates uneasy. Nevertheless talks between the episcopacy and Government at top level, as well as at ministerial level, showed that the Government would not impede such a Church-initiated and Church-supported assistance programme for the private enterprise sector, which even in the case of a take-over by the 'hardliners' would most probably continue to exist, and so the programme would be carried on. The Church was also reassured by a series of Parliamentary laws passed in early 1982 which protected and guaranteed the ownership of private farms and created more favourable terms for the functioning and development of small-scale non-socialized industry, private crafts and services. These new bills guaranteed equal economic and social conditions for all sectors of the economy and considered the private sector as a permanent component of the political and economic system.

The Church's sponsored Polish Recovery Programme is without precedent in its scope and boldness of approach. It was the brainchild of Archbishop Glemp who was personally involved in a series of negotiations with prospective participants. The task was enormous. He not only had to convince the Polish regime but also sceptical Western banks and governments of the viability of such an undertaking at a time when Poland already owed Western creditors some $30,000 million and was continuously negotiating the rescheduling of its debts. Another problem was of course the fact that the Church lacked a legal status in Poland, something that the regime was still reluctant to grant, and which would be required if the Church was to assume the administration of the Programme. The Primate nevertheless persevered with his endeavours on all fronts and by July 1982 there was tangible evidence that he was making some progress. His emissaries' representations in both Bonn and Brussels met with a positive response from Church and political quarters, and his exchange of letters on the subject with General Jaruzelski indicated a favourable response from the regime. In an added effort to speed up the negotiations he travelled to West Germany at the beginning of September to outline the Programme in a more detailed form to West German bishops and other prospective contributors to the Programme.

There is, of course, a clear parallel between the Church's continued attempt to acquire a legitimate legal status and the formal independence once enjoyed by Solidarity. Such recognition would bring the ideal of a formally pluralistic Poland one step further. Hence at the same time the Church continued its search for the reinstatement of Solidarity. In July 1982 the bishops presented the authorities with new proposals suggesting a meeting between the Government's Committee for Trade Unions and five members of Solidarity's national leadership including Lech Wałęsa.[33] The task of such a meeting was to discuss the Statute of Solidarity and the permissible forms of its activity. It was envisaged that after the initial contact full scale negotiations with the participation of all members of Solidarity's leadership could take place. At the same time the Episcopate hoped the underground leaders of Solidarity would extend their moratorium, issued on 26 June,[34] until the end of August, to enable such an initiative to go ahead.

The Church had hoped that positive moves in this direction could be created in connection with the forthcoming second papal visit to

Poland which had been under negotiation for some time.[35] It was a visit that became a dominant feature of Church-State relations from then on. The Pope was expected to come to Poland in August 1982 to participate in the 600th anniversary of the arrival of the icon of the Black Madonna at the monastery in Częstochowa. The regime strongly objected to the timing of the visit which would have closely coincided with the second anniversary of the foundation of Solidarity. With no progress in the negotiations on the visit the bishops decided to bring the issue into the open. On 8 June 1982 the Main Council of the Polish Episcopate met in Warsaw for an extraordinary session and produced a telegram to the Pope informing him of their continuing expectation of seeing him in Częstochowa during the August celebrations. Two days later during the Corpus Christi celebrations in Warsaw Archbishop Glemp stated that 'the visit by the Holy Father is planned for 26 August . . . we invited him last year and he gladly accepted our invitation'. At the same time Archbishop Luigi Poggi unexpectedly arrived in Warsaw for further consultations.[36]

The Church was clearly not prepared to give up the visit in August 1982 and had hoped that the Pope's arrival would produce a suitable environment in which their proposals for the solution of Poland's problems could be further advanced. But at the same time the hierarchy which regarded the Jaruzelski group as a 'lesser evil' to the Olszowski group of hardliners who were considered the most likely successors if the General was pushed too far, was not prepared to undermine his already desperate position further. On 11 June the Political Bureau of the ruling Polish United Workers' Party held an unexpected meeting and on 13 June the Polish Press Agency PAP accused the bishops of making 'unilateral decisions' not yet cleared by the Vatican and the Polish Government: 'The visit should be preceded by thorough organizational arrangements for which adequate socio-political conditions are indispensable. These conditions depend on the progress of normalization in Poland.'

In the meantime another series of street demonstrations erupted on 13 June in Gdańsk, Wrocław and Nowa Huta; on 25 June (sixth anniversary of the 1976 price rise demonstrations) demonstrations took place in Warsaw and Radom; and on 27 and 28 June another series of protests took place in Poznań (twenty-sixth anniversary of the events in 1956). These disturbances were at first played down by the official media but later given more attention in an obvious attempt to demonstrate that the situation in Poland was not yet ripe for a papal visit. These reports found an immediate echo in Prague and Moscow, where they served as a pretext for sharp attacks on the Church, which was reportedly 'providing rallying points for the opponents of martial law'.[37] A more outspoken attack followed on 18 June, when a Tass dispatch from Paris reporting on President Ronald Reagan's visit to the Vatican on 7 June, accused Reagan of prompting the Pope to go to Poland in August 'under the pretext of religious ceremonies', and offering him financial aid for the opposition there, to be channelled through the Church. The report, reprinted in the Soviet Party daily *Pravda* on 19 June provoked an unusually strong denial from the Vatican on 23 June.[38]

Archbishop Poggi returned empty handed to the Vatican on 29 June, after two weeks in Poland. During his stay in Warsaw he met the Polish Foreign Minister and member of the PUWP Political Bureau, Józef Czyrek, and the Minister for Religious Affairs, Adam Łopatka, but the subject of the visit was only briefly touched on during these discussions.

Since the Poggi mission had proved fruitless the Pope now asked Archbishop Glemp, Cardinal Franciszek Macharski and Archbishop Henryk Gulbinowicz to come to Rome for direct talks. The dignitaries arrived on 6 July 1982 and after a series of talks with the Pope and his foreign policy advisers decided that at that stage no progress could be made. The Pope was clearly dissatisfied with the situation. On 19 July Warsaw dispatched to the Vatican Józef Czyrek, a member of the PUWP Political Bureau and Foreign Minister. His unexpected arrival was clearly not to the Vatican's liking. The Pope eventually received Czyrek at Castel Gandolfo on 20 July for some two hours. By all accounts the meeting was far from pleasant. Czyrek also held two longish meetings with Cardinal Agostino Casaroli and several conversations with Archbishop Glemp. The implicit message of this visit and negotiations with other officials at the Vatican, was that although the Polish authorities would be happy to see John Paul II in Częstochowa for a short, perhaps two-day visit, the Soviets would be far from pleased, and might even intervene directly to prevent it. It was also considered that an attempt to force the General to accept the August date would only strengthen the position of the hardliners within the Polish leadership. Some compromise formula had to be sought making the papal visit possible without loss of face for both the Church and the regime in the process. Czyrek's journey to Rome was clearly intended as Jaruzelski's courtesy gesture towards the Pontiff. Pope John Paul II could at least not be simply confronted with a *fait acompli*, but allowed to reach a decision of his own accord.

That decision, obviously reluctantly taken, was not announced by the Pope himself but by Archbishop Glemp, who speaking at a mass in the chapel of the Black Madonna under St. Peter's Basilica on 21 July stated that 'the Holy Father himself, reflecting on the circumstances, decided to postpone his visit to a later date, but always within the framework of this jubilee year'.[39] The same day Glemp told the Independent Television News (ITN) that the celebrations of the jubilee year which were to end on 26 August 1982 had been extended and would continue until the Pope's arrival, even if it took years. The postponement of the visit was a great personal disappointment to the Pope who had very precise ideas about this specific mission. On 21 July he withdrew at the last moment the prepared text of his address he was to deliver during his weekly general audience and instead delivered a prayer to the Virgin Mary for the Church in Poland.

The postponement, however, meant that the Church had to accept finally, at present and in the future, albeit reluctantly, the facts of martial law with all its implications: these left considerable room for manœuvre but only on the regime's terms. The fundamental issues that remained open were how the faithful could also be persuaded to accept the realities of the situation, and to what degree the Church's *de facto* legitimization of martial law would undermine the hierarchy's position *vis-à-vis* radical priests and the vast majority of the society. One other question that had remained permanently present in this sophisticated bargaining process was the scope and number of concessions that could be extracted from the regime that would make the acceptance of the realities both possible and manageable. The Pope and the Polish bishops were obviously fully aware of the importance of these issues and their subsequent actions were aimed at finding acceptable resolutions to these problems. At the same time it should also be emphasized that these dilemmas were not new to the Roman Catholic Church in Poland but perhaps now more than ever before its credibility and standing within the society began to be undermined. The conflict between the temporal and the spiritual was all too obvious.

The authorities were also fully aware of the Church's dilemma. Their view was eloquently put by the well-known Polish sociologist, and former member of the Council of State, Jan Szczepański.

It must be remembered that [the Church] is a Catholic or global Church and that its interests do *not completely* coincide with those of the Polish nation, that in spite of the involvement in Polish affairs it must consider its own interests which result from its universality and its involvement in many continents, lands and political systems. . . Besides, 'My kingdom is not of this world'. The Church must as a consequence look far into the future while at the same time taking into account current power groupings, and it cannot involve itself completely either for the benefit of the authorities or Solidarity, or in the opposition's favour. It must weigh up all arguments with a view to what is essential for its fundamental function, i.e. for the preservation and development of religion.[40]

Although there is obviously a great deal of truth and realism in this assessment, the Church in Poland, as a part of the Universal Church, had always seen itself as an historically much more significant institution than the PUWP. Nevertheless, its unique position in the country had never allowed it to concentrate only on its global organizational dimensions. At the same time, however, there were obvious limits. The other—and perhaps the most important—factor, was the Polish Pontiff. The question which was often asked in Poland was, if the Pope could not help them, who could? And, from the perspective of the Polish Church, if the Polish Pope could not help Poles, then this raised awkward questions about the potential role of the Church world-wide. If the Pope could not help to produce any tangible results in Poland, could he as the head of the Universal Church, substantively influence the resolution of the problems in other troubled parts of the world: South Africa, Asia or Latin America? That is why the internationalization of the Polish problem played such an important part in the Roman Catholic Church's strategy.

In a long awaited speech to the Sejm on 21 July (the eve of Poland's national day) General Jaruzelski announced the release of the majority of internees, including all women,[41] and the easing of curbs on foreign travel, post and telecommunications. Although he did not mention any plans for amnesty for those convicted of martial law violations, he did, however, offer to accept back Polish citizens who had remained illegally abroad since 13 December 1981, provided that they had not been deliberately engaged in anti-State activities. He also stated that provincial governors had been authorized to lift the suspension on the activity of a 'significant group of associations' and suggested that 'conditions permitting', martial law might be suspended before the end of the year.

The General's speech, which fell well short of expectations, also contained some pronouncements on the papal visit. In order to provide the illustrious guest with the reception he deserved, Jaruzelski stressed, 'peace and calm must reign in the country', and all 'activities threatening the security of the State' had to cease. 'An important part in bringing about the desired appeasement was expected to be played by the Church, in accordance with talks that are currently underway.' Should the 'proper conditions' be attained, the Government would 'do all in its power to make it possible for Pope John Paul II's visit to take place next year during the jubilee celebrations at Jasna Góra. The ecclesiastical authorities have informed us that these celebrations will last until September 1983.'

The Pope, speaking on 28 July, repeated the Church's earlier demands.

Again I repeat the words pronounced by the Polish Episcopate in the month of February. The bishops, together with the whole community, expect martial law to end as quickly as possible, those interned to be released, amnesty to be given to those sentenced for actions connected with martial law, safe conduct to be guaranteed to those in hiding, and nobody to be dismissed from work for union affiliation. Full freedom for religious life and the development of culture must be secured. I repeat these words before all those on whom their fulfilment depends, I unite them with the prayer of the jubilee year. If, in this prayer, there is gratitude for what, from among the bishops' words, has been fulfilled, then, at the same time, there is an even more fervent appeal for the fulfilment of that which has not been fulfilled.

In the event, on 26 August 1982 traditional celebrations took place at Jasna Góra, presided over by Archbishop Glemp, during which he again asked for a return to the negotiating table.[42] Recalling the approaching second anniversary of the signing of the Gdańsk, Szczecin and Jastrzębie agreements, which he described as 'a victory of reason, maturity and wise resistance . . . a victory—not on the street barricades but behind the dialogue table', the Primate stated that:

> The Church is constantly calling and asking for such a dialogue and constantly receiving an answer that conditions are not right for it. Let us begin to create the conditions. Here are the proposals: free Lech Wałęsa, or assure him at least temporary conditions in which he can speak as a free person; renew, even if by stages, trade-union work; free the rest of the internees and start work on the preparation of an amnesty; specify the date of the arrival of the Holy Father to Poland.[43]

These proposals were clearly addressed to the authorities rather than to the population. The divided regime, which had no clear idea what to do in the circumstances, vascillated. There was no clear structural conception on any of the proposals raised by Glemp in his sermon[44] and it is therefore not surprising that the anger, humiliation and sheer frustration of society manifested itself in demonstrations and other forms of protest, such as the creation of an 'underground society',[45] which both the Church and the Jaruzelski group wanted to avoid.

On 26 August, in anticipation of the anniversary, the bishops issued a Pastoral Letter to be read in all Polish Churches on Sunday 29 August. The letter, echoing Archbishop Glemp, stressed that only through dialogue was it possible to release tension and to resolve basic issues in public life. The bishops appealed to the authorities and to social groups for 'wisdom in their actions' and recalled that when martial law was declared the Military Council specifically promised that 'trade unions, including Solidarity, will be able to resume their statutory activities. We want to believe that action will follow the words'. Referring to the approaching anniversary, the bishops called for calm and emphasized: 'It would be a great mistake, evil and sadness if the anniversary of the social agreements was used by anyone for violent clashes which might cause fraternal blood to be spilled'.[46]

On 28 August, three days before the anniversary, the army daily newspaper *Żołnierz Wolności* reported that joint manœuvres by Polish and Soviet troops were taking place near Warsaw. But none of these warnings was able to prevent a major outburst of social discontent.

According to official statistics[47] demonstrations occurred in sixty-six 'urban centres' in thirty-four of Poland's forty-nine provinces. In seven cities there had been violent confrontations between the demonstrators and the police in which four people had been shot and killed, hundreds seriously hurt and several thousands detained or arrested.[48] The treatment of the demonstrators showed clearly that the regime, rather than seeking dialogue, was ready and able to act ruthlessly to crush all those who ventured to express their frustration at its policies. There was now little doubt that the authorities were not prepared to take up the Church's advice and suggestions.[49]

In a further, albeit rather desperate, show of strength the Government announced the arrest of four members of the former Social Self-defence Committee KOR: Jacek Kuroń, Adam Michnik, Jan Lityński and Henryk Wujec (all in internment since 13 December 1981), on charges of 'preparing the violent overthrow of Poland's socio-political system'. At the same time 'wanted' warrants were issued against other KOR leaders who remained in hiding, while legal action *in absentia* was taken against Jan Józef Lipski and Mirosław Chojecki who were abroad.[50]

The Church's response to the regime's brutality came in a powerful sermon preached by the Bishop of Przemyśl, Ignacy Tokarczuk, in Częstochowa on 5 September 1982.[51] 'Brute force solves nothing, but only complicates a situation and makes it worse', he told his listeners. And he gave a graphic description of the events that took place in Przemyśl on 31 August, when a peaceful demonstration by workers was met with a violent reaction by the police:

> A man was returning to the suburbs from his garden allotment carrying vegetables in his bag—this is a true story—when he was assaulted, beaten up and thrown to the ground, and this man, opening his battered eyes, shouted 'Hitler wouldn't have done this!' On another street women standing with prams had tear gas cannisters fired at them but they threw themselves weeping over the prams, trying to defend their babies with their own bodies, since they could have suffered a shock which would have made them cripples for life.

The Bishop appealed to 'those brothers who are doing the beating' not to do this and not hide behind others, if they 'want to remain part of our nation'. 'In the past, there were those who relied on orders and who to this day put forward as their defence in trials that they obeyed orders, but no national or international court recognizes this as a defence. Each man's responsibility lies beyond orders. Let us remember that', he stressed.

Reminding his audience about past protests by the workers in 1956 and 1970, Tokarczuk called for a start to a process of reconciliation among various groups within society:

> The good of the people, the good of the State and the good of the authorities themselves demand: the restoration of trade-union activities, Solidarity first and foremost; the release of Lech Wałęsa first of all; proclamation of an amnesty for all those detailed and sentenced; renunciation of brutality; dialogue with the people.

But again there was no evidence that the authorities were prepared to listen. Instead, a campaign of vehement criticism against the Church was launched in the Polish media with the brunt of these attacks concentrating on Bishop Tokarczuk.

That there had been no real attempts at starting talks was confirmed in the 16 September communiqué of the Episcopal Conference.[52] Around the same time the authorities began giving the first indications of the content of the new trade-union bill to be debated by the Sejm on 8 and 9 October, which was to delegalize all trade unions.

The date for the parliamentary session was chosen to coincide with the canonization ceremonies of Father Maximilian Kolbe, who gave his life for a fellow prisoner in the Auschwitz concentration camp and is revered in Poland as one of the country's great heroes. The regime was clearly trying to exploit the canonization by giving prominence to the canonization[53] and thus implying its 'positive' attitude towards the Church, while hoping at the same time to use it as diversion from the dismantling of Solidarity.

The Primate, who together with some forty Polish bishops, was expected to travel to Rome for the celebrations[54], and immediately afterwards to visit Polish communities in Canada and the United States where he was also due to meet President Ronald Reagan and ask for the lifting of Western sanctions, cancelled his trips and also refused to meet General Jaruzelski on 6 October as previously planned. Glemp's decision not to meet Jaruzelski was greeted in official circles with alarm. Various attempts were now made to defuse the situation and finally some offers of a solution were put forward. One of them involved the postponement of the parliamentary session for a week and another the introduction of some changes in the legislation. It would appear that Archbishop Glemp opted for the latter. To what extent he was able to influence the final draft of the bill is unclear. But he had access to the drafts. Some sixteen hours before the Sejm was to debate the bill outlawing Solidarity, Glemp still had four drafts of the legislation.

Only twelve members of the Polish Parliament out of the 430 present voted against the legislation which formally ended the two-year experiment in workers' democracy. Ten deputies abstained in the voting.[55] The new Trade Union Bill, through an indirect clause which simply stipulated 'the registration of any trade union made before this law goes into force loses its validity',[56] terminated the legal existence of all trade unions including Solidarity and Rural Solidarity. At the same time the legislation provided a framework for the establisment of a new labour movement in the future by allowing for the setting up of one small union for each factory scheme. The union would have to register in local courts and would have to pledge support for the leading role of the PUWP and the Polish Constitution.[57]

In his speech at the end of the two-day debate on the legislation General Jaruzelski defended the banning of Solidarity and offered an olive branch to the Church, saying that the existing differences of opinion between the regime and hierarchy should not lead to conflict: 'both sides would lose by it . . . There is a prominent place for the Church in the social life of socialist Poland. We meet half way her requests and postulates, which are related to the discharge of her pastoral mission.' He also stressed that the regime saw a possibility of widening the 'constructive co-operation' with the Church and revealed that 'the Consultative Economic Council affiliated to the Council of Ministers has recently embarked on discussions with members of the Primate's Social Council.' It thus appeared that with Solidarity out of the way the authorities were prepared to discuss some less controversial topics with the Church.[58] In another part of his speech, the General reaffirmed the authorities' 'unequivocally positive stance' on the second papal visit to Poland, and stressed readiness to finalize the arrangements.

Jaruzelski's platitudes were addressed not only to the Catholic hierarchy and faithful but were also aimed at President Reagan who always insisted that in order to lift Western sanctions the Polish regime must show itself to be engaged in dialogue with the Church. The General could not have been more explicit about that. His arguments, however, did not seem to be persuasive enough, and in fact had the opposite result. In a swift reaction to the delegalization of Solidarity, on 9 October 1982, President Reagan suspended Poland's 'most favoured-nation' status.

The workers reponded to the delegalization of their union by staging another series of mass strikes and demonstrations which continued in Gdańsk, Warsaw, Szczecin, Nowa Huta and Wrocław for several days. The Lenin Shipyard in Gdańsk was brought under control after the workforce was put under military discipline.[59]

The Church responded to the delegalization of Solidarity as forcibly as it could. Archbishop Glemp told his congregation on 10 October,

> We are aware . . . that it is very painful for many believers to know that Solidarity as a trade-union organization has been delegalized. But we know that what is good and right cannot simply disappear. Structures may disappear but the idea of good, of struggling for what is right, must not be allowed to vanish.

On the same day the Pope at the end of the canonization ceremonies of Saint Maximilian Kolbe in a spontaneous statement which surprised even his immediate entourage referred to the legal banning of the trade union as 'a violation of the basic rights of man and society' which was giving rise, in many quarters, to resolute objections and to protests in international public opinion.[60] He also showed his displeasure by not receiving the official Government delegation for the ceremonies in a private audience.

But that was all the Church could do. It felt betrayed and disappointed. But this was the price it had to pay for its involvement in the bargaining process with the regime and for making its demands publicly known. In retrospect there appears to have been no other posture that the Church could have adopted. If it did not speak up for the reinstatement of Solidarity it would have isolated itself from its power base. It would have negated the long tradition of the Roman Catholic social teaching and association with Polish nationalism of which Solidarity was the most recent manifestation. Now at least it could put all the blame squarely on the desperately unpopular and shaky regime. However, there is little doubt that the delegalization of Solidarity had undermined the Church's credibility as an effective social spokesman and was a considerable blow to its authority and to that of Archbishop Glemp in particular. In the words of one of his close advisers he had 'lost the present battle' and consequently his popularity at home and abroad, already tarnished, tumbled even further. For many people he was seen as being too accommodating with the military regime. Many viewed his sermons as an uneven cocktail of soft criticism and appeal for calm and tolerance. His often clumsily expressed views fitted conveniently into the authorities' propaganda campaign. Polish wit, a sometimes cruel but well-established form of withdrawal from oppressive realities, even concocted a new word derived from the Archbishop's name: 'Glempic' was the word, which meant 'to say nothing at length in soothing terms'. There was a clear discrepancy between his moderate line and appeals, and those of a great many of the parish clergy who had to and did reflect much more closely the feelings of the ordinary people. It was they who had to cope with the real, everyday sufferings of the faithful, the miseries of life in prisons and internment camps, where they went to offer spiritual solace; they who experienced the plight of families deprived for long months of their fathers and of any means of livelihood; they who had to celebrate memorial masses for those killed and injured during the rallies and strikes; and who sheltered the fugitive Solidarity supporters. The priests were increasingly involved not only in pastoral work which they had to carry out with very limited resources in lieu of the distrusted and in any case bankrupt social agencies of the regime. They willingly took upon themselves the difficult task of distributing Western charity shipments among the most needy. The experience of their work had led many to adopt an increasingly militant position *vis-à-vis* not only the regime but also the Episcopate. They often called the Primate 'Comrade Glemp' for showing too much moderation and for not criticizing Government policy more openly. They had neither the faith nor the time to politicize with the country's rulers. It is therefore not surprising that churches often became rallying points for pro-Solidarity expressions of feeling. There was ample evidence that the Church at the grass-roots level was more representative of the people's feelings than the level negotiating with the regime.[61]

There could be no doubt about Archbishop Glemp's patriotism, dedication and devotion to his people and duties. But there were those who sometimes wondered whether the enormous problems of Poland, the task of getting the country out of its present political, economic and moral predicaments were not beyond his capacities; whether the office of the Primate of Poland, which carried authority and prestige as well as responsibilities unmatched by any other in the land, was not too big for this soft-spoken, affable but ambitious man. Although in the eyes of many people he suffered from unfavourable comparisons with his predecessor, the late Cardinal Wyszyński, in fact his policies were a continuation of Wyszyński's social and political teaching, according to which the sovereign existence of Poland was paramount and the Church must not lend itself to any actions that could undermine it. Only when sovereignty was guaranteed was the Church able to safeguard and contribute effectively to the nation's intellectual, religious and cultural traditions which are the basis for its development and expansion. Political parties and for that matter trade unions, come and go—the nation remains. In other words, social structures reflect only the current phase of the nation's development, a transitory nature of man's work. The Church, which embodies the nation's interests, must operate in different dimensions and time scales to those used by contemporary social groups. Therefore, while not denying the right of social groups to their own assessment of the situation and their own activity, it must not become involved in a struggle between them. In a nutshell, the Church's aspirations are above the political plane, the Church must remain itself and cannot allow itself to become a political partner. There is no doubt that this long-term philosophy was difficult to grasp both for people in Poland exhausted by everyday struggles and desperate for tangible signs of relief, and for those outside Poland, who, although eager to help, saw the situation from a different perspective. To such outsiders, the Church seemed very much involved in politics, which of course it was. However, the justification for this involvement was the very cornerstone of the Church's philosophy, the sovereignty of Poland.

Whether anyone in the Vatican, besides the Pope himself, was able to grasp the peculiarly Polish aspects and the intricacies of the situation is a matter for conjecture. Certainly there were discreet but unmistakeable rumours amongst the Roman curia that after the delegalization of Solidarity, Archbishop Glemp might be moved from Warsaw to Rome in order to make way for someone else.[62]

The Polish Episcopate persevered discretely in their endeavours on the Polish Recovery Programme. On 7 October 1982 Cardinal Franciszek Macharski discussed the matter at a symposium of European bishops in Rome and reported considerable progress in the negotiations between the Episcopate and Polish Government on the scheme. He now obtained an assurance from the Commission of the Episcopates of the European Community (COMECE) of its willingness to participate wholeheartedly in the project and assume the responsibility for it in the West provided the Polish Government gave it unequivocal consent. It was now left to the Polish Episcopate and the regime to work out mutually acceptable arrangements.

First, however, both the Polish regime and Church badly needed to recover ground lost with the dismantling of Solidarity. There was a convergence of opinion that the country badly needed a morale booster. The only conceivable event likely to do this was a papal visit. On 25 October Glemp travelled to Rome to arrange the date for the Pope's arrival. The agreed date was eventually released after the Primate's meeting with Jaruzelski on 8 November. A communiqué issued after their talks stated that: 'The State authorities of the Polish People's Republic and the Conference of the Polish Episcopate will officially invite His Holiness to begin his pilgrimage to Poland on 18 June next year.' During the meeting Archbishop Glemp also again asked for the release of Lech Wałęsa.

On 10 November the Secretary General of the Soviet Communist Party Leonid Brezhnev died and the following day the Primate was informed by a representative of the Ministry of Internal Affairs that Lech Wałęsa would be released, thus fulfilling at least one of the Church's demands.[63] Undoubtedly the release of Wałęsa and the subsequent suspension of martial law on 31 December, together with the progress made in negotiations on the Polish Recovery Programme, were all important factors in facilitating the papal visit.

The Polish Recovery Programme was slowly becoming reality. At the end of November Archbishop Glemp wrote to General Jaruzelski in order to ask formally for his agreement to the Programme. The

General's reply was favourable but indicated the need for setting up a Joint Working Group in order to work out the proposals and their ramifications in detail. Subsequently at the beginning of December the Joint Working Group was set up consisting of experts nominated by the Polish Episcopate and Government experts. The regime's commitment to the scheme is best exemplified not only by the fact that between the beginning of December 1982 and January 1983 four meetings of the Working Group were held in quick succession, but also that Deputy Prime Minister Zbigniew Madej, who is also Poland's representative to the Council for Mutual Economic Assistance, represented the Government in addition to other eminent polititicians. During the deliberations of the Working Group an agreement was reached on the creation of a Foundation for the Modernization and Development of Private Agriculture, Handicrafts and Private Sector Economy in Poland. The Foundation, its aims and scope of operation would be approved by a decree of the Council of State and given full authority to function within the framework of Poland's economy. Furthermore the Foundation would be able to utilize the existing private structures as well as fall back on some under State control. The Working Group also agreed on the following distribution of the Foundation resources. One-third to be steered directly towards private farmers for the improvement of their conditions of production, regrouping of land and incentives for specialization in output. One-third would be put at the disposal of small privately owned workshops in order to create the infrastructure for the manufacturing of some small parts of agricultural machinery, and of servicing centres as well as of new shops in order to improve the rural retail network. The remaining third would be used for the creation of self-help co-operatives for the purchase or rent of agricultural machinery, fertilizers, pesticides, medicines for animals and other products necessary for the improvements in agricultural and animal production. The Government gave a commitment to re-direct customs duties for products relating to the Programme (collected under its agreement with GATT) to the Foundation. The Working Group also envisaged the setting up of either a special bank under the Foundation's control or preferably a special account in the Narodowy Bank Polski (Polish National Bank), or Polska Kasa Oszczędności (Polish Savings Bank), to deal with the Foundation's financial matters. The Working Group also reached an agreement in principle on the creation of a partner institution for the Foundation in the West under the control of the Commission of Episcopates of the European Community. As far as the funds were concerned, the Working Group accepted that 50 per cent would be contributed by the governments of the member states of the European Community, as outlined in the initial Memorandum issued in June. However, since then the Episcopate has been able to solicit the participation of the governments of Canada, Japan and Australia. A notable absentee on this list was the government of the United States of America. Nevertheless, among the 25 per cent promised from private funds and foundations, some would emanate from American based or owned foundations including the Rockefeller Foundation. The remaining 25 per cent would be contributed by church organizations and episcopates in the West, including the United States.

The Working Group also agreed that in order to reach a final decision on the best use of the Programme, a few pilot programmes in five or six villages in one or two areas should be set up and monitored carefully for a year in order to obtain the best possible results for the Programme as a whole. In the meantime the Working Group decided to hold a series of negotiations in Warsaw with COMECE on the Programme, its preliminaries and conditions. In January 1983 Father Alojzy Orszulik, who was appointed by the Primate to be in charge of the Programme, held further discussions in Rome, Paris, Brussels and Bonn. At the same time work continued on the statutes of the Foundation and detailed outlines not only of the pilot schemes but also of yearly inputs and their expected results for the duration of the programme.

All these negotiations were conducted in considerable secrecy. On the surface the topic which appeared to dominate Church-State relations for the next six months was that of the forthcoming papal visit. There followed a series of long and complex negotiations on the details of the visit. The Church submitted a proposal of sixteen towns to be included in the Pope's itinerary, including Gdańsk, Szczecin, Olsztyn, Poznań, Bydgoszcz and Lublin as well as Częstochowa, Wrocław, Łódź, Katowice, Kraków and Warsaw. The regime refused to consider any part of northern Poland in the Pope's plans. At the beginning of January 1983, it also requested the Vatican to give it prior access to the texts of the homilies the Pope intended to deliver in Poland. The Vatican refused.

As the negotiations continued the Church decided to announce unilaterally the plans of the visit on 19 January. A pastoral letter from the bishops named the date of the Pope's arrival in Poland as 18 June 1983. The visit was to last seven days and include Warsaw, Częstochowa, Łódź, Kraków and Lublin. Significantly the announcement was made without a formal invitation having been sent from the Government in Warsaw. The bishops were clearly pushing the issue. In the same pastoral letter the bishops appealed to the State authorities to 'grant an amnesty and to undertake other suitable measures to reestablish full social justice' in the country, measures that might serve as a basis for general forgiveness and national unity. In their opinion, such national reconciliation could be regarded as a proper common 'gift for the Holy Father' on the occasion of his visit.

It required yet another meeting between Glemp and Jaruzelski (9 March 1983) and extensive consultations which involved Archbishop Glemp, Cardinal Macharski and Archbishop Gulbinowicz in the Vatican, who stayed there between 10 and 16 March, and Archbishop Poggi in Warsaw (10-18 March), for the formal invitation to be issued and a detailed itinerary to be announced. But even then there were last minute hitches and surprises. The invitation was to be handed over on 16 March in the Vatican by Jerzy Kuberski, the minister at the Polish Embassy in Rome with special responsibility for permanent working contacts with the Vatican and published simultaneously in Warsaw and the Vatican, together with the papal acceptance. Eventually, five days later, Kuberski delivered the invitation from the Chairman of the Polish Council of State, Henryk Jabłoński.[64] This was duly published, together with the bishops' invitation, by the Vatican Press Office on 23 March. But there was no official papal response to the invitation. Instead the Secretariat of the Primate of Poland released in Warsaw a statement saying that the Pope accepted the invitation. The Vatican kept silent. The Pope was now to visit Poland between 16 and 22 June and travel to Warsaw, Teresin (the Niepokalanów Franciscan monastery near Warsaw, founded by Poland's newest saint, Father Maximilian Maria Kolbe), Piekary Śląskie (A Marian shrine near Katowice, widely known for its annual pilgrimage of miners, and a place the Pope was prevented from visiting in 1979), the Mount of St. Anna (another Marian shrine near Opole, commemorating the Silesian uprisings of 1919, 1920 and 1921), Częstochowa,

Wrocław, Poznań and Kraków. At the same time the Church also expected that it would be able to negotiate a papal visit to Lublin, where he was to receive an honorary doctorate of all faculties from the Catholic University of Lublin where he taught for some twenty-five years. While in Lublin he was to lay a foundation stone for an interdenominational chapel at the former Nazi concentration camp at Majdanek. (Even earlier proposals envisaged Lublin as a venue for a national meeting with the farmers.) The University's Rector, Father Albert Krąpiec, disclosed during an interview with ITN on 18 April 1983 that the Pope had sent him a personal letter urging him to make every effort to persuade the authorities to make the visit to Lublin possible. Under this proposal the Pope was to say one open-air mass in the Warsaw suburb of Ursynów, spend one night in Warsaw and for the rest of his stay confine himself to the monastery of Jasna Góra, travelling from there by helicopter to other places to avoid any drives through towns and as little contact as possible with the population.

One of the fundamental problems in these negotiations was the Church's insistence on a general amnesty for those convicted under martial law regulations. In a communiqué issued on 4 May, after their conference, the bishops stated that in the context of the papal visit they hoped for 'the release of prisoners sentenced in connection with the introduction of martial law, the consignment to oblivion of deeds defined by the law in connection with martial law as violations of the legal order, and the restoration to their places of work of persons dismissed as a result of their convictions.'

Also at the beginning of May the Pope sent a private letter to Jabłoński in which he accepted the invitation but at the same time requested the Polish authorities to proclaim an amnesty. This was promptly refused with a polite explanation that the time for granting amnesty was inopportune so soon after the large-scale anti-Government demonstrations on 1 and 3 of May, and also that the granting of amnesty in connection with the visit would be interpreted by Poland's East European allies as a direct interference in Poland's internal affairs. However, an amnesty would be declared at the time when martial law was finally lifted. This, however, could not occur in connection with the visit alone but favourable conditions for the lifting of martial law would be created by the removal of Western economic sanctions.

TRIBULATIONS UNDER MARTIAL LAW: 1981-1983

The Vatican and the Church in Poland expected that the very fact that the arrangements for the papal visit were essentially finalized would meet with a suitable response from the international community, and the United States in particular. After all, several Western governments and their leading politicians had been for some months aware of the Polish Church's long-term thinking and had been involved in the negotiations on the Polish Recovery programme, for which the need had been advanced by the Primate and his close lay and clerical associates with considerable vigour and determination. A dramatic reminder of the need for international co-operation for the solution of the Polish problem came in the form of a front page appeal in the Vatican daily newspaper *Osservatore Romano*. On 11 May the newspaper published, without any explanations, Giuseppe Garibaldi's appeal to the people of Europe: 'Do Not Leave Poland'.[65] This seemingly unexpected revival of Vatican interest in the hero of the Risorgimento, whose anti-clerical views were notorious, was in fact a uniquely expressed plea for help to Poland's friends in the West.

The message, however, evidently fell on stony ground and with no tangible result to be seen there now followed another spell of complex negotiations which involved Archbishop Dąbrowski and Cardinal Macharski virtually commuting between Warsaw and Rome in an added effort to help to smooth out the intricate problems, which had to be faced, because of the fact that the Pope would be arriving in Poland while it was still under martial law. Their discussions involved details concerning the number and venue of open-air masses, drives through towns, the nature of the meeting with State officials in the Belvedere Palace and the papal meeting with Lech Wałęsa.

On 16 May, Cardinal Glemp, Archbishop Gulbinowicz and the Bishop of Katowice, Herbert Bednorz arrived unexpectedly in Rome for further consultations with the Pope which were to last three days. Cardinal Macharski, Bishop Nossol of Opole and one of the bishops from Częstochowa were to join the party the following day. However, with rumours of an expected meeting of the Political Bureau of the PUWP to be held on 19 May and consistent speculations about the removal of Jaruzelski, without waiting any further the Polish Episcopate's Press Office in Warsaw and the Vatican Press Office unexpectedly released simultaneously at 1 p.m. on 17 May the official programme for the papal pilgrimage.

The programme, which included a detailed timetable and a full list of various religious functions and public appearances, differed from the two earlier plans. The visit to Piekary Śląskie was no longer in the itinerary and instead the image of the Madonna of Piekary would be brought to Katowice especially for the occasion. This was obviously the result of a compromise struck between the bishops and the regime, which vetoed a trip to that sanctuary as in 1979. Another compromise solution was reached on the Pontiff's visit to Lublin, which because of its proximity to the Soviet border was now dropped from the itinerary. It was now felt that the visit to Lublin and its undoubted influence on the still deeply religious part of the Ukraine would irritate the Russians, particularly as the Pope, who in the past had addressed himself to the problems of the oppressed Church in the Ukraine, would have to make some references to the other side of the border. In these circumstances it was decided that the Senate of the Catholic University of Lublin would travel to Warsaw and award the Pontiff the honorary doctorate there. Added to these plans was a visit to Nowa Huta (which the Pope was prevented from visiting in 1979), where he would consecrate a newly built church in the town's suburb of Mistrzejowice.[66] According to this programme the Pope was to reside for one night in Warsaw, three nights at Jasna Góra and the remaining two nights in his old residence at Franciszkanska Street in Kraków. Most importantly, however, an eighth day, 23 June, was added to the programme. Under these arrangements the official visit would be concluded around 8 p.m. on 22 June and the remainder of the Pope's stay in Poland would be considered as time for his private activities. The Pontiff expressed a desire to go to his favourite place of retreat, the Kalatówka house, in the Chochołowska Valley in the Tatra Mountains. The regime promised to facilitate this on 23 June. The official timetable provided only for the formal farewell ceremony on that day at 4.30 p.m.

However, even now two outstanding problems still remained unsolved. The nature of the meeting in the Belvedere Palace, where at that stage no public speeches were planned, and the meeting with Lech Wałęsa. The Vatican let it be known that prior arrangements had been made within the Polish Government that the Pope could under no circumstances be prevented from meeting with whomever he wished. At the same time it was felt that the regime might try to restrict Wałęsa's movements instead. After all various spokesmen for the Government had made it perfectly clear that 'Wałęsa was a former leader of the former Solidarity'. On the other hand it was inconceivable that the Pope who entertained Wałęsa in January 1981, communicated with him during his internment and made a number of representations for his release, would not meet one of the most devoted sons of the Catholic Church.

The Vatican suggested a bargain. The Pope would meet Jaruzelski in the Belvedere Palace, deliver a speech and exchange gifts, at the price of being allowed to see Wałęsa as well. But that was not enough. The General now asked for an additional meeting at the beginning of the Pope's private day. After all, Gierek in 1979 met John Paul II only once during the official ceremonies in the Belvedere Palace. Jaruzelski, mindful of this comparison asked for what in effect was a more overt sign of legitimization. After hesitation the Vatican agreed.

On 30 May the Vatican's Undersecretary of State, Archbishop Achiles Silvestrini (commonly regarded as a trouble shooter who negotiated the intricate arrangements with the Nicaraguan regime during the papal visit to Central America in March 1983), unexpectedly arrived in Warsaw at the invitation of the Polish Foreign Minister, Stefan Olszowski. During the official part of the visit, lasting three days, he not only met Olszowski who even gave an official dinner in his honour, but also Jaruzelski, the Chairman of the Council of State, Henryk Jabłoński, and the Minister for Religious Affairs, Adam Łopatka. Silvestrini who brought the texts of three papal 'official' speeches (one to be given on arrival, the second in the Belvedere Palace, and the third during the departure ceremonies), and the agenda for the first meeting with Jaruzelski on 17 June, which included the lifting of martial law, amnesty and the Polish Recovery Programme. He also discussed the details of the second meeting as well as arrangements for the 'papal rest day' on 23 June.

In the meantime, however, Wałęsa was refused holiday leave from the Lenin Shipyard in Gdańsk for the duration of the papal visit. The Pope, dismayed and annoyed, but determined to meet Wałęsa, now called Archbishop Dąbrowski to Rome for further consultations, where he arrived on 11 May, only five days before the papal pilgrimage to Poland was to begin.

There is little doubt that the Pope's second pilgrimage to Poland was the most carefully prepared of all his previous seventeen foreign visits. It was envisaged that the intricate and detailed arrangements would satisfy all concerned with the visit. For the Russians and Poland's Eastern European allies, although they were not particularly happy about the event, it offered a useful sign of 'normalization' in Poland and a help to their campaigns for peace and to keep the new American missiles out of Western Europe. For General Jaruzelski it offered a boost to his otherwise shattered prestige and reputation at home and abroad. He, like the entire Polish regime, was also counting on the visit improving their tattered international reputation, international isolation and leading to the lifting of Western economic sanctions. After all, John Paul II was only the second statesman (apart from the Libyan leader Colonel Qadhafi) to visit the country since December 1981. If the Polish Pope could bring himself to meet with Poland's leaders, the international community ought to do the same.

For Archbishop Glemp, it offered a much needed boost to his authority in the Polish Church, leading to a substantial improvement of his reputation among sections of the disenchanted faithful and radical clergy. To the nation, which was nursing deep grudges against a Communist regime that had crushed hopes of greater political freedom, and which was to exist in economic misery and mental anguish, it offered an injection of life, possibilities for the spontaneous expression of otherwise depressed feelings and a new beginning for the road ahead. Those who did not expect tangible results from the visit were badly informed and underestimated the Church's political pragmatism and potential. The Pope would not have decided to go to Poland if there was no prospect of securing reasonably quick results.

Perhaps the only unknown factor, which of course could not have been negotiated, was the reaction of the crowds. But to prevent any outburst of spontaneous opposition to the regime, huge numbers of militiamen were employed to make their presence felt at every papal event. This was in contrast to 1979 when the crowd control was left entirely to Church appointed stewards. Otherwise the authorities made ample health, sanitation, food provision, and transport facilities available to the millions of pilgrims who were to follow the Pope throughout the seven days, in what must have been one of the largest population movements in Polish history.

The underground leadership of Solidarity appealed to the union members not to demonstrate during the visit, but asked people to wear badges and display other signs of independence of thought, attitudes and actions, arguing that any disturbances would not only be insulting to the person of the Pope but would also preclude the Church's contacts with the authorities and make peaceful attempts to influence their policies impossible. Ultimately this would be in the interests neither of the Church nor of society.

John Paul's second visit to Poland was also potentially the most difficult and politically volatile of all his journeys. The Pontiff's advantage, and for that matter disadvantage, was his intimate knowledge of the country, its people, their culture, history and language, which could convey a multitude of nuances that only Poles could interpret in many different ways. Of course the Pope was aware of the stakes involved, the delicate balancing act he was to perform and that even a simple provocation could enrage the crowds and put the visit in jeopardy. However, he also knew that the anxious expectations of his people were also his own. That in essence was where the assured success of his second pilgrimage to Poland lay.

Notes

1. For complete text see: *Communist Affairs: Documents and Analysis*, vol. 1, no. 3 (July 1982), pp. 689-93.
2. The Polish constitution has no provision for the declaration of a state of emergency or martial law but only for *stan wojenny*, literally translated as 'state of war'. Art. 33 of the constitution stipulates: '1. A decision concerning the declaration of a state of war may be adopted only in the event of armed aggression having been committed against the Polish People's Republic, or if, in pursuance of international agreements, the necessity of common defence against aggression should arise. Such a decision is voted by the Sejm or, if the Sejm is not in session, by the Council of State; 2. The Council of State may, should considerations of the defence or security of the State so require, proclaim martial law in parts or in the entire territory of the Polish People's Republic. For similar reasons the Council of State may proclaim partial or general mobilization.'
3. For text of the proclamation by the Council of State of the Polish People's Republic giving details of all the restrictions applied for the duration of martial law see: *Communist Affairs: Documents and Analysis*, vol. 1, no. 3 (July 1982), pp. 694-6.
4. General Leon Dubicki, former close associate of Jaruzelski, claimed in an interview with *Der Spiegel*, no. 5 (28 December 1981) that the takeover was planned as far back as December 1980. The most decisive proof that the coup was planned at least several months ahead has actually appeared in

print, though its significance was certainly overlooked at the time. It is a short note which appeared in the bulletin of Solidarity's press agency *AS*, No. 44 dated 26 September–12 October 1981. On p. 25, among some other items within the regular column 'Against Solidarity', it reads: 'On 30 September 1981, at a meeting with members of branch trade unions in Krosno, A[lbin] Siwak [member of the Political Bureau of the PUWP] informed those present that a six-man Committee of National Salvation had been formed, with Generals Jaruzelski and Kiszczak (deputy member of the Political Bureau of the PUWP and Minister for Internal Affairs) at the head. Also that special units of the army and militia have been assigned the task of suppressing popular resistance. The leadership of the Party and Government would wait another two months before using these forces, until popular support for Solidarity had weakened. A decision to rescind the registration of Solidarity is to be expected.

5. The 'crisis' team, whose membership has never been made public, consisted in addition to Professor Stomma of at least seven other veteran lay Catholic politicians; Professor Wiesław Chrzanowski, Władysław Siła-Nowicki and Jan Olszewski, three prominent lawyers who also served as plenipotentiaries of Solidarity; Jerzy Turowicz, editor of the Catholic weekly *Tygodnik Powszechny* and secretary of the Kraków Catholic Intelligentsia Club; Andrzej Wielowieyski, leading Solidarity expert and director of its Social Research Institute; Andrzej Micewski, editor of Rural Solidarity's weekly *Solidarność Rolników*; Professor Andrzej Święcicki of the Academy of Catholic Theology in Warsaw.

6. As yet no comprehensive list of strike actions during the first few days after the imposition of martial law has been compiled. Independent sources however, reported resistance in the Lenin Shipyard in Gdańsk, Lenin Steelworks in Nowa Huta, Polish Academy of Sciences, Katowice Steelworks, URSUS tractor factory in Warsaw, Żerań car-plant in Warsaw, Poznań, Wrocław, Białogard, Swidnik, and the Institute for Nuclear Research in Świerk. In addition the Polish radio and television between 14 and 17 December reported summary court proceedings for 'illegal trade-union activities' (strikes) in Elbląg, Koszalin, Radom, Dąbrowa Górnicza, Będzin, Jaworzno, Głogów, Częstochowa, Przemyśl, Tarnowskie Góry, Gorzów Wielkopolski, Bydgoszcz, Lubin, Racibórz and Lubliniec. By all accounts these reports were also only selective. Officially the regime admitted that 199 strikes took place. An interesting insight into the feelings expressed by the striking workers is provided by the Appeal from the Szczecin Shipyard Strike Committee. For its complete text see: *Communist Affairs: Documents and Analysis*, vol. 1, no. 3 (July 1982), p. 697.

7. For an eyewitness account see: *Communist Affairs: Documents and Analysis*, vol. 1, no. 3 (July 1982), pp. 713–14.

8. For complete text see: *Communist Affairs: Documents and Analysis*, vol. 1, no. 3 (July 1982), pp. 704–5.

9. The copy of the letter sent to Wałęsa at his private address in Gdańsk was accompanied by a short note: 'I want to assure you that in this very difficult moment with all my heart I am with you and your family and all those who suffer!'

10. Archbishop Poggi's five-day fact finding mission to Poland proved to be quite frustrating. Although he held a series of talks with the Polish Primate

and other Church officials he was unable to travel outside Warsaw and contrary to press reports at that time he did not visit any of the internment camps. In fact the only first hand account of the situation inside an internment camp was given to him by two priests when he was already on the train bound back for Vienna. The priests described to him in French the condition in the Białołęka camp which they had recently visited. Their meeting with Monsignor Poggi lasted only twenty minutes. He was, however, received on 24 December for an hour and a half by General Jaruzelski, when he handed the Pope's letter to the Polish leader, who promised to 'study with attention the opinions contained in the letter'. Archbishop Poggi returned to Rome on 27 December while Monsignor Bolonek remained in Poland for another two weeks. Jaruzelski's reply to the Pope's letter was delivered on 12 January 1982 by Kazimierz Szablewski, Resident Minister Plenipotentiary in charge of working relations with the Vatican, during his private meeting with the Pontiff.

11. For complete text see: *Communist Affairs: Documents and Analysis*, vol. 1, no. 3 (July 1982), pp. 718-19.
12. The requirement to sign the loyalty pledge was introduced through a circular letter issued on 17 December by General Michal Janiszewski in his capacity as both head of Jaruzelski's civilian Government office and a member of the Military Council for National Salvation. For the complete text of the circular see: *Communist Affairs: Documents and Analysis*, vol. 1, no. 4, (October 1982), pp. 808-9. Apparently there were numerous versions of the loyalty pledges. The translation of one of these, which is reproduced below, is taken from *Communist Affairs: Documents and Analysis*, vol. 1, no. 4 (October 1982), pp. 809-10: 'I hereby declare that I have today acquainted myself with the statement of the Chief of the Ministerial Council's Office dated 17 December 1981 and I fully confirm the knowledge of the fact that I bear the duty to behave according to the principles of the people's rule of law. Guided by public interest and the principles of the building of socialism I undertake at the same time to defend by all my actions the authority of the People's authorities, strictly carrying out the instructions of my superiors at work, always having regard to the socialist development of the Polish People's Republic and keeping faith with the People's State. Taking account of the fact that many organs of NSZZ Solidarność leadership have in recent months openly stood up against the constitutional organs of power and administration, working with a counter revolutionary aim for the overthrow of the socialist system, I declare that I resign from this union.'
13. For complete text see: *Communist Affairs: Documents and Analysis*, vol. 1, no. 4 (October 1982), pp. 810-13.
14. For example in his Angelus address on 1 January, the Pope put the full weight of his personal authority behind Solidarity. In a clear sign that the reinstatement of the union and the release of its leaders formed a basic demand of the Church's mediation effort in Poland, he said: 'The word solidarity speaks of the great effort which working people in my homeland have made in order to ensure the genuine dignity of working people. Working people have the right to create independent unions whose task is to guard their social, family and individual matters. . . Solidarity belongs to the modern heritage of working people in my homeland and I would go so far as to say in other nations too. . .'

TRIBULATIONS UNDER MARTIAL LAW: 1981-1983

15. This also became apparent during the meeting of the Joint Church-Government Commission, held on 18 January 1982. Perhaps the only positive result of the Glemp-Jaruzelski meeting was an agreement on the resumption of broadcasting of Sunday Mass. However, in order to get this approved by the authorities the Church had to agree to censorship of the sermons delivered during the broadcast. The regular transmission of Sunday Mass resumed on 17 January 1982.
16. On 7 January 1982 the Polish Government formally announced that 5,906 individuals had been interned. Subsequently the same spokesman said that by 9 January 1982, 1,433 people had been arrested. Later, the Minister for Internal Affairs and member of the Military Council for National Salvation, General Czesław Kiszczak revealed that by 26 February 1982, 6,647 persons had been placed in internment camps. On 8 December 1982, the Deputy Minister for Internal Affairs, Bogusław Stachura informed the Sejm that till that date 10,131 persons 'had been through internment camps'.

A 'Note Concerning Repressions in the Lower Silesia Region' issued by the Archbishop's Charity Committee in Wrocław on 29 September 1982, gives the number of internees from the archdiocese of Wrocław as 'more than 2,000'. It also gives a list and description of the following camps where internees from the archdiocese were held: Wrocław, Nysa, Grodków, Gołdap, Kamienna Góra (during the Second World War a branch of the Gross Rosen concentration camp), Głogów, Darłówek, Nowy Łupków, Załąże, Uherce and Strzelin. For a map showing internment camps see: *Communist Affairs: Documents and Analysis*, vol. 1, no. 3 (July 1982), pp. 625.

The most comprehensive data concerning repressions between 13 December 1981 and 31 December 1983 is included in a mimeographed memorandum entitled *Prawa człowieka i obywatela w PRL w okresie stanu wojennego (13 XII 1981-31 XII 1983)* (Human and Civil Rights in the Polish People's Republic during the State of War (13 XII 1981-31 XII 1983) compiled by the Polish Helsinki Committee and submitted by the Interim Co-ordinating Commission of Solidarity to the Conference for Security and Co-operation in Europe in February 1983. The memorandum gives the following breakdown of arrests: 13 December 1981-15 February 1981, 964 persons; 16 February 1982-22 October 1982, 1,396 persons; 23 October 1982-8 December 1982, 1,256 persons; 9 December 1982-31 December 1982, approx. 50 persons. According to the memorandum, during the same period courts had issued more than 30,000 prison sentences 'related to charges of a political nature'. More than 60,000 persons had been fined for 'participating in various forms of protests'. In addition the memorandum listed numerous other forms of repression for political activities: twenty-eight deaths, dismissals from work, expulsion of students from colleges and universities, and others.
17. The Independent Student's Union, which was officially registered on 17 February 1981, was disbanded by the military regime on 5 January 1982. This was the first legally registered union to be dismantled under martial law, other unions merely being suspended.
18. For the text of another of Cardinal Macharski's powerful sermons, 'The Candlemass Sermon', see: *Communist Affairs: Documents and Analysis*, vol. 1, no. 4 (October 1982), pp. 815-18.
19. Thus for example the Archbishop's Charity Committee in Wrocław has

existed since the first week of martial law. In its 'Note Concerning Repressions in the Lower Silesia Region' the Committee list the following sections: for communications with parishioners, help for the internees, help for the sentenced, for immediate 'on the spot' help, medical aid, medical requirements, financial aid, legal aid and aid during court proceedings.
20. *Trybuna Ludu*, 16 February 1982.
21. For complete text see: *Communist Affairs: Documents and Analysis*, vol. 1, no. 4 (October 1982), pp. 818–20.
22. It should be remembered that a similar list of Solidarity leaders and members of the former Committee for the Defence of Workers (KOR) was drawn up in advance of the proclamation of martial law. When on 16 December 1981 the military authorities announced a list of fifty-seven internees it contained three names (Seweryn Blumsztajn, Mirosław Chojecki and Wojciech Karpiński) of persons who had been abroad for some considerable time prior to the martial law declaration. This suggests that the list was prepared well in advance.
23. The Primate's Social Council was formed by Archbishop Glemp in November 1981. Its membership consists of twenty-eight prominent Catholics representing varied disciplines and professions. Some of the members were invited personally by Glemp while others were suggested by diocesan bishops. The first meeting of the Council was held on 12 December 1981 and some of its members were interned on the way home from that meeting. The Council membership is as follows: Professor Stanislaw Stomma, Chairman; Dr Julian Aulaytner (Warsaw), sociologist, employee of the Ministry of Labour, Wages and Social Affairs; Dr Olgierd Baehr (Poznań), lawyer, Chairman of the Poznań Club of Catholic Intelligentsia; Bogdan Bońkowski (Olsztyn); Rev Dr Bronisław Dembowski (Warsaw), parish priest of St. Martin's church; Grażyna Dziedkiewicz (Sosnowiec), barrister, Chairwoman of the Katowice Club of Catholic Intelligentsia; Joanna Fabisiak (Warsaw); Przemysław Fenrych (Szczecin), historian, Chairman of the Szczecin Club of Catholic Intelligentsia; Professor Jerzy Kanik (Kraków), professor of physics at the Jagiellonian University; Maria Kokot (Opole); Dr Jerzy Krzewicki (Kielce), surgeon; Professor Józef Łukaszewicz (Wrocław), professor of mathematics at Wrocław University, former Chancellor of the university; Rev. Józef Majka (Wrocław), Dean of the seminary, Andrzej Micewski (Warsaw), writer and editor of Rural Solidarity's weekly *Solidarność Rolników*; Jerzy Pietrzak (Ostrów Wielkopolski), historian, teacher at a secondary school; Bogusław Piskorski (Szczecin), engineer; Professor Aurelia Polańska (Gydnia), professor of economics; Jan Rejcza (Radom), engineer; Professor Stefan Sawicki (Lublin), professor of Polish literature at the Catholic University of Lublin and its Deputy Vice-Chancellor; Professor Krzysztof Skubiszewski (Poznań), professor of international law at Poznań University; Andrzej Smułkowski (Gydnia), Solidarity activist; Dr Bolesław Suszka (Kórnik), curator at the local museum; Leonard Szymański (Poznań), Solidarity activist; Professor Andrzej Święcicki (Warsaw), professor of sociology at the Academy of Catholic Theology in Warsaw, Chairman of the Warsaw Club of Catholic Intelligentsia; Jerzy Turowicz (Kraków), editor of the Catholic weekly *Tygodnik Powszechny*; Andrzej Tyc (Toruń), engineer, Chairman of the Toruń Club of Catholic Intelligentsia; Dr Andrzej Wielowieyski (Warsaw), leading Solidarity expert and director of its Social Research Institute,

secretary of the Warsaw Club of Catholic Intelligentsia; Professor Czesław Zgorzelski (Lublin), professor of Polish literature at the Catholic University of Lublin. Besides its full members, the Council also involves a number of specialists from various fields who aid its work with their expert advice. Similar advisory bodies also operate at diocesan level.

24. The release of the 'Theses' was accompanied by the Primate's letter addresseed to all Polish bishops which in effect was his commentary on the proposals. In it he emphasized that the document prepared by lay Catholics was the expression of 'their concern about the fate of our homeland and their own reflections concerning the ways in which normal functioning and development may be restored to our State community. This document deserves the deepest reflection, all the more so since in its import it departs from the proposals of renewal or reform worked out by persons or institutions elsewhere'. The Primate's letter stressed in four parts some of the reasons why the Church in Poland addressed itself to subjects vital in the public life of the country.

The first part, under the heading 'The historical reason of the Church's presence in the nation', emphasized that 'The Church in Poland was with the nation in the days of its glory and its pain. Today it is and wishes to remain with the nation at the time when it is torn apart, uncertain and searching for a solution'. In the second part 'The basis of service', the Primate stressed that the Church considered its pronouncements on public affairs as a service in the name of truth and love. Objective truth required humility and should correspond to the dictates of one's conscience. Humility allowed for the possibility of errors, while service in the name of love required courage. Passivity would be more comfortable. The third, headed 'The service of the hierarchy and lay Catholics' expanded the Primate's view on the Church's role in society. Its standing within the nation did not depend upon its current political influence, even if this was an assumption made by people not familiar with the Church. At the same time, lay Catholics had not only the right but also the duty to participate in social and political life. Unfortunately there were not enough Catholics prepared for responsible public activity, since in the past there had been too few opportunities for them to gain experience by participating in public life. Those groups of lay Catholics which had been formally recognized by the authorities had been frequently invigilated, manipulated and used. Consequently, they could not always be considered to be instrumental in shaping Catholic attitudes. In the fourth point, entitled 'The meaning of social accord' the Primate stated that such an accord should be regarded not just as a single act but as a process, consisting of a multitude of activities aimed at a formal act of accord. Firstly, however, the necessary social climate had to be created. This climate was, above all, a minimum of trust in other human beings and social groups, in the mass media and, finally in the authorities. So far the authorities' attempts to gain credibility had been unsuccessful, not only because of the existence of certain moods or prejudices within the society, but primarily because of the detrimental activities of lesser officials, and of decisions of the authorities which society failed to understand. A national discussion on the country's basic problems would, more than anything else, influence the process whereby this climate was created. The discussion could not at its conception contain the final thesis, for the start of this discussion should aim at achieving a compromise. 'In the final instance',the Primate continued, 'we wish for such a Poland, which as a mother for all Poles, would be organized in a State which is lawful, just, democratic, tolerant, respectful of the past and its culture, but also open to the future and to friendship with other nations, especially immediate neighbours.' The letter ended with a reminder to lay Catholics, and especially non-believers, of an old Latin maxim, *Primum vivere, deinde philosophari* (survive first, philosophize after, or in other words: first existence and later the creation of superstructure and disputes about details).

25. This fact was subsequently revealed by the Minister of Internal Affairs, General Czesław Kiszczak in his speech to the Sejm on 16 September 1982. According to him the initiative to make contact was taken by the Ministry of Internal Affairs which 'made use of the mediation of people of goodwill, including representatives of the Church and lay Catholic activists'. The Ministry, he said gave the fugitive leaders a guarantee of safe conduct to and from the meeting place, no matter what the outcome. 'But the only answer to our proposal was silence or public pronouncements . . . and their final reaction was the organization of more riots..

26. Radio Free Europe Research, Munich, Background Report 114, 11 May 1982, p. 8.

27. See: *The Church, Solidarity and the 'State of War'*, Keston College News Service, no. 154, pp. 9-10.

28. For complete text see: *Communist Affairs: Documents and Analysis*, vol. 2, no. 1 (January 1983), pp. 105-6.

29. For selection of articles see: *Uncensored Poland News Bulletin*, no. 14/82, London (30 July 1982), pp. 13-17.

30. The one day visit to Geneva was initially scheduled for June 1981 when John Paul II wanted to present to the sixty-seventh session of the International Labour Organisation (ILO) his encyclical *Laborem Exercens*. The visit, however, had to be postponed because the Pope was still convalescing from the assassination attempt on his life. In June 1982 in addition to attending the inaugural session of the ILO the Pontiff also visited the headquarters of the International Committee of the Red Cross (ICRC) and the headquarters of the European Organization for Nuclear Research (CERN).

31. Emphasis as in the original text provided by the Bureau de Presse et d'Information pour la visite du Pape Jean Paul II à Genève.

32. At present 80 per cent of the agricultural land in Poland is used by private farmers, 18.5 per cent by the State and 1.5 per cent by co-operative farms.

33. Quoted after *Uncensored Poland News Bulletin*, no. 14/82, p. 12.

34. Solidarity's Provisional Co-ordinating Committee's appeal was to refrain from strikes and street demonstrations until the end of July 1982 in order to give the Government the opportunity to lift martial law. For the text of the appeal see: *Uncensored Poland News Bulletin*, no. 13/82, pp. 3-4.

35. The possibility of the second papal visit to Poland was first mentioned by Cardinal Wyszyński during the farewell ceremony, concluding his visit, at Kraków airport on 10 June 1979. Later Bishop Bronisław Dąbrowski, the Secretary of the Polish Episcopal Conference confirmed that the Pope had accepted, Cardinal Wyszyński's invitation to visit Poland for the 600th anniversary of the arrival of the icon of Black Madonna at the monastery of Jasna Góra in Częstochowa.

TRIBULATIONS UNDER MARTIAL LAW: 1981–1983

On 23 October 1980 Jerzy Kuberski, the then Minister for Religious Affairs (subsequently moved to the Polish Embassy in Rome as a Minister Plenipotentiary for permanent contacts between the Polish Government and the Holy See), told Western journalists that Pope John Paul II was to visit Poland again in 1982. Although no exact date was mentioned, it was suggested that it was most probable that the Pope would like to attend the celebrations of the 600th anniversary of the Black Madonna icon at the shrine of Jasna Góra. It was suggested that the visit should take place in May or August 1982, but could be moved to any Marian feast.

In September 1981, when the First Congress of Solidarity sent a cable to the Pope, they stressed their deep desire for his presence at the celebrations in August 1982. In November 1981 the Polish Episcopate officially invited the Pope to visit Poland, and he accepted the invitation. Speaking to a delegation of priests from Częstochowa diocese, he told them that he would join them at the national celebration scheduled for 26 August 1982.

The imposition of martial law on 13 December 1981, cast serious doubts on the feasibility of a trip to a country under martial law. However, to abandon plans for the visit would have amounted to tacit acknowledgement of the irreversibility of the situation. The visit was not discussed during the January 1982 meeting of the Joint Episcopal–Government Commission which was meeting for the first time since martial law was declared. At the same time various pronouncements made by individual bishops and the Episcopal Conference emphasized that the Church expected the visit to take place as planned. The Episcopate and the Pope decided to proceed with preparations for the visit, emphasizing on a number of occasions the necessity for a major alteration in the current situation in Poland, to include the release of all internees and prisoners arrested under martial law, as well as a revival of the suspended Solidarity union, as a pre-condition for the visit.

36. It is perhaps worth noting that in 1981 the Vatican expected that its relations with the Polish Government would improve to the extent that full diplomatic relations would be established by 1982. The 1982 edition of the Vatican's official handbook *Annuario Pontificio* lists Poggi's address as a nuncio in Warsaw: Aleja I Armii Wojska Polskiego 12 (an address of the pre-war nunciature building which has remained partially empty).

37. Soviet journalist Grigulevich, in an interview for the periodical *Journalist* quoted the Czechoslovak Party daily newspaper *Rude Pravo* as saying that the Church in Poland found itself on the side of counter-revolutionaries and extremists. Grigulevich also questioned the role of the Church as a factor in attempting to achieve a genuine social contract. It was impermissible, he said, that priests should intervene in disputes between State and trade unions. Also on 22 June 1982 the Soviet periodical *Literaturnaya Gazeta* joined the criticism, accusing some churchmen of trying to assume the role of the suspended Solidarity union. The paper said that churches served as rallying points during the demonstrations in Wrocław and Gdańsk, after priests had preached against martial law. Another instance of Soviet displeasure with the papal visit and the Church in Poland was the attention devoted by the Soviet mass media, including TASS, to an article by the Slovak Party daily *Pravda* published on 11 July 1982. The newspaper, after restating the official Polish position that the Pope's visit was possible only when calm had been re-established in the country, observed that: 'Unrest

TRIBULATIONS UNDER MARTIAL LAW: 1981-1983

in many Polish towns began immediately after Church services . . . the services themselves were being directed against the people's power . . . Churches are a place where anti-socialist forces meet openly and find support from the pulpit in the form of instigatory sermons. In this way the Church is embarking on the path of practical political activity . . . Certain Church dignitaries want to take over from the discredited Solidarity and replace the 'independent trade unions' in influencing public opinion. . . A political organization in opposition to the socialist system. . . . It was the Catholic Church that, after August 1980, together with KOR, the Confederation for an Independent Poland and other anti-socialist forces, was present at the birth of Solidarity and then joined it in creating what amounted to a coalition against the Polish Party and socialism in Poland. . . . The Church acts against martial law regulations, defends the interned leaders of Solidarity and other anti-socialist elements. . . The Polish Church leadership, headed by the Pope in Rome, wants to turn the developments in the country back to the period before 13 December 1981. It is reckoned that the visit of John Paul II to Poland could serve this end.

38. On 24 June the Vatican daily *Osservatore Romano* took the almost unprecedented step of publishing in the English original the exchange between Reagan and the Pope during the official audience. Furthermore the Vatican Press Office issued a statement denying that in the public speeches and the talk between the Pope and the President 'the subject of the Holy Father's planned pastoral journey to Poland was never mentioned'.

39. A somewhat different message on this subject emerged from a Pastoral Letter of the Polish Episcopate issued on 3 August and read in churches throughout Poland on 8 August, where the bishops stated: 'We have been reiterating our expectation of the Holy Father's arrival on 26 August 1982 considering that implementation of the Pastoral visit at that date was possible. However, the view of the State authorities was different. These authorities have not given their consent for the arrival of the Pope this year. On the other hand they have expressed their readiness to receive him next year'.

40. Jan Szczepański, 'Alternatywy' (The Alternatives), in *Odra*, January-August, 1982, pp. 6-9.

41. The release from internment was, however, somewhat academic in the circumstances. It is worth recalling that on 1 May 1982 the regime freed 1,000 internees, only to haul an even larger number back into detention after street riots in Warsaw a few days later. Many of those released from internment in July were charged with anti-State activities and simply transferred to prisons. On 12 August the Polish Press Agency PAP reported that a number of people released from internment during the previous months had been re-interned because those concerned had resumed activities described as incompatible with State security.

42. For text see: *Communist Affairs: Documents and Analysis*, vol. 2, no. 2 (April 1983), pp. 252-4.

43. On the same day the Pope said Mass for Poland in his private chapel at Castel Gandolfo which was beamed to Poland by Vatican radio's most powerful transmitter, normally used for broadcasting to the Far East. During the service the Pontiff said that as a Pole and a patriot he considered it to be his duty to go to Poland.

44. For example, on the question of the reinstatement of Solidarity the regime appears to have been contemplating three possible alternatives advanced by various groups in the leadership. First suggestions involved the revival of the trade union but under new statutes which would have allowed stricter Party control over its activities. This clearly would not have been acceptable to Solidarity's leadership which always stressed its independence from State authorities but not opposition to them. If such a union were to come into existence it would have resembled the old trade union which Solidarity rebelled against. The second suggestion was the creation of two parallel trade-union structures. One under the direct control of the PUWP, the other under the auspices of the Church as a Christian Democratic Union. This would not have been acceptable to the Church which never wanted to become an instrument in the hands of either social groups or the State. The third suggestion was the dissolution of Solidarity altogether, regardless of the internal and external consequences.
45. Because the balance of brute force was so obviously in favour of the regime, Solidarity leaders suggested in the summer of 1982, that union members should ignore the regime and construct their own alternative society. The real Poland, they argued, should simply go underground. It should run its own information network and alternative education system, organize support for the victims of martial law and set up workshops and co-operatives. Protest actions in the form of demonstrations, leaflet campaigns etc., should continue, but there should not be a direct assault against the regime. For details see: 'Underground Society. Draft Manifesto of the Interim Co-ordinating Committee of the NSZZ Solidarność, 28 July 1982', in *Communist Affairs: Documents and Analysis*, vol. 2, no. 2 (April 1982), pp. 250-1.
46. A considerable degree of apprehension surrounding the anniversary was evident in Government circles. In what must have been deliberately exaggerated warnings General Kiszczak claimed on 25 August that his men had discovered steel rods, sticks, petrol bombs, sharpened rods and other dangerous tools prepared for that occasion. On 26 August Kazimierz Barcikowski warned of the possibility of an armed uprising: 'The calls for demonstrations on 31 August and the demonstrations themselves are to be a stage in the preparation for a general strike which in turn will be a stage in preparation for an armed uprising, if this should be required, for the overthrow of the political order of the Polish People's Republic'.
47. Information given to the Polish Parliament by the Minister of Internal Affairs, General Czesław Kiszczak.
48. According to Solidarity sources, altogether seven people were killed or died as a result of their injuries. Three in the mining town of Lubin, one person in Wrocław, Gdańsk, Nowa Huta and Toruń, respectively. The demonstrations in Lubin appeared to have been contained with particular brutality. For revealing account see: *Newsweek*, 11 October 1982.
49. On 3 September 1982 the Government press spokesman, Jerzy Urban, announced the authorities' rejection of any possibility of negotiations with Solidarity's leadership about conditions under which the trade union could resume its activities publicly.
50. Jan Józef Lipski, who was in London for medical treatment at that time, had subsequently returned to Poland to face the charges. See his 'Why I

return to Poland' in *Uncensored Poland News Bulletin*, no. 18/82, pp. 9-11. See also in the same issue of the Bulletin (pp. 11-12), a Communiqué of Solidarity's Co-ordinating Office Abroad.
51. For extensive excerpts see: *Communist Affairs: Documents and Analysis*, vol. 2, no. 2 (April 1983), pp. 254-8.
52. The relevant passage in the communiqué reads as follows: 'The bishops repeatedly appealed to all sides involved in the current social conflict for accord, agreement, for resuming the dialogue interrupted by martial law. So far no proper steps have been taken despite the fact that the overwhelming majority of the public expects agreements and accord and the working people wish to have their own independent representative bodies: trade unions, including the Independent Self-governing Trade Union Solidarity and the Independent Self-governing Trade Union Solidarity of Private Farmers. Young people at higher educational establishments also expect to have a proper organization of their own.'
53. An official State delegation consisting of Jerzy Ozdowski (Deputy Speaker of the Sejm), Zenon Komender (Deputy Prime Minister and Chairman of the PAX Association), Kazimierz Morawski (member of the Council of State and Chairman of the Christian Social Association), Adam Łopatka (Head of the Office for Religious Affairs), and Jerzy Kuberski (Minister at the Polish Embassy in Rome responsible for permanent working contacts between the Polish Government and the Holy See) participated in the ceremonies. The ceremonies were also broadcast (but not live) by the Polish radio and television.
54. The occasion was also used as the *ad limina apostolorum* ('return to the roots') bishops' visit to the Pope, which normally takes place every five years, and during which they submit official reports on the state of their dioceses. The only bishop who was prevented from making the trip was Ignacy Tokarczuk to whom the authorities refused a passport.
55. The following members of the Sejm voted against the outlawing of Solidarity: Rudolf Buchała, Janusz Zabłocki, and Zbigniew Zieliński (representing the Polish Catholic Social Union), Maria Budzanowska, Jan Jankowski, Halina Mankisiewicz-Latecka, Dorota Simonides and Hanna Suchocka (representing the Democratic Party); Edmund Osmańczyk, Anna Pławska, Ryszard Reiff and Professor Jan Szczepański (non-Party members). Abstentions were recorded from the following: Jannina Banasik, Władysław Kupiec, Genowefa Rejman and Szymon Bala (representing the United Peasant Party); Jadwiga Giżycka-Koporowska, Zbigniew Kledecki and Szczepan Styranowski (representing the Democratic Party); Halina Koźniewska, Witold Zakrzewski and Ryszard Bohr (non-Party members).
56. See 'Act Respecting Trade Unions Adopted by the Sejm of the Polish Peoples' Republic on 8 October 1982' in *Communist Affairs: Documents and Analysis*, vol. 2, no. 3 (July 1983), pp. 363-71.
57. In preparation for the new trade-union scheme some 60,000 loyal activists were trained in the Soviet Union and in Czechoslovakia. How relatively unsuccessful the scheme was is best illustrated by the official statistics according to which by the end of April 1983 13,642 applications for registration were received by provincial courts. Of these 12,176 (86 per cent) were considered by them and 12,065 factory based trade unions were registered. On 22 June 1983 the Polish radio reported that 37 per cent of

the working population belonged to the new trade unions. In comparison in 1977 95 per cent of the working population belonged to the Government sponsored Central Council of Trade Unions.

58. A particularly interesting example of this, as well as of the continuing work and impact of the Primate's Social Council, is a ten-page document presented in April 1983 to the Sejm's Committee working on a new Local Government Bill. The document entitled 'Proposals to Reconstitute Local Government in Poland', points to the inefficiency of the present local government system and to the fact that until now conflicts of interest between local communities and local People's Councils could not have been prevented. This is seen as a result of contradictions inherent in present regulations in force since 1950, under which local councils are given the dual role of implementing orders for the central authorities while representing local interests and performing functions of self-governing bodies at the same time. In the course of time, the document underlines, local councils have ceased to fulfil the latter role but have become a blind instrument in the hands of the State authorities. In practice, the denial of any divergence of interests between local and central government, has led to the situation in which, in the extreme cases, those who have defended local interests have been denounced as enemies of the State. In effect, there has been no initiative at the local level and all local needs were expected to be satisfied by the State. In addition, the fact that local councillors have been appointed and not elected has resulted in a lack of social control over the work of local authorities and has facilitated a rise of networks involved in frequently illegal exchanges of goods and services. The document cites specific examples of the harmful results of the present system in such areas as housing and social services, and expresses the opinion that the process of urbanization of the whole country has been negatively affected. Under the heading 'Proposals' the document puts forward a number of suggestions with regard to reintroduction of local self-government. Independent representation of local interests is seen as a necessary condition for the success of economic reforms and for national accord. Local government, the document states, cannot perform the dual role prescribed for it until now, i.e. councils cannot serve as the direct extension of the State administration. Local authorities, the document underlines, must have their own executive organs, their own sources of income and the rights to manage their own property. In certain instances local government should be subject to control and intervention by the central authorities, but such instances should be clearly defined in the Bill and cannot restrict or replace local initiative. The document concludes that the package of new legal regulations prepared by the Sejm should aim at bringing far-reaching changes in the present local government system. With reference to the Electoral reform Bill which is under consideration, the document states that elections to local councils must be based on personal abilities and qualifications, which in turn means that non-Party members and representatives of Catholic organizations should have the right to contest local seats. Only if such conditions are met, the authors say, can the population regain a sense of participation in the running of their local affairs.

59. For the text of the Order of Militarization of Gdańsk Shipyard see: *Communist Affairs: Documents and Analysis*, vol. 2, no. 3 (July 1983), p. 262.

60. These remarks, during a public audience on 11 October attended by a Polish Government delegation, were even more explicit when he said: 'When I was passing through the hall, I heard and saw many tears. Things cannot be good if our fellow countrymen arrive here for the canonization of a compatriot with their eyes brimming with tears. These were not tears of joy... Along with them we have had words and shouts, and that is why I wish to reply to them. Through you present here, I wish to reply to those who are absent, above all those who find themselves in internment camps and prisons. I wish to answer those who suffer in the land of Poland in one way or another. I also wish, from this place here, to address my words to the authorities of the Polish People's Republic. I wish to ask them: "Let there be no more tears. Polish society, my nation, does not deserve the fate of tears of despair and resignation".'
61. The gap between some of the bishops and militant priests widened quite considerably after the delegalization of Solidarity and in the long run could lead to the emergence of an underground Church similar to that which exists in Czechoslovakia and also in a sense in Hungary. In an apparent attempt to bridge this gap Archbishop Glemp held, in the autumn of 1982, two meetings with the Warsaw diocese clergy, during which he went to considerable lengths to present the rationale for his decisions and dispel their misgivings. For details see: *Uncensored Poland News Bulletin*, no. 22/82, p. 19, and no. 1/83, pp. 22-5.
62. In fact a forced resignation from the Primacy of Poland was not without precedent in the turbulent history of the Polish Roman Catholic Church. In modern times two primates had to resign for political reasons. In 1863 Cardinal Mieczysław Ledóchowski was moved to Rome by Pius IX and in 1883 the Archbishop of Warsaw, Zygmunt Feliński, was forced to resign his post after twenty years of political exile. See: Norman Davies, *God's Playground. A History of Poland*, vol. 11, *1795 to the Present*, Oxford, Oxford University Press, 1981, pp. 127-220.
63. However, the release of Wałęsa was quite a complex story. Throughout his internment he had been visited on behalf of Archbishop Glemp at regular, about six weekly intervals, by Father Alojzy Orszulik. The last such visit took place on 7 October 1982. On that occasion Wałęsa appeared to be relaxed and calm and among other things he asked Orszulik that the Episcopate should no longer demand his release. He would stand firm until martial law was abolished in order to be released together with all internees. Afterwards he would try to go back to his old job in the Lenin Shipyard and failing this he would work as sacristian for his parish priest in Gdańsk. As for his further activity in the trade union he wanted first to ascertain the situation after his release. Wałęsa also told Father Orszulik that on a number of occasions he was urged by his guards to write to General Jaruzelski asking for release and was assured that should such a letter be sent he would be released immediately. He had always refused to write pointing out that since he had not asked Jaruzelski for his arrest he would therefore not ask him for release.

Father Orszulik promised Wałęsa another visit on 31 October and consequently on 27 October asked the Ministry of Internal Affairs for permission to visit Solidarity's leader. This permission was duly granted, but withdrawn two days later. On 8 November after the date for the papal visit was announced Wałęsa was persuaded to write a letter to Jaruzelski which said, 'It seems to me that the time has come to clarify some issues and to work for an agreement. Time was needed for many to understand what could be achieved, and to what extent, on either side. I propose a meeting and a serious discussion of the problems, and I am sure that with goodwill on both sides a solution can be found.' The letter was significantly signed 'Corporal Lech Wałęsa', as he did not want to sign it simply as a private person and at the same time did not want to provoke by signing it as Chairman of Solidarity's National Co-ordinating Commission. On 11 November the Primate was informed by a representative of the Ministry of Internal Affairs that Wałęsa would be released, at the same time bringing with him a tape purporting to be a recording of conversations between Wałęsa and his brother during their meeting on 30 September 1982. During this conversation Wałęsa was supposed to have discussed how the sum of $1 million which he had received from various awards in the West should be used, and suggested its distribution among the family. Moreover, in this conversation Wałęsa is said to have reproached the Pope, the Primate, the Polish Episcopate and Orszulik for having abandoned him and Solidarity. The security agent also explained that the tape was recorded by Wałęsa's brother without his knowledge in order that it could be used in family discussion as evidence of Wałęsa's thinking. The recording was supposed to have been found on Wałęsa's brother during a search.

This was an obvious attempt to destroy Wałęsa's personal credibility and his relationship with the Church. The tape was subsequently submitted through official governmental channels to the Pope who refused to hear it. At the same time the tape was passed on to the New York based National Broadcasting Company (NBC) with information that the recording had also been passed to the Pope and Archbishop Glemp.

Furthermore, attempts were also made to implicate Father Orszulik and the Vatican in this sordid afair deliberately set up by the Polish Secret Service. On 12 November he was called to the security agent's private apartment, shown a transcript of the tape and told that Wałęsa wanted to use him to deposit the money with Archbishop Paul Marcinkus, who of course by then was implicated in the Calvi affair. Needless to say the attempt at discrediting Wałęsa and the Church proved fruitless. The Primate and other senior Church officials simply refused to discuss the tape and Wałęsa categorically denied its authenticity. It was the credibility of the regime rather than its intended victims that tumbled even further.

64. The text of the invitation read as follows: 'Your Holiness, I still remember the day of 10 June 1979 when in the course of the ceremonial farewell in Kraków, the Primate of Poland Cardinal Stefan Wyszyński, invited Your Holiness to participate personally in the jubilee of the 600th anniversary of the image of the Mother of God at Częstochowa. Unfortunately, the prime mover of this pilgrimage did not live to see the year of the jubilee celebrations. On behalf of the supreme authorities of the Polish People's Republic, and in my own name, in agreement with the Polish Episcopate, I invite Your Holiness to visit your homeland once again, during the agreed period of 16-22 June 1983.

At the same time I express the conviction that both the announcement itself of the visit of Your Holiness this year and the further preparations for it, and in particular the course it takes and its results will prove beneficial to the good of the homeland, the socialist Polish State, the national agreement begun in Poland and the further normalization of relations between the State and the Church.

The Polish nation, mindful of the experience of history and of the threats to humanity, expects that the visit of Your Holiness will promote the efforts of the nations of Europe and the world to preserve peace, check the arms race and avert a nuclear catastrophe. Awaiting the meeting with Your Holiness in Warsaw with these hopes, I beg you to accept my expressions of deep respect.'

65. The appeal was in a form of a letter addressed to the People of Europe on behalf of Poland written by Giuseppe Garibaldi on 15 February 1863, a month after the beginning of the January 1863 uprising in Russian-occupied Poland. In it, Garibaldi appealed to the people of Europe for help in liberating Poland from Russian tyranny.
66. The church of St. Maximilian Kolbe is only the second church to be built in Nowa Huta's history. Its construction began in 1976 and was completed at Easter 1983. In 1983 some 280,000 people lived in the town.

5 A New Coalition?

Throughout his eight days in Poland the Pope preached the Christian doctrine of redemption and renewal while at the same time reminding his compatriots of what they had lost since 13 December 1981 and how it might be regained through dialogue and solidarity based on human work. His mission was one of peace, and in support of peaceful endeavours, not strife or conflict. At the same time his pronouncements were based on the acceptance of the internal and external realities of the Polish situation. He rekindled hope among his people for the eventual elimination of their misery and suffering without undermining the legitimacy of the regime or calling for the relegalization of Solidarity's structures.

On arrival, in an apparent reference to the parts of Poland excluded from the itinerary, the Pope said that he had come 'to the entire homeland and to all the Poles, from north to south and from east to west'.[1] He considered it a duty to be with his compatriots in 'this sublime and at the same time difficult historical moment' of the country, and in a clear expression of solidarity with those who were suffering he asked them to be particularly close to him: 'I ask this in the name of Christ's words: I was sick and you visited me, I was in prison and you came to me.' He elaborated this support later that evening during the memorial Mass for the late Cardinal Wyszyński, once a prisoner himself, saying: 'Together with all my compatriots—especially with those who are most acutely tasting the bitterness of disappointment, humiliation, suffering, of being deprived of their freedom, of being wronged, of having their dignity trampled upon, I stand beneath the Cross of Christ'. These two statements set the tone for his pilgrimage, to heal wounds and give hope, rather than condemn or seek revenge.

On the second day during a meeting with State officials in the Belvedere Palace he reminded all the dignitaries, including General Jaruzelski, as he did in 1979, that 'a prosperous and happy Poland is in the interest of peace and good co-operation among the peoples of Europe' and that this was demanded by 'a healthy European *raison d'état*'. The country's prosperity could be achieved through 'social renewal, the beginning of which is established by the social agreements concluded by representatives of State authorities with representatives of the working people'. He urged the return to these agreements 'so painstakingly worked out during the epoch-making days of August 1980' and emphasized that these agreements were reached through dialogue:

> People are capable of overcoming divisions, conflicts of interests and even, it would seem, medical contradictions, if only they come to believe in the power of dialogue and if they agree to search like human beings for a peaceful and rational solution to the conflicts. . . . Taking into account the interests of various groups, it is possible to attain peaceful settlement through dialogue, through democratic observance of freedom and through everyone fulfilling his duties, and thanks to structures that ensure the participation of all and thanks to the many means of reconciliation between employers and workers—with due respect for the cultural, ethnic and religious groups which make up a nation. When unfortunately dialogue between a government and a nation is absent, social peace becomes threatened or even disappears; it is like a state of war. But history and contemporary experience show that many countries have succeeded or are succeeding in working out lasting agreement. . .

The Pope thus used his whole authority to back unequivocally the Gdańsk, Szczecin and Jastrzębie agreements of 1980, and the processes that led to their conclusion and emphasized that the way out of Poland's predicaments was not through the use of force but a genuine dialogue between the rulers and ruled. The same suggestions had of course often been advanced in the past by the Polish bishops. At the same time he linked dialogue not only with Polish but also European *raison d'état* and stressed that it is essential for the maintenance of Poland's good reputation in the world. Significantly also the appeal for dialogue was coupled in the papal speech with another, for cooperation of 'all the nations of the West in our continent, as well as in the Americas, above all with the United States of America' and Poland. Here the call for the lifting of western economic sanctions was unmistakable.

A NEW COALITION?

The meaning of national freedom and sovereignty was the central theme of his homily during the central celebrations in Częstochowa on the fourth day of his visit.

The nation is truly free when it can mould itself as a community determined by the unity of culture, language and history. The State is really sovereign if it governs the community serving at the same time the common good of society, and allows the nation to realize its own subjectivity, its own identity. Among other things this involves the creation of suitable conditions of development in the fields of culture, economic and other spheres of life of the social community. The sovereignty of the State is closely linked with its capacity to promote the freedom of the nation, that is to create conditions which will enable it to express the whole of its own historical and cultural identity, that means conditions which will allow it to be sovereign to the State.

Here, there was a clear appeal to the rulers of Poland and her neighbours to allow the free expression of the multitude of social, cultural and political currents predominant in Polish society and a reminder that the plurality of freely expressed views would safeguard the stability of the State and its sovereignty. In effect what the Pope was saying was that the stability of the authorities and the sovereignty of Poland is directly related to the degree to which the identity of the nation's social groups can express themselves and not to a claim to the universality of a single ideology. In terms of the conventional conception of democratic centralism, which is still the dominant principle around which the Communist states organize their political structures, these views represent an attempt to fundamentally redirect the patterns of political authority. While they stop short of a demand for political pluralism as institutionalized in Western liberal democracies, they must be seen as providing a potential model for change in Eastern Europe. As far as the Church is concerned this potential change represents the first stage in creating the political conditions in which the Church could once again enjoy the full formally acknowledged authority as the leading social and spiritual force in society.

At the meeting with the Polish Episcopate held on 19 June in Częstochowa, the Pope stated that the long experience of history confirms 'that the Church in Poland is intimately bound up with the life of the nation', and expressed support for the communiqués of the Episcopal Conferences which 'respond to the need to hear the truth ... so acute in society. The truth is the first and fundamental condition of social renewal.' This was a clear allusion to the bishops' constant calls for general amnesty for all those sentenced under martial law regulations. But significantly there was no specific call for this in any of the papal public pronouncements. In the same address the Pope also only alluded to Solidarity saying: 'The Christian doctrine of work postulates both the solidarity of workers among themselves and the need for honest solidarity with workers'. He thus argued that the question of the spirit of human work is also a question of its social form.

On the fifth day of his visit to the mining centre of Katowice the Pope, in what was obviously a strong defence of Solidarity's record, spoke of the events 'before December 1981' which were 'primarily concerned with moral order ... and not just ... increasing remuneration for work'. Reminding his audience that 'these events were free of violence', he emphasized that 'the duty to work corresponds to the rights of a working man', and these included: the right to a just salary, to be insured against accidents connected with work, and work-free Sundays. Then quoting Cardinal Wyszyński the Pope repeated the late Primate's defence of free trade-union organizations:

> When the right of association of people is at stake, then it is not the right bestowed on people by some person. This is people's own inherent right. That is why the State does not give this right to us. The State has merely the right to protect that right so that it is not breached. This right has been given to people by the Creator who made man a social being.

And again in the industrial heartland of Pland the Pope returned to the need for dialogue which is 'the right of the working people'. It is their right, he stressed, 'because the working man is not just an instrument of production but a subject, a subject who in the whole production process has primacy over capital... He is also ready to make sacrifices, so long as he feels himself to be a genuine joint steward with an influence on the just distribution of goods jointly produced.'

During all the papal events throughout Poland the people displayed an overt and unmistakable support for Solidarity. Banners and victory signs were to be seen everywhere the Pope went and his allusions to both rural and industrial Solidarity were often applauded by the crowds, something he always tried to restrain asking for no interruptions. At the same time the large contingents of militiamen did not intervene and allowed people an uninhibited display of their feelings. In that sense there was perhaps a first minute but nevertheless visible sign that some kind of dialogue after the papal visit would be possible.

The Pope of course knew after his two meetings with General Jaruzelski that a tangible and direct result of his visit would be the lifting of martial law to follow only within a matter of weeks after his departure. In this respect what is quite significant is that on only one occasion did he tone down the content of his pre-released speech.[2] The wide-ranging discussions with Henryk Jabłoński and Wojciech Jaruzelski on 17 June and with General Jaruzelski in the evening of 22 June centred primarily on two sets of issues. Firstly on the mechanics of the lifting of martial law, the nature of amnesty to be declared, and constitutional guarantees for private farmers. And secondly, perhaps more importantly, on the role the Church was to play after martial law was lifted. One of the main objects of these discussions was the legal status of the Church particularly in view of its sponsorship of the Polish Recovery Programme. The Church, as much as its prospective creditors being mindful of the experience of Solidarity when the regime's administrative decision had wiped out solemnly signed agreements, expected its position to be acknowledged in a more formal act of Parliament. Such an act would of course admit the plurality of not only social but political forces in Poland and to a considerable degree undermine even the formalistic claims of the Party. Another stumbling block appears to have been the organizational structure required to administer this Programme. In addition to the establishment of the Foundation for the Modernization and Development of Private Agriculture, Handicrafts and Private Sector Economy, controlled by the Episcopate, for the allocation of financial and material resources under the Programme, the donors also envisaged the setting up of a parallel body in Western Europe which would retain overall control of the Programme. This in turn raised a series of delicate and intricate ideological problems not only for the regime internally but also for Poland's relations with the 'socialist camp' and the Council for Mutual Economic Assistance in particular. One of the main problems still unresolved appears to have been the statutes of the Polish aspect of the Foundation and its counterpart in the West, the level of their interdependence and scope of operations. In spite of numerous, seemingly insurmountable problems, the conclusion of these meetings was that the Programme was visible, advisable and necessary and that the attempt to find mutually acceptable solutions should continue through the Joint Government Episcopate Working Group established in December 1982 for that purpose. It was expected that perhaps an agreement on the Programme could be initialled before the Pope returned to Rome and the fact that this did not occur should not be taken as an indication of a lack of genuine commitment on both sides.

The Pope did meet Lech Wałęsa, not as planned on 19 June in Częstochowa, but on the last day of his visit, in the Chochołowska hostel in the Tatra Mountains. The meeting was postponed until the last day at the Church's request since it was felt that the encounter might take too much attention away from the content of the visit in view of the disproportionate media attention it was attracting in the West. It is quite probable that the Pontiff would have told Wałęsa about the new realities of the Polish situation and that a position would be found for him within the structure of the Polish Recovery Programme.

The Pope's second pilgrimage to his homeland epitomized the Church's unique role in contemporary Polish politics. Unique because it intertwined moral and political authority with national, historical and cultural traditions and with the current demands and expectations of national survival. As long as there exists a sovereign Poland the Church can and will promote the nation's interests. The Church's total identification with this paramount national interest, so often threatened in the country's history and so vivid in its historiography of which the Black Madonna of Częstochowa is one, albeit the best known, example, is unique in Communist Party states and makes the Communist ideology almost redundant. Marxism–Communism in Poland has never been anything more than a formal ideology, despite its clear-cut identification with the interests of the working class. The fact that the country lies in the centre of the continent in the direct security zone of a world socialist power, the Soviet Union, makes it a necessary and prudent formal ideology.

The Roman Catholic Church in Poland has always accepted this Polish *raison d'état* and has drawn its strength from that. At the same time, since 1945, it has consolidated its position and acquired its present role through the conflicts and coexistence with its political opponents, through its astute sensitivity and identification with the social and political aspirations of the vast majority of the population, through the careful encouragement of these aspirations and expectations and through participating and sharing in the people's triumph and tribulations. The Church, unlike the ruling Party, has never had to legitimize itself and its position in Polish society. But it took the Communist regime in Poland some thirty-eight years to acknowledge, in the words of the Minister of Religious Affairs, Adam Łopatka, the simple fact apparent to many for so long, that 'if anyone tries to imagine socialism in Poland without the Church, he shows his lack of knowledge of Polish reality'.[3]

So it was left to the Polish Pope, and the irony of that could not be greater, to come to Poland again to legitimize this new political entity based on the intertwined interest of national Catholicism with residual Communism, their sharp contours blended in order, at least for the present, to sustain Poland, her unhappy people with an unhappy history in an unhappy geopolitical location; none of this can be fundamentally changed in the short term despite the newly formed authority of the Polish Church.

As the Pope bade farewell on the tarmac of Kraków airport one of the monks from Częstochowa called out 'We invite you Holy Father to come back in three years time'. Before the Pope could answer, President Henryk Jabłoński intervened to insist, 'The sooner the better.'

Notes

1. This and all subsequent quotes from the Pope's speeches are taken from official texts released by the Vatican Press Office.
2. In his homily on the Błonia Meadow in Kraków the expression 'arrogant use of power' in the original version was substituted in the actual delivery by 'the use of violence'.
3. Polish Interpress Agency, 15 June 1983.

Appendix I

AREA OF DIOCESES AND POPULATION
(as on 1 January 1979)

Diocese	Area (sq. kmm)	Percentage of total area of Poland	Population	Population per square kilometer
Białystok	6,000	1.9	422,186	70.4
Chełmno	17,600	5.6	1,417,590	80.5
Częstochowa	8,500	2.7	1,145,000	170.0
Drohiczyn	4,300	1.4	182,477	42.4
Gdańsk	1,900	0.7	605,000	318.4
Gniezno	9,900	3.2	986,472	99.6
Gorzów	15,600	5.0	1,076,000	69.0
Katowice	4,200	1.3	2,200,000	523.8
Kielce	9,900	3.2	1,000,000	101.0
Koszalin	19,300	6.2	979,000	50.7
Kraków	8,200	2.6	2,238,600	273.0
Lubaczów	1,600	0.6	80,000	50.0
Lublin	16,900	5.4	1,645,810	7.4
Łomża	12,300	3.9	620,000	50.4
Łódź	6,100	1.9	1,450,000	237.7
Olsztyn	24,300	7.8	1,330,000	54.7
Opole	9,700	3.1	1,670,000	172.2
Płock	14,400	4.6	875,000	60.7
Poznań	15,400	4.9	1,800,000	116.9
Przemyśl	13,900	4.4	1,508,754	108.5
Sandomierz	12,400	4.0	1,217,000	98.1
Siedlce	13,800	4.4	851,814	61.7
Szczecin	12,800	4.1	985,000	72.0
Tarnów	8,900	2.8	1,180,000	132.6
Warszawa	12,500	4.0	3,429,000	274.3
Włocławek	11,900	3.8	1,091,500	91.7
Wrocław	20,400	6.5	2,850,000	139.7
Total	312,700	100.0	35,136,203	112.4

Source: *Kościół katolicki w Polsce, 1945-1978* (The Catholic Church in Poland, 1945-1978) p. 17.

APPENDIX I

PARISHES AND NUMBER OF FAITHFUL
(1972)

Diocese	up to 1,200	1,201–2,500	2,501–5,000	5,001–10,000	10,001–20,000	20,001–30,000	30,001–40,000	above 40,000	Total
Białystok	7	14	19	12	1	–	–	2	55
Chełmno	65	157	63	33	25	4	–	–	347
Częstochowa	28	73	80	47	14	8	–	–	250
Drohiczyn	6	17	11	6	–	–	–	–	40
Gdańsk	9	17	14	7	9	3	1	–	60
Gniezno	61	116	46	29	8	3	–	–	263
Gorzów	13	73	57	25	9	2	2	–	181
Katowice	24	81	92	46	42	8	1	1	295
Kielce	15	99	93	27	7	3	–	–	244
Koszalin	2	57	45	15	11	5	–	–	135
Kraków	31	120	128	50	16	8	2	2	357
Lubaczów	4	8	5	1	–	–	–	–	18

APPENDIX I

Lublin	11	61	108	51	12	4	1	—	248
Łomża	13	20	55	11	6	—	—	—	105
Łódź	6	29	60	16	25	5	3	1	145
Olsztyn	37	105	52	20	15	2	1	1	233
Opole	70	162	80	36	21	6	2	—	377
Płock	10	83	102	14	9	2	—	1	221
Poznań	69	134	110	39	22	6	1	—	381
Przemyśl	10	20	17	1	3	—	—	—	51
Sandomierz	22	91	99	28	11	1	2	—	254
Siedlce	42	60	71	27	8	4	1	—	213
Szczecin	1	35	35	21	18	3	2	1	116
Tarnów	51	127	103	25	11	1	—	—	318
Warsaw	14	79	122	54	32	10	2	2	315
Włocławek	14	95	96	32	6	4	1	—	248
Wrocław	59	260	118	57	36	4	—	—	534
Total	694	2,193	1,881	730	377	96	22	11	6,004

Source: *Kościół katolicki w Polsce, 1945-1972*. (The Catholic Church in Poland, 1945-1972) pp. 15-18.

APPENDIX I

PARISHES CHURCHES AND CHAPELS
(as of 1 January 1979)

Diocese	Parishes	Churches	Chapels	Total Churches and Chapels
Białystok	67	82	2	84
Chełmno	389	450	35	485
Częstochowa	264	281	167	448
Drohiczyn	36	40	23	63
Gdańsk	64	105	16	121
Gniezno	320	365	9	374
Gorzów	205	666	1	667
Katowice	288	345	–	345
Kielce	264	288	125	413
Koszalin	181	567	30	597
Kraków	327	534	115	649
Lubaczów	33	79	1	80
Lublin	272	335	62	397
Łomża	139	159	8	167
Łódź	157	183	15	198
Olsztyn	282	428	81	509
Opole	445	689	325	1,014
Płock	247	290	–	290
Poznań	433	554	112	666
Przemyśl	484	707	–	707
Sandomierz	273	309	25	334
Siedlce	244	259	68	327
Szczecin	168	544	25	569
Tarnów	359	471	98	569
Warsaw	333	356	188	544
Włocławek	272	309	2	311
Wrocław	590	1,136	149	1,285
Total	7,118	10,531	1,682	12,213

Sources: *Kościół katolicki w Polsce, 1945-1978* (The Catholic Church in Poland, 1945-1978) pp. 18, 25.

APPENDIX I

PRIESTS MONKS AND NUNS

Diocese	Priests* In Poland	Abroad	Total	Monks**	Nuns**
Białystok	283	12	295	6	120
Chełmno	745	30	775	125	829
Częstochowa	648	13	661	89	950
Drohiczyn	82	24	106	1	66
Gdańsk	152	8	160	83	206
Gniezno	570	13	583	80	643
Gorzów	288	2	290	142	292
Katowice	799	62	861	105	1,535
Kielce	542	12	554	52	532
Koszalin	263	1	264	110	295
Kraków	977	14	991	651	3,020
Lubaczów	126	22	148	7	46
Lublin	697	14	711	149	927
Łomża	337	15	352	17	200
Łódź	404	11	415	124	815
Olsztyn	466	12	478	198	389
Opole	666	–	666	211	1,511
Płock	455	9	464	61	542
Poznań	865	30	895	240	1,824
Przemyśl	904	8	912	110	1,260
Sandomierz	603	11	614	79	858
Siedlce	471	10	481	50	457
Szczecin	218	1	219	122	164
Tarnów	1,006	35	1,041	143	1,358
Warsaw	951	38	989	475	3,358
Włocławek	510	21	531	111	681
Wrocław	944	44	988	436	2,834
Total	14,972	472	15,444	3,977	25,712

* As on 1 January 1979
**In 1978

Source: *Kościół katolicki w Polsce, 1945-1978* (The Catholic Church in Poland, 1945-1978) pp. 28, 48, 58.

APPENDIX I

SEMINARIANS AND ORDAINED PRIESTS
1970–1982

Year	Seminarians Diocesan	Seminarians Monastic	Seminarians Total	Newly Ordained Priests Diocesan	Newly Ordained Priests Monks	Newly Ordained Priests Total
1970	3,131	n/k		260	n/k	
1971	3,097	991	4,088	356	124	480
1972	3,057	1,073	4,130	471	133	604
1973	3,035	1,139	4,174	450	107	557
1974	3,091	1,125	4,216	486	152	638
1975	3,130	1,265	4,395	455	151	606
1976	2,410	1,295	3,705	319	158	477
1977	3,607	1,451	5,058	341	97	438
1978	3,784	1,541	5,325	420	149	569
1979	4,179	1,666	5,845	407	182	589
1980	4,449	1,836	6,285	470	162	632
1981	4,727	1,987	6,714	482	206	688
1982	5,018	2,207	7,225	571	204	775

Source: Annual Reports of the Secretariat of Polish Episcopate.

Appendix II: Cardinal Stefan Wyszyński to the Members of the Main Council of the Polish Episcopate, Warsaw, 22 May 1981

The following is Cardinal Wyszyński's last address to the members of the Main Council of the Episcopal Conference delivered six days before his death. It is not only a farewell message but also a testament to his fellow bishops.[1]

I will not talk about myself, for Bishop Dąbrowski[2] knows the state of my health, or more accurately, my illness, which—according to medical opinion—is permanent, so that God's Church can place no great hope in me. Instead it must place it in you, my dear brothers of the Main Council, in which we have all worked together for so many years. Once long ago, the General Councils also took place here and thus, in a circle, Our Lord has plucked one after the other from this company. I think, since I am approaching 80 years old, it is high time for me.

I will not say much. I have already said that I will leave no programme behind me because my counterpart must not be hindered by any such programme. He must be able to recognize the situation of Poland and the Church from day to day, and to lay out his programme of work accordingly. Such a programme cannot in Poland be a rigid one. Our steadfastness finds expression in the 'Credo', in the 'Our Father' and the 'Hail Mary', in the vows of Jasna Góra pledged by our Holy Father himself. The rest is fluid. Our greatest worth is found in the faith of our people, their ties with the Church, their bond with the Church in Christ and His Mother, in your faith, in your burning love and in your own uncommon apostolic fervour. I can expect no more. The Church must remain here where it is. For without any exaggeration, it is the bulwark of Christianity. From here, the Church goes East.

Our Holy Father! We have no need to tell him of our sentiments

APPENDIX II

nor speak of this plainly unusual coincidence in our lives up until this moment, and especially in the last few years. This concomitant binds me personally to our Holy Father, and I accept this responsibility consciously, with full understanding and compliance.

I stated, during the ceremonial moment of my acceptance of the Sacrament of the Sick, that I have never sinned by any act of faithlessness during my life, against God, who is the giver of life, and has full rights to it, especially when he has given it so many years. I have never sinned against Jesus Christ, who is—as the Perpetual Pastor—the giver of my own chaplaincy, and has full rights to it. I have never sinned against the Church as an institution, though very often in my work I have been obliged to represent the position of the Episcopate and the Church in Poland, as representing the proper understanding of the mission of the Church in a complicated situation in Poland, which had to be discriminately discerned according to our circumstances. This I undertook boldly, though always with humility.

I acknowledge deeply the necessity for understanding in this situation, especially by our Holy Father Pius XII and Paul VI, and also by John XXII and by both John Pauls. I say nothing of the standpoint of our Holy Father today, who suffers happily and serves the Church. This you all know my brothers. For this is your friend, your colleague, who understands you best. It augurs a certainty that it will be thus in the future. I believe that our most Holy Mother, to whom he pledged his vow at Jasna Góra, will raise him through his experiences.

Of myself, I say nothing, for I know, that the Mother of God can do all things, but I am only her servant and have entrusted everything to her. I shall lay no pleas for my intentions at our Holy Mother's feet, for I know that it is her affair, a fantastic affair of heroic prayer, which will reach her through your hearts and those of your devoted people. I have always marvelled at your living faith and your apostolic fervour, which I have not always been able to equal.

I am so indebted to all of you. Especially to Bishop Bronisław, our Secretary, in whom I see the most loyal executor of the programmes and plans on which we have been working day in day out. I give my heartfelt thanks to His Eminence the Cardinal,[3] for taking upon himself the responsibility of the Presidency of the General Council and the Episcopal Conference, and who performs this task with dignity. I am

APPENDIX II

grateful to the Bishop of Gdańsk[4] for his splendid handling of the problems at the Gdańsk shipyards, of 'Solidarity', and those of our own country at Rome. To say nothing of my successor at Lublin,[5] who has to enter so delicately into the entire spirituality of my work in the territory of this academic and Catholic city. To say nothing of the heavy burden placed upon our father the Archbishop of the metropolis at Wrocław,[6] who knows what has to be done in order to bond the Recovered Territories forever to Poland and her Church. Not to mention my closest neighbour, the Archbishop of the city of Poznań,[7] who knows supremely well the traditions of this proud region, honoured by country and by Church alike. I know these people, anyone can trust them and place confidence in their ideals day and night. They have their own hopes, but also an instilled responsibility. To you, my dear Bishop of Przemyśl,[8] and not only of Przemyśl, but of all the rich land opening out to the south and to the east of Poland, will fall a heavy responsibility for the extension of the Church in Poland, towards those horizons. But at the same time there is the conscious need for the development of Latin and national culture in those directions. We do not have with us the Bishop of industrious Łódź,[9] which is in a way the heart of the industrial structure of Poland, whose people have given an example within their own spheres of labour of how to solve communal problems in a Christian way, so as to remain in the spirit and according to the justice of the Gospel.

I have feelings only of gratitude—against no one have I the smallest complaint. There is no one I would deceive. To everyone, I bequeath my heart, which takes with it no reservations in relation to any Polish bishop, or any chaplain or child of God. All our hopes rest in our Holy Mother, and if there is any programme—it rests in her.

Should you meet the Holy Father on the 7th June, as I trust you will, please give him from me a brotherly embrace and an assurance that my sufferings, which are the expressions of protracted illness, are allied to his even greater sufferings. My sickness requires patience without pain—his, great pain and great suffering.

I fall with all humility as Primate of Poland at your bishops' feet and embrace them. Remember, that the very traditions of Polishness are linked by the primacy to Gniezno, despite anyone's brooding or intentions to the contrary. Poland became strong through this, when Baltic lands and Baltic people felt the conscious proximity of the

APPENDIX II

primacy to their dioceses. It was then that their power grew. And this territorial strategy must be respected as a cornerstone of the building up of the Church in Poland. Poland in the south will be forever strong, unswerving, Poland in the north and west will constantly require the spiritual fortification of those who through historic acts of greatness have been made to endure the incursions of Swedes, Teutonic knights and Germans. Of the east I will say nothing, because the east is open in its entirety, to be won by the Church in Poland.

And let this be enough, my brothers. Let this be enough. I have served the Church for thirty-five years, and in my present post for thirty-three. That is enough. May God repay you. Maintain always, a trust for this house. It is open for you, or for public conferences. For this reason, this house was built, downstairs you may feel free here, and as relaxed as in your own offices. Maintain the traditions of the house, and similarly the traditions of the Secretariat of the Polish Episcopacy, as those also which arise out of the great difficulty and with your help, through the essential work of the Church in Poland.

Thanks be to God, that you wanted to come and that you wanted to be witnesses to my ineffectiveness. It is necessary, this conscious knowledge, so that it be obvious, that in Poland only God governs, not man. For this reason a man, who imagines that he has done something, must depart, so that people know that in Poland God alone reigns— *quis ut Deus. He* remains strong in Poland, people are weak. Such are the acts and thoughts of God. In Poland there are no great people, all of them are servants, all of them on their knees before the tiniest child, baptized by the Church in Poland. Love them. May God reward you!

Give your blessing to me, my brothers. I ask you most humbly. [All the bishops present join in bestowing a blessing upon the Primate.]

You have the programme, my brothers, waste no time, go to your work. *Et omnipotentem Deum etiam pro me orate.*

Bishop Dąbrowski: 'We ask for a blessing upon our work'.
Primate Wyszyński: *'Pater et Filius, et Spiritus Sanctus cum Maria Madre Dei.* Do not forget me in Rome on the 7th June. All decrees for the future—until my return to health—will be signed *de mandato* by Bishop Bronisław Dąbrowski.'

APPENDIX II

[At this point, Primate Wyszyński asks a nursing sister to wheel him to the window and for a long while he remains, in silence, looking at the garden before him.]

Notes

1. The text is taken from Monsignor Piasecki's book: *Ostatnie dni Prymasa Tysiaclecia.* pp. 73–6.
2. Bronisław Dąbrowski, Secretary of the Polish Episcopal Conference.
3. Franciszek Macharski, the Archbishop of Kraków.
4. Lech Kaczmarek.
5. Bolesław Pylak.
6. Henryk Gulbinowicz.
7. Jerzy Stroba.
8. Ignacy Tokarczuk.
9. Józef Rozawdowski.

Appendix III: 'Theses of the Primate's Social Council in the Matter of Social Accord'

The decision of 13 December 1981 created a new historical situation in Poland. In the period after August 1982, an immense hope was born in Polish society: the hope that our State, within the framework of the existing political system and the binding international treaties, would become a country in which society would regain its subjectivity, would have a real part in public life and a real influence on the functioning of the State, would have the power to control the activities of the authorities and would take advantage of the scope of civil liberties widened after August 1980.

The introduction of martial law and the suspension of fundamental civil rights was felt by a considerable section of society to be the collapse of that hope and caused bitterness and a state of depression. As always in similar historical circumstances, society expects from the Church spiritual help, moral strength and the salvation of the nation's cultural traditions. The Polish Episcopate assembled at the 183rd plenary conference, in a communiqué of 26 February 1892,[1] out of concern for the fate of the nation, pointed out the vital need to strive for social accord. This communiqué was received in Poland with the greatest emotion. People in Poland see in it a direction for themselves and the indication of a way out.

The Primate's Social Council was set up by the Primate, Józef Glemp, referring back to the former tradition of the times of Primate Hlond. The Council is an opinion-giving and ancillary body attached to the Primate of Poland, to whom it presents the results of its work. The idea put forward by the Episcopate of a new, internal social accord based on the model of the social agreement concluded in August 1980 demands development and specification. The Primate's Social Council puts forward its proposals on this matter.

1. If that social accord or agreement between the authorities and society is to be a way out of the present political impasse, it will have

APPENDIX III

to gain broad social acceptance. Achieving this acceptance will be possible only when society comes to believe and receives the guarantee that its hopes have not been definitively shattered. This social accord could be concluded between the authorities and the appropriate independent representatives of organized social groups. Representatives of real social and opinion-creating forces should participate in these agreements. This means representatives of trade unions, including in particular the most numerous Independent Self-Governing Trade Union Solidarity, the trade unions of private farmers and craftsmen, representatives of science and culture, and of creative guilds and youth unions. In our particular conditions, the presence of the Church at the reaching of this agreement would also be necessary. The subject of national accord, or the detailed agreements which will make up that accord, should be the conditions, course and deadline for reactivating the suspended trade unions and other organizations; the conditions, course and deadline for removing the restrictions imposed by martial law and restoring civil rights, some of the more important legislative proposals and the general programme of reform and renewal of social and economic life.

The political and legal significance and the format of such agreements would be special; they would be untypical, extraordinary acts and, depending on needs, could have a wider or narrower scope. They would not have to regulate everything. It should be stressed however, that since the situation in Poland is after all extraordinary and tragic it demands extraordinary measures. The great and deepening rift between the authorities and society, and the intensifying signs of hostility and outright hate in the situation of deep crisis demands a form of social agreement which would convince people and guarantee a process of renewal which would be capable of awakening hope. On the other hand, the accord should strengthen the position of the State authorities and enable them to combat the crisis effectively, taking into consideration that martial law was caused in fact by weakness and the threat to the structures of the State and the system, although it was not the only way to save them and brought much evil. To operate effectively, social accord should fulfil two conditions. It should be concluded between the authorities and persons with social standing, having in this case also the significance of a symbol, and representing social groups which count for something. In its footsteps, conditions should be created and guarantees given that the road of accord and national agreement will be a lasting factor in the normalization of life in Poland. An important condition for the effectiveness of accord should be a declaration of adherence to all social agreements concluded in 1980, without which the negotiation of a new accord would be completely lacking in credibility. Respect for those agreements was stressed by the Chairman of the Military Council for National Salvation in his first speech on 13 December and also by the Sejm of the Polish People's Republic in its resolution of 25 January 1982.

2. The basis of accord is to be recognition by the authorities of the subjectivity of society, respect for the fact of the existence of independent public opinion, and understanding and recognition by the authorities that without dialogue and agreement with society on important issues there is no way out of the crisis. On the other hand, however, an unavoidable pre-condition for internal stabilization is understanding on the part of society of the demands of the system and the objective situation of the State as determined by the existing international structures. The communiqué of the 183rd session of the Episcopate speaks of the need for realism in assessing the consequences of our country's geo-political situation. These are words of great significance. The real problem of the nation must be solved within the framework of historical structures. No authorities in Poland would have unrestricted freedom in solving of problems; and the present Government has not got it either. This must dictate to society caution and moderation.

3. The communiqué of the 183rd session of the Polish Episcopate listed particularly urgent social demands, which are certainly conditions for internal peace. A rapidly progressing process of freeing internees and ensuring a free return for people who are in hiding for fear of political repression are essential. Society expects an amnesty for people sentenced for deeds which do not appear in the Penal Code but which were regarded as acts of resistance after the introduction of martial law. Pressure, personal repression and dismissal from work for one's beliefs or membership of Solidarity are, of course, in conflict with the demands for social accord and with the demand for justice. These kinds of repression, wherever they are applied, should be stopped and banned. People dismissed from work for such reasons should be reinstated. There must be determined opposition to all pressures aimed

APPENDIX III

at inducing people to leave the country for good—especially if they are applied to the interned, which may constitute an alternative to emigration or imprisonment. Important steps towards the normalization of State life should be the restoration of the free activity of creative and scientific unions. It is also necessary to restore the freedom and activity of all Clubs of Catholic Intelligentsia existing on 13 December 1981 and to permit a resumption of all organs of the Catholic press existing at that date. Solutions such as applied regarding the Association of Polish Journalists[2] runs counter to the demand for social accord and increases bitterness.

4. The basic aim of social accord should be the removal of the barriers that exist between the authorities and society. If social accord is implemented, the matter of social structures that would permit increased participation by citizens in deciding on public affairs, and contact between the authorities and society, will emerge. Within the framework of increasing social participation in State life, it could be useful to create advisory bodies attached to the Government or the Sejm, on condition that such commissions were composed of people delegated by independent social organizations and had the guaranteed right to free representation of their views in the mass media. What is needed is the reorientation of society and the outlining of prospects for the appearance of a new type of civic activity and a democratic direction of change. Self-government in the wide and profound conception of the word can be the only model of this kind. The starting point could be elections to people's councils at lower levels. These should be fully autonomous, not politically determined. For this reason it would not be correct to link those elections with elections to the Sejm or provincial people's councils where the political element could not be eliminated. The people must be given the opportunity of free choice of local authorities. This would necessitate freedom in putting forward candidates. One of the aims of social accord would be to eliminate political play during such elections. Although these self-managed elections should be connected with the lifting of martial law, the matter must be already properly considered and prepared.

5. The spread of hatred is a dangerous phenomenon which poisons the life of the nation. There is no justification for hatred and there can be none, even where understandable resentment and anger have been born. All Christians, and in particular clergymen, ought to oppose this. Social

resistance to martial law may take the form of acts of violence which can turn into a vicious circle of terror and repression. These acts have to be condemned resolutely. They will be countered effectively if there develops in parallel a process of internal easing of tension and national accord. A fundamental condition for the effective struggle against hatred and mutual rancour is a fundamental change in the orientation of official propaganda in the mass media, which by rejecting in essence all the manifestations and achievements of the broad movement for renewal in past months, insults the public and stirs it up against the authorities.

6. The moral problems that result from the present situation are felt particularly keenly by the young. The breakdown of hope and the failure to perceive a way out of the crisis leads to rebellion. The overwhelming majority of the young are of an oppositional frame of mind; they are embittered and set about these notions feverishly. One cannot remedy this by means of repression. That is why the Polish Episcopate correctly raised the problem of autonomous associations of the young. An unusually urgent matter is the formation of independent student organizations, especially self-help ones. The lack of organizations of their own is one of the essential causes of the ferment among the young.

7. One of the most important fields awaiting positive solution is the question of the trade-union movement. It is the general feeling in society that the conditions for implementing social accord and for effective struggle against the crisis will not exist unless there is a reactivation of the existing trade unions and above all the Independent Self-governing Trade Union Solidarity, which enjoys broad social support. It seems, however, that at the present moment, the authorities have not got a clear concept of action as regards Solidarity; the Council of Ministers' Committee for Trade Union Affairs had not put forward contructive proposals in this area. The text published by the Committee gives the impression of evading social dialogue on the topic of national accord. Taking up this issue is an urgent necessity. In the view of broad social circles there is no other way to accord than to adhere to the social agreements concluded in 1980. The first fundamental point of that social agreement was the creation of independent trade unions operating within the framework of the Constitution of Polish People's Republic. On this basis, in accordance with Convention 87 of the

APPENDIX III

International Labour Organization, Solidarity was set up and registered. In the period of martial law, representatives of the authorities many times guaranteed the activity of Solidarity on its statutory principles.

8. The reactivation of the trade unions in a genuine form, in accordance with the will of trade unionists can only be realistic in the present situation of martial law after a critical assessment of the situation that existed before 13 December 1981. There is no doubt that without the workers' protest and the agreements in Gdańsk, Szczecin and Jastrzębie, and also without the subsequent creation of Solidarity and other social and professional organizations, the achievements of the renewal movement would not have been possible. The result of this was the beginning of economic reform and development of workers' self-management as well as the work on new legislation (among others the Bill on Censorship) and the democratization of a number of social organizations. In the field of the defence of workers' rights and social policy, great progress was made. Despite all the difficulties in Poland, a new climate of hope for a better tomorrow existed. Solidarity was not the only factor in these transformations, but it was definitely the most important factor.

Rejecting the enormous number of untrue, exaggerated and unjust accusations which have been made against Solidarity, it must be recognized that, in connection with the broad influence it exerted on social life, it also bears a part of the responsibility for the serious crisis which has happened to our country. Solidarity itself made efforts to limit its activity, to avoid many local conflicts, to ensure control over union bulletins which sometimes undertook political propaganda, and to separate the union clearly from the activity of opposition groups. It also tried to hold back the huge wave of demands from the union masses, especially those concerning living conditions, wages and supply; it sought to calm the trade unionists down. These activities were clearly insufficient however. Although the situation was very difficult, the mistrust of the authorities and irritation with the more and more onerous economic situation grew; many conflicts were provoked. The young mass movement was very difficult to lead. Solidarity, however, should have defended more decisively and consistently the idea of accord and a limited socio-trade union programme.

In a situation of a collapsing economy, of a crisis of weakened authority which threatened the basis of the system of government, and of the expectations of our allies increasingly worried at the state of our country, only mutual understanding and co-operation between society and the authorities offered a chance of perpetuating and securing the achievements of renewal. That understanding and goodwill, as well as imagination and courage, was lacking on both sides. The impulsive and spontaneous reaction of members of the trade union to the conflicts and blatant evidence of injustice emerging partly from many former wrongs, which had been festering for years, hampered—as Cardinal Wyszyński said—the harnessing of the most noble impulses of Solidarity for the good of the Republic. Trade union activity needed and needs the approach of small steps—i.e. the gradual achievement of the desired goals—in a spirit of caution, patience and circumspection. It will not be easy to speak of these issues without mutual reproaches and accusations; but it will be necessary to muster the maximum restraint. At the same time Solidarity must make the effort to take a critial look at its activity and experiences. It is to be thought that a considerable number of trade union activists are ready to do this.

9. The trade unions should retain their independence not only of the administration and the State employer, as the Council of Ministers' Committee for Trade Union Affairs puts it, but also from political organizations. John Paul II writes thus about this in *Labor Exercens*: 'The task of the trade unions is not to practise politics in the meaning of the word generally used today. Trade unions are not in the nature of political parties struggling for power and should not be subject to the decisions of political parties or have too close links with them. In this sort of situation, they easily lose contact with their proper task, the safeguarding of the just rights of working people within the framework of the common good of the whole of society. Instead they become a tool for other ends.'

The non-political nature of trade unions conceived in this way can and must be reconciled with respect for the Constitution and the first point of the Gdańsk agreements. This will require a clear curtailment of the activity of Solidarity on the one hand, and a safeguarding of the autonomy of the union as regards the political authorities on the other.

10. The proposals published by the Council of Ministers' Committee for Trade Union Affairs regarding the trade-union movement assume a discussion of the organizational rebuilding of the trade unions in accordance with the will of the working class and working people

APPENDIX III

in general. In connection with this it is essential to accept the principle of pluralism, which was shown sufficiently clearly over the past dozen months or so by the working people in Poland setting up various trade-union organizations. All interested should be able to participate in this discussion; no other principle will be acceptable to the workers. In our view all trade-union organizations and all workers should be able to express their opinion regarding the reactivation of their trade union. We wish to stress that the proposal for a Bill on Trade Unions has already been discussed by the society last year; it was accepted by the Committee of the Council of State in which representatives of trade unions also participated. The proposal has already been submitted to the Sejm. It should be stated that formulations included in this proposal form an agreement which is in force.

We are well aware that our ideas and proposals will not be easy to implement. We can foresee that those in the leadership who reject the idea of compromise with society and wish to use only force may be against it. There may also be resistance among those members of society who, deeply offended by the use of force, may not be willing to accept any agreement while martial law lasts. In spite of this with the feeling of responsibility for the fate of all Poles we feel we must speak out. Our lot will not be improved through complaints and the use of force. We cannot count on a change in the situation as long as we do not do everything in our power. We must fight against fatalism. The way out is through the mobilization of our forces and common endeavour on the conditon that they are used with prudence. Therefore these suggestions should be submitted to the authorities as well as to every member of society. These proposals are not abstract, they can be met in our circumstances, in our country.

Warsaw, 5 April 1982.

Notes

1. The conference presided over by Archbishop Józef Glemp was held in Warsaw on 25 and 26 February. For the complete text of the communiqué see: *Communist Affairs: Documents and Analysis*, vol. 1, no. 4 (October 1982), pp. 818-20.
2. The Association of Polish Journalists, which was suspended on 13 December 1981, was dissolved by the authorities on 19 March 1982.

Selected Bibliography

Ascherson, Neal, *The Polish August*, Harmondsworth, Penguin, 1982 (second edition).

Boniecki, Adam, *Budowa Kościołów w Diecezji Przemyskiej* (The Construction of Churches in the Prezemyśl Diocese), Biblioteka Spotkań, London, 1980.

Blażyński, George, *Flashpoint Poland*, London, Pergamon Press, 1979.

Cyziński, Bohdan, *Ogniem Próbowane* (Tried by Fire), Rzym, Papieski Instytut Studiów Kościelnych, 1982.

Davies, Norman, *God's Playground. A History of Poland*, 2 vols., Oxford, Oxford University Press, 1981.

Dissent in Poland: Reports and Documents in Translation, December 1975-July 1977, London, Association of Polish Students and Graduates in Exile, 1977.

Dziewanowski, M. K., *The Communist Party of Poland*, Cambridge, Mass., Harvard University Press, 1978.

Halecki, Oskar, *Eugeniusz Pacelli, Papież Pokoju* (Eugenio Pacelli, the Pope of Peace), London, Hosianum, 1951.

Hirszowicz, Maria, *The Bureaucratic Leviathan*, Oxford, Martin Robertson, 1980.

I Krajowy Zjazd Delegatów NSZZ Solidarność. I tura. 5-10, IX, 1981 (The First National Congress of the Delegates of the Independent Self-Governing Trade Union Solidarity. First stage. 5-10 September, 1981), Solidarity's Press Office, Gdańsk, 1981.

John Paul II, Pope, *Redemptor Hominis*, London, Catholic Truth Society, n.d.

John Paul II, Pope, *Laborem Exercens*, London, Catholic Truth Society, n.d.

Kołomiejczyk, Norbert, and Syzdek Bronisław, *Polska w latach 1944-1949* (Poland During the Years 1944-1949), Warsaw, Państwowe Zakłady Wydawnictw Szkolnych, 1971.

SELECTED BIBLIOGRAPHY

Kościół katolicki w Polsce, 1945-1978, Poznań-Warszawa, Pallottinum, 1979
Leslie, R. F. (ed.), *The History of Poland since 1863*, Cambridge, Cambridge University Press, 1979.
McShane, Denis, *Solidarity: Poland's Independent Trade Union*, Nottingham, Spokesman, 1981.
Marek, Ryszard, *Kosciół rzymsko-katolicki na ziemiach zachodnich i północnych* (The Roman Catholic Church in Western and Northern Lands), Warsaw, Państwowe Wydawnictwo Naukowe, 1976.
Mazowiecki, Tadeusz, 'Chrzescijaństwo a prawa człowieka' (Christianity and Human Rights), in *Więź*, no. 2 (February 1978).
Micewski, Andrzej, *Kardynał Wyszyński, Prymas i Mąż Stanu* (Cardinal Wyszyński, Primate and Statesman), Paris, Editions du Dialogue, 1982.
Michnik, Adam, *Kościół, lewica, dialog* (The Church, the Left and Dialogue), Paris, Instytut Literacki, 1977.
Mysłek, Wiesław. 'Kościół i władza' (The Church and the Authorities), *Nowe Drogi*, no. 5 (May 1979), pp. 34-7.
Piasecki, Bronisław, *Ostatnie dni Prymasa Tysiąclecia* (The Last Days of the Primate of the Millennium), Rome, Dom Polski Jana Pawła II, 1982.
Pomian-Srzednicki, Maciej, *Religious Change in Contemporary Poland: Secularization and Politics*, London, Routledge & Kegan Paul, 1982.
Prawa człowieka i obywatela w PRL w okresie stanu wojennego (13 XII 1981-31 XII 1982) (Human and Civil Rights in Polish People's Republic During the State of War (13 December 1981-31 December 1983)), compiled by the Polish Helsinki Committee and submitted by the Interim Co-ordinating Commission of Solidarity to the Conference for Security and Cooperation in Europe in February 1983.
Raina, Peter, *Independent Social Movements in Poland*, London, London School of Economics and Political Science, 1981.
Raina, Peter, *Political Opposition in Poland. 1954-1977*, London, Arlington Books, 1978.
Sabbat, Anna and Stefanowski, Roman (comps), *Poland: A Chronology of Events, July-November 1980*, Radio Free Europe, RAD Background Report/91, March 1981.

SELECTED BIBLIOGRAPHY

Sanford, George, *Polish Communism in Crisis*, London, Croom Helm, 1983.

Szajkowski, Bogdan (ed.), *Documents in Communist Affairs—1977*, London, Butterworth Scientific, 1982.

Szajkowski, Bogdan (ed.), *Documents in Communist Affairs—1979*, London, Butterworth Scientific, 1982.

Szajkowski, Bogdan (ed.), *Documents in Communist Affairs—1980*, London, Macmillan, 1982.

Szajkowski, Bogdan (ed.), *Documents in Communist Affairs—1981*, London, Butterworth Scientific, 1982.

The Book of Lech Wałęsa, Harmondsworth, Penguin, 1981.

The Strikes in Poland: August 1980, Munich, Radio Free Europe Research, 1980.

Tomsky, Alexander, *Catholic Poland*, Keston, Keston College, 1982.

Who's who, What's what in Solidarność (book issued at the time of its First Congress in Gdańsk in September 1981. No place or date of the publication given).

Wiśniewski, Ludwik M. 'Chrześcijanie wobec walki o sprawiedliwość' (Christians and Fight for Justice), in *Spotkania*, no. 2, Lublin (January 1978), pp. 98-107.

Wyszyński, Stefan, *Zapiski więzienne* (Prison Notes), Paris, Editions du Dialogue, 1981.

Zaborowski, Jan, *The Catholic Church on the Odra and Nysa*, Warsaw, Novum, 1976.

Index

Academy of Theology in Warsaw, 112
Adzhubei, Alexei, 23
Amnesty
  economic sanctions and, 200
  expected, 188
  partial declared, 188
  second papal visit and, 200
Ascherson, Neal, 109
Association of Catholics, 14
Auschwitz, 68, 191
Australia
  participation in Polish Recovery Programme, 198

Barcikowski, Kazimierz, 93, 103, 122, 127, 156
Bednorz, Herbert, Bishop, 201
Believers' Self-defence Committees, 35, 61-2, 75
Belvedere Palace, 67, 201, 202, 203
Białołęka internment camp, 169
Bielsko Biała, 116-17
Blachnicki, Franciszek, 177
Black Madonna
  anniversary, 184
  Częstochowa motorway project and, 75-6
  millennial celebrations and, 21, 22
  miracle in the Vistula and, 2
  symbol of resistance, 2
Bolonek, Janusz, Monsignor, 163
Bonhoeffer, Dietrich, 46
Boniecki, Adam, 78
Brezhnev, Leonid
  death, 196
  letter from John Paul II, 111-12
Bujak, Zbigniew, 175
  received by Wyszyński, 104
Bukowski, Romuald, 169
Bydgoszcz, 198
  incident, 119-20

Canada
  participation in Polish Recovery Programme, 198
Capitular Vicars, 15, 18
Caritas, 13, 14
Casaroli, Agostino, Cardinal, 23, 34, 53
  meets Stefan Olszowski, 37, 39
  officiates at Wyszyński's funeral, 128
Cathechetic points, 20
Catholic Church
  Accord (1950) with government, 13-15
  acts as mediator and shock-absorber, 102
  acts as guarantor of striking peasants' demands, 116
  after Stalin's death, 16
  appreciated by Prime Minister Pińkowski, 101
  appraised by Szczepański, 187
  at December 1980 commemorative ceremonies, 114
  attacked by East European media, 185
  attempts at re-creation of Catholic Workers' Party, 10
  backing for Flying University, 55-6
  calls for amnesty, 199
  communication difficulties with Vatican, 10, 156
  communism and, 3
  criticism of under martial law, 178-9
  delegalization of Solidarity and, 193-4
  demands abolition of censorship, 59
  demands access to mass media, 58-9
  demands full legal status, 54
  demands reinstatement of Solidarity, 164, 171
  demands release of internees, 164, 171

INDEX

Catholic Church (*cont.*)
  demands return to normal functioning of the State, 168
  dissident movement and, 48-9
  dissolution of seminaries and holy orders, 16
  during the Second World War, 9
  economic sanctions and, 165
  expects crackdown, 172
  facilitates contacts with underground Solidarity, 175
  fading of moderating influence on Solidarity, 134
  gains from first papal visit to Poland, 78-9
  Gdańsk and Szczecin agreements and, 98-100
  gives guidelines for work under martial law, 170
  government seizure of Church land, 13
  impact of John Paul II elections, 61
  impact of John Paul II first visit to Poland, 72-4
  initial reaction to 1980 strikes, 90-1
  KOR and, 46
  martial law and, 186
  nationalism and, 57
  on 1976 workers' riots, 43-4
  on Częstochowa motorway project, 75-6
  on dialogue, 167, 173
  on government seizure of welfare institutions, 13
  on proposed constitutional changes, 40-2
  on Recovered Territories, 12, 13-14
  on socialist education of school children, 36-7
  on sovereignty, 195
  options under martial law, 165
  police brutality and, 190
  political direction and, 3
  Primate's Social Council and, 173-5
  radical priests, 194
  reconciliation and, 191
  responds to martial law declaration, 157-8
  return of its property by the Government, 34
  restrictions on activities, 12
  Solidarity annual demonstrations and, 190
  strength, 2-3
  see also: Glemp, Józef; Jaruzelski, Wojciech; Wyszyński, Stefan
Catholic deputies
  (1957) elections, 18, 19
  (1980) elections, 78
Catholic Faculties at Universities
  dissolution, 16
Catholic Labour Party, 20
Catholic University of Lublin
  formation of independent student movement, 37
  pressure on, 16
  second papal visit and, 200, 202
  under 1950 Accord, 14
Catholic Workers' Party, 10
Censorship
  demands for abolition, 59
  during John Paul II visit to Poland, 65-6
  John Paul II first Christmas Letter of, 63
Charter 77, 74
Chochołowska
  hostel, 226
  valley, 202
Chojecki, Mirosław, 190
Christian Social Association, 78
Church-State Accord of 1950, 13-15
Church-State Agreement of 1956, 17-18
Ciechan, Zbigniew, 132
Clubs of Catholic Intelligentsia, formation, 20-1
Cold War, 10
Collectivization, 3
Commission of Episcopates of European Community (COMECE), 196
  and Polish recovery Programme, 198
Committee for the Defence of Workers 'KOR'
  1980 strikes and, 88
  calls for amnesty, 47
  co-operation with Church, 45-6
  formation, 44
  former members arrested, 190
  on John Paul II visit to Poland, 64-5

INDEX

St. Martin's Church hunger strike and, 49
Committee of the Unjustly Persecuted, 74
Communist Party of the Soviet Union
  first letter to PUWP, 129-30
  second letter to PUWP, 135
Concordat
  termination of, 9
Conference on Security and Cooperation in Europe, 37, 41
Conscription of seminary students, 36
  ended, 78
Constitution
  bishops' reaction to proposed changes, 40-2
Construction of new churches, 21, 34, 35, 37
Council for Mutual Economic Assistance, 197, 225
Council of State, 197
  decree of February 1953, 15-16
  annulled, 18
  declares martial law, 156
Cyrankiewicz, Józef
  meets Wyszyński (1957), 18-19
Cywiński, Bohdan, 49, 94
Czechoslovakia
  closes borders with Poland, 106
Częstochowa, 156, 184, 185, 198, 199
  motorway project, 75-6
Czyrek, Józef, 127
  confers with Glemp, 185
  confers with John Paul II, 137
  confers with Casaroli, 137, 185
  meets Poggi, 185
  second papal visit and, 186

D'Amato, Alfons, 111
Dąbrowski, Bronisław, Archbishop, 47, 92, 101, 106, 126, 129, 164
  during Wyszyński's illness, 125
  involvement in settlement of Bydgoszcz incident, 120
  meets Solidarity representatives, 103, 104
  negotiates with Rakowski, 128
  personally guarantees settlement of farmers' strike demands, 116
Democratic centralism, 223
Demonstrations (1982), 190, 193

Dissident movement
  and Catholic Church, 48-9
Dziś i Jutro, 11
Dziwisz, Stanisław, Monsignor, 92, 126

Ecclessiam Suam, 23
Economic sanctions
  amnesty and, 200
  Church's opposition to, 165
Elbląg, 30
Elections to the Sejm
  (1957) 18, 19
  (1980) 77-8
Episcopal letters, communiqués and memoranda
  December 1970, 32-3
  January 1971, 33
  January 1976, 40
  March 1976, 40
  September 1976, 43-4
  November 1976, 46
  June 1977, 50
  December 1977, 53-4
  March 1978, 55
  September 1978, 58-9
  October 1978, 62
  February 1980, 77
  May 1980, 79
  June 1980, 90
  August 1980, 97
  October 1980, 103-4
  December 1980, 112-13
  August 1981, 133
  November 1981, 138
  December 1981, 161-2
  January 1982, 167
  February 1982, 170
  August 1982, 189
  September 1982, 191
  January 1983, 199
  May 1983, 200
Episcopate's Press Office, 201
European Community, 183
Excommunication of communists
  government's reaction, 13
Extraordinary powers demanded, 139

Falanga, 12
Final Act of the Helsinki Conference, 75
Fiszbach, Tadeusz, 90
Flying University, 95

255

INDEX

Foundation for the Modernization and Development of Private Agriculture, Handicrafts and Private Sector Economy in Poland, 197, 225-6
Frasyniuk, Władysław, 175
Free Trade Union of the Coast, 90
Front of National Accord, 136, 138, 175
   Episcopate's attitude to, 139

Garibaldi, Giuseppe, 201
GATT, 197
Gdańsk, 156, 161, 198
   demonstrations, 184, 193
Gdańsk Agreement, 98-100, 105, 107, 189, 222
Gdańsk workers' riots
   (1970) 29-30, 31
   (1976) 42
   commemorative ceremonies, 114
Gdynia, 29, 155
   commemorative ceremonies, 114
German Episcopate, 21-2
German Democratic Republic, 15, 172
   closes borders with Poland, 106
   closes borders to Western attachés, 109
German Federal Republic
   treaty with Poland, 35
Gierek, Edward, 58, 60, 61, 76, 94
   and 1980 strikes, 88
   attempts to separate Church from dissidents, 48
   elected PUWP leader, 30
   implores Wyszyński's help, 94
   meets Wyszyński
      (1977), 50-1, 54
      (1979), 64
   meets John Paul II, 67-8, 203
   on Church–State relations, 44
   on papal visit, 62
   ousted, 101
   visits the Vatican, 51-3
Gieremek, Bronisław, 94
Glemp, Józef, Cardinal
   addresses Solidarity's National Congress, 134
   appeals for calm, 163
   appeals for dialogue, 188
   conditions for, 189
   asks for Wałęsa's release, 196
   authority undermined, 194
   compared with Wyszyński, 195
   complains of lack of initiatives, 167
   complains of social polarization, 133
   confers with John Paul II, 137
   delegalization of Solidary and, 191, 192, 193
   differences within the Episcopate and, 171
   forms committee for help to internees, 160, 169
   given assurances on martial law, 159-60
   informed of Wałęsa's release, 196
   letter from Anka Kowalska, 178
   meets Jaruzelski
      (11 July 1981), 131
      (21 October 1981), 37
      (9 January 1982), 167
      (25 April 1982), 175
      (8 November 1982), 196
      (9 March 1983), 199
   meets Jaruzelski and Wałęsa, 139
   meets Kania, 133
   new style of leadership, 131
   nominated Primate of Poland, 130
   patriotism of, 195
   Polish Recovery Programme and, 183
   postpones travels, 191
   Primate's Social Council and, 173
   radical priests and, 194
   receives congratulations from State authorities, 130
   receives Solidarity officials, 133
   refuses to meet Jaruzelski, 191-2
   resignation rumours, 196
   responds to martial law declaration, 158-9, 160
   second papal visit and, 184, 186, 189, 199, 204
   sends appeal letters, 139-41
   sends protest letter to Jaruzelski, 165-6
   sets up crisis team, 160
   told of martial law declaration, 156
   withdraws bishops' communiqué, 162
Glempic, 194
Gniezno, 68

INDEX

Gomułka, Władysław, 17, 20, 22, 29, 30
Government of National Unity
  termination of Concordat, 9
Grabski, Tadeusz, 122
Groblicki, Julian, Bishop, 107
Grudziądz, 42
Gucwa, Stanisław, 127
Gulbinowicz, Henryk, Archbishop, 170, 185, 199, 201

Helsinki Final Act
  message to all signatories from John Paul II, 102
Hlond, August, Cardinal
  dies, 12
  invested with special powers, 10
Holy Cross Church
  hunger strike, 74-5
Hunger strikes
  Holy Cross Church, 74-5
  St. Martin's Church, 49

Inter-factory Strike Committee
  Gdańsk, 92, 93
  Szczecin, 93
Independent Self-Governing Trade Union Solidarity
  see Solidarity
Independent Students' Union, 116
Independent Television News (ITN), 186, 200
International Covenant on Human and Civil Rights, 75
International Labour Organization
  John Paul II address to, 179-81
Invasion of Czechoslovakia, 74
Invasion threats of Poland, 109, 110-11

Jabłoński, Henryk, 61, 127, 199, 203, 227
  congratulates Glemp on appointment, 130
  sends message to John Paul II, 126
Jagielski, Mieczysław, 89, 93
Jankowski, Henryk, 91
Japan
  participation in Polish Recovery Programme, 198
Jaroszewicz, Piotr, 30, 42, 43, 61
  meets Wyszyński, 34

Jaruzelski, Wojciech, General, 119, 127, 129, 169, 172, 173, 174, 221
  attitude to Primate's Council Theses, 175
  becomes Party leader, 137
  becomes Prime Minister, 118
  calls on Cardinal Wyszyński, 120-1
  congratulates Glemp on appointment, 130
  declares martial law, 156, 157
  delegalization of Solidarity and, 192
  gives assurances on martial law, 160
  Glemp refuses meeting, 191-2
  hardline faction and, 167, 172, 184
  July 1982 speech, 187-8
  martial law declaration and, 155
  meets Glemp
    (11 July 1981), 131
    (21 October 1981), 137
    (9 January 1982), 165
    (25 April 1982), 175
    (8 November 1982), 196
    (9 March 1983), 199
  meets Glemp and Wałęsa, 137
  meets John Paul II, 203, 225
  meets Silvestrini, 203
  on Church-State relations, 132, 192
  on second papal visit, 188, 192
  Polish Recovery Programme and, 183
  Primate's Social Council and, 192
  receives letter from John Paul II, 162
  second papal visit and, 186, 196
  sends 'get well' message to John Paul II, 126
  speculation of removal of, 201
  strategy of martial law, 161
Jasna Góra monastery
  1982 celebrations, 188
  during first papal visit, 69
  raided by police, 20
  second papal visit, 200, 202
  site of millennial celebrations, 22
Jastrzębie, 189, 222
John XXIII, Pope, 23, 57, 118
John Paul II, Pope
  addresses ILO, 179-81
  appeals for compromise, 122
  assassination attempt on, 126-7
  impact on Poland, 126-7

257

INDEX

John Paul II, Pope (*cont.*)
  comments on martial law, 163, 164
  departs from Angelus text, 111
  first visit to Poland, 67-73
  formulation of *Ostpolitik*, 70-2
  holds meeting with Dąbrowski, 164
  holds talks with Wyszyński and bishops, 106
  impact on Church-State relations, 61
  inauguration ceremonies, 61
  informed on martial law declaration, 155
  invites himself to Poland, 63-4
  letter to Macharski, 131-2
  meeting with Gierek, 67-8, 203
  meeting with Jaruzelski, 203
  official reaction to election, 61
  on amnesty, 188
  on delegalization of Solidarity, 193
  on dialogue, 222
  on economic sanctions, 222
  on Gdańsk, Szczecin and Jastrzębie agreements, 222
  on martial law, 188
  on sovereignty, 223
  on the role of St. Stanisław, 63
  plea for 30-days' national mourning, 128
  personal message to Wyszyński, 92
  popular reaction to election, 60
  reaction to the Gdańsk strikes, 92
  receives Czyrek, 185
  receives Ozdowski, 108
  receives Solidarity delegation, 115
  responds to martial law declaration, 157-8
  role in world's trouble spots, 187
  second visit to Poland, 199-205, 221-7
  sends letter to Brezhnev, 111-12
  sends letter to Wałęsa, 163
  sends message to signatories of Helsinki Final Act, 102
  sends personal envoy, 163
  sends request for amnesty, 200
  speaks on Poland's right to independence, 102
  see also: papal visits to Poland
Joint Episcopal-Government Commission, 22, 79
  after martial law, 173
  restitution, 103
Joint Working Group on Polish Recovery Programme, 197, 198, 226

Kaczmarek, Lech, Bishop, 103, 134
  briefs Wyszyński, 92-3
  issues proclamation, 93
  mediates during Gdańsk strikes, 91
Kąkol, Kazimierz
  on Church-State relations, 42
Kania, Stanisław, 94, 106, 107, 119, 127, 129, 134
  becomes Party leader, 101
  congratulates Glemp on appointment, 130
  meets Glemp, 133
  meets Wyszyński, 104
  relinquishes Party leadership, 137
  sends message to John Paul II, 126
Katowice, 162, 198, 199, 201, 202
Kielce, 110
Kiszczak, Czesław, 160
Klasa, Józef
  on prospects of Soviet intervention, 109
Klus, Kazimierz, Bishop, 134
Kolbe, Maksymilian, 199
  beatification, 34
  canonization, 191, 193
Kołodziejczyk, Mirosław, Bishop, 107
Konstancin, 162
KOR, *see* Committee for the Defence of Workers
Kościelniak, Zdzisław, 105
Kościół, lewica, dialog, 46-7
Kowalik, Tadeusz, 94
Kraków, 198, 199, 200, 202, 227
Krąpiec, Albert, 200
Krol, John, Cardinal, 128
Kuberski, Jerzy, 103, 156
Kuczyński, Waldemar, 94
Kukołowicz, Romuald
  and Bydgoszcz incident, 119, 120
  as Wyszyński emissary to strikers in Gdańsk, 98
  as Wyszyński emissary to Political Bureau, 98
  called to Central Committee building, 129

258

INDEX

negotiates settlement in Rzeszów, 118
Kulikov, Viktor, 157
Kuroń, Jacek, 114, 190

Laborem Exercens, 135
Lama, Luciano, 115
Lay Catholic Organizations, 11-12
Legal Status for the Church, 54
Legitimization of communism, 1-2
Lenin Shipyard, 29-30, 203
  1980 strikes, 90
  demands, 90
  militarization of, 193
  strike committee, 90
  martial law declaration, 160-1
Letter from CPSU Central Committee, 129-39
Letter from Glemp to Students' Union, 141
Letter from Glemp to Jaruzelski, 140
Letter from Glemp to Wałęsa, 141
Letter from Glemp to Sejm deputies, 139-40
Light and Life Movement, 36
Lipski, Jan Józef, 190
Lis, Bogdan, 175
Litski, Witold, 103
Lityński, Jan, 190
Łódź, 31, 42, 198, 199
  university strike, 116
Łopatka, Adam
  meets Poggi, 185
  meets Silvestrini, 203
  on Church and socialism, 227
L'Osservatore Romano, 78, 91, 201
Lublin, 89, 198, 199
  and second papal visit, 200
  commemorative ceremonies, 114
Lublin Manifesto, 9
Luxemburg, Rosa, 2

Macharski, Franciszek, Cardinal, 103, 107, 125, 128, 129, 131, 160, 163, 170, 185, 199, 201
  speaks on martial law, 165, 166, 168
  and Polish Recovery Programme, 196
Madej, Zbigniew, 197
Majdanek, 200

Majdański, Kazimierz, Bishop, 107
Małkowski, Stanisław, 177-8
Martial law, 179
  bishops' guidelines for work under, 170
  declaration, 155-7
  ratified by Sejm, 169
  first date for, 122-3
  lifting of, 225
  restriction under, 157
Marxism-Leninism, 2, 129
Mass broadcasting
  first transmission, 103
  petition for, 76
  see also: Mass Media Sunday
Mass Media Sunday, 50, 58
Mater et Magistra, 118
Mazowiecki, Tadeusz, 49
  becomes adviser to Gdańsk strikers, 94
Merker, Alexander, 103
Message to Working People of Eastern Europe, 134-5
  East European reaction, 135
Michalski, Jan, Bishop, 120, 128
Michnik, Adam, 46-7, 60, 114, 190
Military Council for National Salvation (WRON)
  formation, 156
  see also: WRON
Military manœuvres, 189
Military task force, 138
Millennium celebrations, 21, 22
Mistrzejowice, 202
Mount of St. Anna, 199
Movement for Defence of Human and Civil Rights, 89

National Co-ordinating Commission of Solidarity, 129
  and Bydgoszcz incident, 120
  call for national warning strike, 120
  calls for referendum on government, 141
  last meeting, 141
  rounded up, 155
  warned by Wyszyński, 121-2
National Democratic Party, 12
National identity, 1
National traditions
  and Roman Catholic Church, 1

259

INDEX

Ney, Roman, 122
Niepokalanów, 199
Novena, 21
Nowa Huta, 21, 65, 70, 184, 193, 202
Nowe Drogi
   on Church-State relations, 64
Nowy Targ, 42

Olszowski, Stefan, 122, 172
   and hardliners, 184
   coup planned, 159
   meets Casaroli, 32, 39
   meets Silvestrini, 203
   visits Vatican, 37
Olsztyn, 198
Opole, 199
Orszulik, Alojzy, 103, 113, 114
   appointed in charge of Polish Recovery Programme, 198
   criticizes Jacek Kuroń, 114
   involved in settlement of Bydgoszcz incident, 120
Orthodoxy, 1
Ostpolitik, 22-4, 37-9, 47-8, 53, 61, 128
   John Paul II formulation, 70-2
Ozdowski, Jerzy, 127
   received by John Paul II, 11, 108
   appointed Deputy Prime Minister, 108

Pan-Slavism, 68, 74
PAP, 184
   see also: Polish Press Agency
Papal visits to Poland
   Paul VI
      discussed (1972), 34
      (1972), 34
      (1975), 37
      prevented (1966), 22
      proposed (1979), 62
   John Paul II
      first (1979): arrival, 67; at Auschwitz-Birkenau concentration camp, 69; at Mogiła, 70; gains of, 78-9; impact of, 72-5; Mass on Victory Square, 68; meeting with State authorities, 67; meets students, 69; negotiations, 62-5; on *Ostpolitik*, 70-2;
      organization of, 73; repercussions on participants from Czechoslovakia, 75
      second (1982), 183, 204-5: amnesty and, 199, 200; approved, 196; arrival, 221; at Katowice, 224; departure, 227; dialogue and, 224; expected, 184; first itinerary, 199; formal invitation issued, 199; importance of, 226-7; Jaruzelski and, 204; Jaruzelski's view of, 188; list of towns proposed, 198; Lublin and, 200, 202; meeting with Jaruzelski, 203, 225; meeting with State authorities, 221-2; meeting with Wałęsa and, 201, 202-3, 226; negotiations for, 185-6, 199; official programme released, 201, 202; plans for announced, 199; Polish Recovery Programme and, 203, 225-6; postponed, 186; second itinerary, 199-200; Solidarity record and, 224; Soviet objection to, 185; support for Solidarity, 224-5; talks with State authorities, 203
Pastoral care in hospitals
   under 1950 Accord, 14
Pastoral care in penal institutions
   under 1950 Accord, 14
Partitions of Poland, 1
Patriotic priests, 16
Paul VI, Pope, 22, 23, 62, 125
   summons Wyszyński, 39
   receives Gierek, 51-3, 54
   see also: papal visits to Poland
Pax, 11-12, 16, 78
Peasant movement, 117-18
   see also: Rural Solidarity
Peasantry, 3
Piasecki, Bolesław, 12
Piekary Sląskie, 65, 199, 202
Pińkowski, Józef, 106, 107
   on Church-State relations, 101
Pius XII, Pope, 10, 12, 22
Pledges of loyalty, 166
Płock, 42

260

INDEX

Pluta, Wilhem, Bishop, 107
Poggi, Luigi, Archbishop, 47-9, 163, 184, 185, 199
Polish Committee for National Liberation, 9
Polish Communist Party, 2
Polish National bank, 197
Polish Press Agency, 65, 66, 97
  see also: PAP
Polish Recovery Programme
  approved by Jaruzelski, 196-7
  discussed by European bishops, 196
  discussed by John Paul II, 225
  Joint Working Group, 197, 198
  Foundation for set up, 197
  Memorandum on, 181
  proposed Foundation in the West, 198
  contributions to, 198
  scope, 181-3
Polish Savings Bank, 197
Polish Students' Association, 37
Polish United Workers' Party, 12, 19, 62, 105
  Central Committee appeal, 109
  Eighth Congress, 77
  first CPSU letter and, 129-30
  Political Bureau, 184, 201
  second CPSU letter and, 135
Polish Workers' Party, 9, 12
Polityka, 57-8
  on Church-State relations, 64, 66-7
Poznań, 198, 200
  demonstrations (1976), 43
Poznań riots (1956), 16-17
  anniversary of, 184
  commemorative ceremonies of, 114
Pravda, 185
Primate, office of, 1
Primate's Committee for Help to Internees
  activities, 169
  formally established, 169
  formed, 160
Primate's Social Council, 179
  and Jaruzelski, 192
  Theses of, 173-5, 240-7
Propositions of the Primate's Social Council, 176-7
Protestantism, 1
Prussia, 1

Przemyśl, 37
Pyjas, Stanisław, 49

Radical priests, 194
Radom, 42, 43, 184
Rakowski, Mieczysław, 136
  negotiates with Dąbrowski, 128
  negotiates with Solidarity Commission, 120, 123
  on Church-State relations, 57-8, 64, 66-7
Reagan, Ronald, 165, 181, 191, 193
  accused by Tass, 185
Recovered Territories, 12, 13-14, 18, 22
  government's ultimatum, 15
  recognition by Vatican, 34
Red Army, 2
Redemptor Hominis, 64
Religious education in schools
  bill on socialist education, 36
  eliminated, 20
  forbidden, 16
  under 1950 Accord, 14
Rockefeller Foundation, 198
Rozwadowski, Józef, Bishop, 107
Rude Pravo
  accuses Solidarity, 133-4
Rural Solidarity, 118
  arguments for and against registration, 117
  demands registration, 116-17
  Presidium received by Wyszyński, 123-4
  supported by Wyszyński, 118, 119
Russo-Polish war, 2
Rzeszów, 116, 118

St. Martin's Church
  hunger strike, 49
St. Stanisław, 62-3, 167
Samizdat publications, 56-7
Sapieha, Adam, Cardinal, 11, 166
Sejm, 168, 169, 174
Silvestrini, Achiles, Archbishop, 203
Skarżyński, Aleksander, 34
Skrzypczak, Edward, 132
Slipyi, Josyf, Cardinal, 23
Słupsk, 30
Socialist Rural Youth Union, 37
Socialist Union of Polish Students, 49
  bishops' objection to, 37

261

INDEX

Socialist Youth Union, 37
Society of Academic Courses
   bishops' backing for, 55
   formation, 55
   see also: Flying University
Solidarity trade union, 102, 157, 164, 165, 169, 171, 172, 177, 183, 184
   bishops' demand for reinstatement, 189, 191
   bishops' support for registration, 104
   calls for protest rallies, 139
   Church's moderating influence and, 134
   delegalization of, 191, 192
      Church's reaction to, 193
      reaction to, 193
      workers' reaction to, 193
   delegation meets Dąbrowski, 104
   First National Congress, 133
      Church's presence, 134
   first national warning strike, 103
   Presidium received by Wyszyński, 104
   Primate's Social Council and, 173, 174
   radical priests and, 194
   registration, 105, 107
   second anniversary demonstrations, 190
   underground leadership of, 175
      accepts Primate's Social Council proposals, 177
      and protest moratorium, 183
      second papal visit and, 204-5
      uneasy about Church's involvement, 177
   see also: Glemp, Józef; Jaruzelski, Wojciech; Message to Workers of Eastern Europe; National Co-ordinating Commission of Solidarity; Wałęsa, Lech; Wyszyński, Stefan
Solidarity without frontiers, 179-81
Sopot, 30
Soviet military intervention prospects, 160
Soviet naval exercises, 133
Soviet Union, 2
   and martial law declaration, 157

Soyuz 81 manœuvres, 119-20
Spotkania, 56-7
   activists co-ordinate strike in Lublin, 89
Staniszkis, Jadwiga, 94
Starachowice, 43
Stomma, Stanisław, 160
Strike Information Bulletin—Lenin Shipyard, 98
Stroba, Jerzy, Archbishop, 103, 129
Student Solidarity Committees, 49
   bishops' support of, 78
Sundić, Milika
   warns of 'Czechoslovak type' invasion, 108
Swięcicki, Andrzej
Wyszyński's personal representative to Gdańsk Inter-Factory Strike Committee, 98
Szablewski, Kazimierz, 39
Szczecin, 30, 31, 193, 198
   commemorative ceremonies, 114
Szczecin Agreement, 98, 222
Szczepański, Jan
   on Catholic Church, 187

Tass, 98, 110
   attack on the Vatican, 185
   reports Solidarity's *putsch*, 122
Tczew, 88
Teresin, 199
Theses of Primate's Social Council, 173-5
   criticism of, 177, 178
   text of, 240-7
Tokarczuk, Ignacy
   construction of churches without permits, 37, 41
   on police brutality, 190
   on reconciliation, 191
   on state capitalism, 41
   on workers' rights, 41
Tomasek, Frantisek, Cardinal, 74
Toruń University, 74
Tripartite meeting (Glemp, Jaruzelski, Wałęsa), 137
Trybuna Ludu, 66, 97, 131, 169
Tygodnik Powszechny, 11, 18, 19, 20, 63
Tygodnik Wojenny, 177-8

INDEX

Ukraine, 202
Ukrainian Uniate Church, 23
Underground society, 189
United Nations Charter, 41
United Peasants' Party, 117
United States, 183
   economic sanctions and, 165, 201, 222
   non-participation in Polish Recovery Programme, 198
   Polish Recovery Programme, and, 182
   State Department invasion warnings, 109
Ursus Tractor Plant, 42, 43, 88
Ursynów, 200
Ustrzyki Dolne, 116

Vatican, 9
   and Government in exile, 35
   and John Paul II letter to Brezhnev, 111
   attacked by Tass, 185
   communication difficulties with Polish Church
      after World War II, 10
      after martial law, 155
   excommunication of communists, 13
   Gierek's visit, 51-3, 54
   new formulation of *Ostpolitik*, 70-2
   Ostpolitik, 22-3
   Recovered Territories and, 12, 34-5
   Yugoslavia and, 23
   see also: papal visits to Poland; Wyszyński, Stefan
Vatican Press Office, 201
Vatican Radio, 158, 162
   broadcasts guidelines to priests, 170

Wałentynowicz, Anna, 90
Wałęsa, Lech, 106, 114, 116, 121, 123, 128, 162, 181, 183, 203
   arrested, 156
   becomes leader of Gdańsk strike, 90
   cautioned by Wyszyński, 107
   criticized by GDR press, 106
   demands for release of, 189, 191
   meets John Paul II in Poland, 226
   received by Glemp, 133
   received by Wyszyński, 100
   registration of Solidarity and, 105
   release asked for, 196
   released from detention, 196
   second papal visit and, 202
   sets condition for broadcast, 163, 164
   signs Gdańsk agreement, 98
   visited by Orszulik, 163
   visits John Paul II, 115
Wambierzyce, 91-2
Warsaw, 43, 184, 193, 198, 199, 200, 202
Warsaw Pact, 19, 74, 129, 157
   Foreign Ministers' meeting, 104
   manœuvres, 120
   Moscow summit, 109
Wielowieyski, Andrzej, 94
Wojtaszek, Emil, 155
Wojtyła, Karol, Cardinal, 166
   elected as Pope John Paul II, 60
   on the death of Stanisław Pyjas, 49
   see also: John Paul II
Workers' riots
   (1956), 16-17
   (1970), 29-31
   (1976), 42-3
   (1980), 87-99
Wrocław, 184, 193, 198, 200
WRON, 157, 160, 164
   see also: Military Council for National Salvation
Wujec, Henryk, 114, 190
Wujek colliery, 162, 172
Wyszyński, Stefan, 128, 131, 166, 195
   acknowledged as eminent patriot, 53
   and Accord (1950), 15
   appeals for calm, 17
   appointed Primate, 12
   arrested, 16
   backs KOR's call for amnesty, 47
   briefed by Kaczmarek on strikes, 92-3
   calls for improvement in living standards, 50
   cautions Wałęsa, 107
   commends workers' strikes, 100
   criticizes mismanagement of economy, 76-7
   demands enquiry into police brutality, 46
   denied passport, 22

INDEX

Wyszyński, Stefan (*cont.*)
dies, 127
national mourning and funeral, 127-8
farewell message of, 235-9
Gierek visit to Vatican and, 51-3
holds talks with John Paul II, 106
illness, 125-6
implored by Gierek to help, 93
invested with special powers, 12
mediates in settlement of peasants' strikes, 116
meets Cyrankiewicz, 18-19
meets Gierek,
 (1977), 50-1
 (1979), 64
meets Jaroszewicz, 34
meets Kania, 104
nominates successor, 126
on 1976 workers' riots, 43
on construction of churches, 35
on Częstochowa motorway project, 75-6
on millennium of Christianity, 21
on *Ostpolitik*, 23
on Recovered Territories, 12
on right of peasants to trade union, 124
on right to trade unions, 224
on Rural Solidarity, 118
on socialist education, 36
on workers' riots in 1970, 30-1
papal letter to Brezhnev and, 111-12
pressurized to accept Vatican-Warsaw talks, 38-9
reaction to 1980 strikes, 91-2
receives Founding Committee of Solidarity, 100
receives Jaruzelski, 120-1
receives message from John Paul II, 92
receives Presidium of Rural Solidarity, 123-4
receives Rural Solidarity delegation, 118-19
receives Solidarity Presidium, 104
reconfirmed in post, 47
released, 17
sends emissary to PUWP Political Bureau, 98
sermon on 26 August 1980, 95-7
submits resignation, 47
tribute from *Polityka*, 66
warns Solidarity, 121-2
see also: Episcopal letters, communiqués and memoranda; Solidarity; Vatican

Zawieyski, Jerzy, 19
Zbrosza, Duża, 35
Zieja, Jan, 45
Znak, 11, 18, 19
Znak Parliamentary Circle, 19, 20, 78
Żołnierz Wolności, 157, 189
ZOMO, 155, 161, 162
Życie Warszawy, 131